# From

## The

# Holocaust

## To The

# Highlands

By

**Walter Kress**

Published by

**Cauliay Publishing & Distribution**
PO Box 12076
Aberdeen
AB16 9AL
www.cauliaypublishing.com

**First Edition**

**ISBN 978-0-9554964-1-7**

Cover design. Christine Molden.

A CIP catalogue record for this book is available from the British Library.

## Acknowledgements

To those wonderful people in Aberdeen who are more than just friends and of course not forgetting my friends here in England who are too numerous to mention.

I would also like to thank Michael William Molden for his invaluable help. Finally I would like to dedicate this book to my family who have given me endless support.

I thank you all

Walter Kress
March 2007.

# Introduction

Every now and then the world hears about an ordinary person who has lived an extraordinary life. This book is about one such person, Walter Kress. Not only has he lived an incredible life—the kind of life that novels are based on—he has managed to record it in a unique style and in a way that allows his wonderful personality to shine out from every page. The book you are about to read is heart-warming and humourous, romantic and dramatic. It is the story of a man who grew to love and serve the country which gave him and his family sanctuary when they fled the horror of the Nazi holocaust. Walter Kress is an amazing character and I count myself very fortunate to have known him. After reading this book, you will know him too.

# CHAPTER 1

Now seventy years of age and retired, time to think back. So here is a true story of our times.

The time must have been, I guess, being just nine years of age, about 5.00am on that summer's morning. What woke me was that the train had slowed down and was click-clicking to a somewhat different sound. When I came to, I remember it as if it were yesterday; we were going across a wide waterway, high up indeed on this fantastic bridge. I had never seen or been on any structure similar. Of course, at that age, I was simply awe-struck. It was at a much later date that I was told that this structure was the Forth Bridge, which is still regarded by many as a miracle of engineering.

I must have nodded off again, as we had with my mother and father left London Kings Cross station the night before as sitting passengers, and I was, I assume, rather weary.

My father woke me with a call, "We are here, come on!"

So picking up my little bag—it was my old school bag actually—we walked along the platform, my father holding my hand. Of course, we only knew the English phrases, 'please' and 'thank you,' and I think that was it, as we had arrived in Britain from Vienna about two weeks previously.

I stopped at the engine which I believe had pulled the train from Edinburgh. It was black and to a small boy like me, it looked absolutely huge with its massive wheels and those connecting parts of mechanism, hissing steam and every now and then giving a sigh-like sound. I made up my mind there and then, that one day I was going to be an engine driver.

But I am way, way ahead of myself here. We must

now go back from our arrival in Aberdeen, Scotland to a time when I began to focus as a very young child. It is all very relevant I feel to the story I am about to tell.

I was born in Vienna, Austria on 24th April 1930. My parents had emigrated from Poland to the city of dreams, the city of music, culture and true civilisation. But just like dreams, we were all to have them shattered, and much worse—much unbelievably so worse.

One of my earliest memories includes rocking my pram until it tipped over. I can still recall my mother and older sister coming to help me when they heard the crash. I am not sure exactly how old I was at the time. Probably a year and a half—who knows?

My mother and father had both worked at the biggest bakery in the country and my father was still working there when the SS took him away to Dachau Concentration Camp. That was in 1937. The world trembled; looked on. Synagogues, Jewish schools, shops, factories, businesses, anything Jewish was systematically destroyed. The euphoria taken in destruction had to be seen to be believed. We were terrified.

The present generation is probably not aware, although I daresay some know the facts. People of other nations did not want to say a word against the tyrant, Hitler.

One remembers the words of Mr Chamberlain when he unashamedly stated, with remarks regarding Poland, that what was happening in a far-off country was no concern of ours. Absorb that, and you might take in a very deep breath also, and stop to think that such a statement is possible from a man in that position. There again, that is now known as history—ahem and aha.

Well, my father being a baker, offered to cook and bake for those despicable *people*. They had him up at 5.00am and he was never finished until around 11.00 at night. But it was thanks to his workmates and the management at the bakery of the Anker Brotfabrik who somehow or other got him out of that hellhole. My father never told us or spoke to us about his experiences until we were much older and living in Aberdeen.

So as I am now in reflection, as things of far-off bygone days come to mind, I wonder if anyone would believe when I state that such dreadful things at that time were taking place. We nearly did not leave Austria, as my father's friends at the bakery assured us that, as working class people, we would be ok, etc, etc and etc. My father nearly fell for it, but my mother insisted that we must go without delay.

People often ask me, 'How can you possibly remember those things all those long, long years ago?' Take it from me; there are things that even in sleep will not go away. As I said previously, I even remember as far back as tipping the pram over.

At school, even when I started at the age of five, I already felt uneasy at some of the things that were said. I was even pushed and kicked. I did have friends, and I hasten to add that these were of the Christian faith.

I was told by my parents that I should consider myself, lucky to be alive—and I do. But that one for quite a different reason; evidently, I turned on the gas on the cooker, with the result of a terrific explosion which blew out the door of the cooker and made a great gash on a wall. That was while we were still in Vienna, of course.

Another milestone of survival was when I was about four years old. I had a mastoid operation on an ear, and I have a scar to this day. I praise the surgeons of the day, as in the 30s, this kind of operation had a 50/50 chance of success, so I must have been fated to survive. The nurses in that hospital were nuns and they evidently told my parents that I was a bit of a character and when they showed me a picture of Jesus Christ—a large one it was I believe—all I did was to cry furiously. What does a small child know about these things? I was, for some reason, obviously frightened by it.

Here again I can recall without hesitation the details; my father had a brother in Budapest, Uncle Josef, whom I had met when he came to Vienna to visit us. He was a big man—very smartly dressed, gold rings and watch and a big cigar of course. He was a serious businessman and owned a furniture manufacturing business. He also had a small boat hire business on the River (Danube, of course). So somewhere between the ages of four and five came yet another milestone, that became a serious passion in my life. It was his beautiful motorboat.

However, my passion for boats began before that, as Vienna is on the Danube, and I simply became hooked. In fact, jumping a few years on and in Aberdeen again, while fellows of my age were swinging with girls, (some of them getting into serious trouble as well) with the girls, I was taking my apprenticeship seriously, and, being a Sea Cadet, I got to know the local boat people. I will cover that phase in due course, but I thought I would mention it as it comes to mind, that some people perhaps thought, *Funny boy; boats, not girls, very peculiar!* But people are entitled to their thoughts. I may have had other interests, but as I will prove later, I did not put girls out of my mind—not at all.

So my dear departed Uncle, murdered in a concentration camp; I think of him and my Aunt and all the others of our family. And sadly, they include Uncle Josef and his wife and the many, many others that went and never came back. Yes, my Uncle and Aunt in Budapest had no children of their own, therefore I was—I assume—with all the love they gave me, their surrogate son, so to speak.

Anyone who gave me the slightest sign of friendship and help or encouragement or love, I would immediately reciprocate these feelings without, I hasten to add, stiff upper lip or restraint. My mother instilled this in me. As the song goes, to love me and be loved in return; yes indeed.

So the boat in Budapest, in which we would regularly go upriver to a cut-out from the main river channel to this short narrow cut, where Uncle and Aunt had a beautiful summer house amid fields where huge watermelons grew; I simply loved it. The lovely yachts glided slowly past all day as we enjoyed the good life, little realising what the near future would hold.

My uncle at that beautiful place had a large shed which was supported on long heavy uprights, where he kept the motorboat in case it rained, as it was, except for a small area at the front, an open boat.

So I now relate a tale of just what can happen when one becomes besotted with, in my case, a boat.

On the first day there, I got into the shed and shut the door, sat myself in the boat and there I was in a boat on my own, and my mind took off. However, I soon heard people calling, "Walter, lunchtime! Where are you?" I did not move or dare breathe. I was in a boat and I was staying here; not realising of course that a general alarm went out and the police were on their way shortly, as they feared that I had either fallen in, got lost, or worst of the worst that the gypsies had taken me away. It was rife in those days, kids being taken away. I could hear the klaxons of the police cars coming, but never gave it a thought.

Well, when they found me, did I get a pasting! My uncle had to restrain my father—as I was between him—as did a policeman. I remember my uncle handing out cigars and brandy to the four police officers. One patted my head and gave me some advice. I remember this episode and the drama of it all as if it were only yesterday.

So time goes on and Jewish kids in Vienna are now channelled into a Jewish kid's only school. It was miles away; two changes on a tram. I recall it was at least three to four miles away from where we lived. One day while waiting at a crossing on a busy road, on my way home from school, a large ESSO petrol tanker stopped. I immediately recognised the driver as a neighbour in a Czechoslovakian's house we were now living in—as we had been turned out of our lovely state-owned flat. He kindly helped me into this high-up cab and drove me home. Yes, there were a few decent ones around, very few indeed.

Then another neighbour, a very wealthy man—I assume he was Jewish, but that is only an assumption—had this beautiful big Afghan hound. I took this great big animal for walks. He was as big as I was. I was about seven years old, and I can still see myself today. I felt proud and big. I felt that no one would dare touch me when I was out walking this beautiful, great creature. I was immune to danger!

I must now, as it comes to me, relate the time not too long before we left Austria. One day—I am not exactly sure of the days before or after my father was sent to Dachau Concentration Camp—the SS came and bundled my mother and father into the back of a truck. I remember most vividly my sister, who was eleven at the time, crying bitterly. My parents were forced to take brooms, scrubbing brushes, soap, soap powder, liquids, metal polish, etc, and they were gone well into the evening. A kindly Christian lady we knew looked after us until our parents came home. Walking in, they looked—and to this very day I can still see them—absolutely like people on the verge of death. They were covered in grime. They had also been kicked and punished, and my mother—I was told this much later in life—had been subjected to a dreadful experience—come to your own conclusion without a lot of imagination.

I ran around and played with other kids, mostly of the Christian faith. It made no difference to me. In fact, on recollection, I was not what one would describe as your true little Yiddish boy—far from it—although at that tender age, one cannot really grasp the meaning of it all. I went to religious class and actually, one day just before we left Austria, the lady teacher told me to stay behind, as she said I had not behaved myself during the lessons. So I asked to go to the toilet and took my chance to run home without waiting until my father or mother, whoever had brought me, to come and collect me. Running home, I went over some of the busiest roads in Vienna. I never went back to that school. I told my parents that the teacher was a bully, and that is the absolute truth.

Yes, I suppose if ninety percent of people looked back as far as they could remember, their tales would also make very interesting reading.

The religious class was in a hall next to our beautiful Temple. That is what they were called, not Synagogues. And next to this hall was a small house where the caretaker, not of our faith, lived. The penny dropped (to coin a phrase) when this chap, by the name of Schweigoffski, appeared one day in his SS uniform. He had always, as far as I was concerned, had this deathly grey pallor, and was forever being gruff with us kids. The gifts and money that the more upper class of us Jews—and many were extremely well-off—gave to this cretin regularly was extortion in every sense of the word! I think he even sort of watched over their cars—that was one of his claims anyway.

We did not have such a luxury, not even a motorbike. My father had hankered after a motorbike and sidecar; alas, he never got one. My father's friends at his place of work, some of whom had a motorbike, would take my sister and me for little trips round the block. The way we wheeled on bends and corners, the thrill was great. I will never forget it.

Well, by now things were going from bad to worse for us. We were spat on and shops refused to serve us. Oh yes, believe it or not, while the whole world looked on in abject terror. I was shot in the right knee by a powerful air pistol dart—not the lead type, but a small pointed dart. I was grateful they did not shoot me in the eyes. Yes, that is what it meant to be Jewish. This sort of treatment prompted many Jews to become Christian, but that did not help them in any way whatsoever, as later events proved.

Again, my thoughts have just focussed on other acts in this seminal part of my life. Having been turned out of our lovely state-council flat, I can only describe those workers' flats by comparison to those that know the lovely privately owned flats near Lord's Cricket Grounds in London, the ones overlooking the park. Yes indeed, that is the luxury that workers lived in, in Vienna.

Luckily, we had some friends of Czechoslovakian nationality, and at that time Czechoslovakia had not been invaded. So this dear family let us have rooms at the top of their house. I do not know what we would have done otherwise, I am sure. The lady of the house thought diplomatically, as Czechoslovakia was not at war with Germany, that she and her property were safe, but one day six SS brutes turned up, went through everything we had and took what they fancied. Terrible scenes like these can never, ever be erased from the mind. At one stage, my mother protested and attempted to grab something back. She was given a hefty push, and I thought they had killed her. She fell back on a fireplace and with the pain, she semi-blacked out and fell in agony to the floor.

It was at that moment that the Christian lady, wife of

the aforementioned ESSO tanker man, arrived from her flat next door, and in language I had never heard before, laid into those bastards. They gave her the height of abuse, patting their guns and mouthing, "Ein Tag," which means, 'One day,' implying that one day they would shoot her; one day for sure. My sister once again was uncontrolled in her tears and screaming, but I just looked on helplessly, my mind a complete blank. What can a child of that age do?

And now there comes to mind a little episode which got my name on police records in Vienna. Yes, I am not ashamed to admit it, but of course, being Jewish it could have had terrible repercussions for us all.

I was running around with some kids and went to a free show. The centre point was this fellow doing a demonstration with hot molten lead, making various patterns, etc. So after the show, one of the bright older lads suggested he knew where we could get some lead, and off we went to where the goods trains were in the sidings. There were literally hundreds of wagons, full and sealed, the seals being of the much sought-after lead. I think I was the only Jewish kid amongst them, and was possibly set up.

Suddenly one of the lads yelled out that two people were coming. The other kids took off, but the two men were railway workers and grabbed me, with six or eight seals in my pocket. They took me to their hut and within minutes, a policewoman arrived. I was in a desperate situation. Eventually, I was taken to a police station, and I think also at the time my father was in Dachau, because I remember vividly that my mother came for me at eleven at night. It was by then quite late, and she cried all the way home. We thought that we were in deep trouble. Also, I could not name the others, as I simply did not know those kids. That's why, with hindsight, I believe I was set up.

Then comes the day that we had to go to an office at Police headquarters, or maybe it was a room, perhaps even a juvenile court? I am not exactly clear on that point. I think my mother passed over a fair bit of cash and a watch as a kind of under-the-counter fine. The man gave me a terrible dressing down. I think he might even have been Gestapo.

Well, comes the morning—once again, I use the phrase 'As clear as yesterday'—we are to go to the 'Bahnhof,' the railway station—a 'Bahn' being a train and a 'hof' being a station. I knew we were going away forever, and my mother, when I think back to that morning, was in a dreadful state. She could not hide her feelings.

Yes, Vienna to her had meant so much, oh so much. She cried and cried and cried. My father somehow managed to contain himself, but there was the start of a tear or two on my face. My sister had gone weeks before us, on what was known as 'kindertransport,' or children's transport, to England.

So the train starts. I can see it all and feel it all. I think my mother would have jumped off if it was not for her devotion to the rest us. The scene was terrible. My beloved Aunt Martha—I was her *little boy*, and may God rest her poor tortured, murdered soul, along with her husband, Uncle Bernard. She ran along the platform calling, "Regina"—my mother's name—"you should stay! Don't go away. What can they do to us? Oh, Regina.! Chaim"—my father's name—"Chaim! Stay, please come back!"

My mother's chilling last words to these two people so dearly loved by me, and never out of mind, seem now so simple, as the train was now reaching the end of the platform, those words were just, "Wait and see. Just wait and see." I have remembered these words every day of my life ever since. Yes, I even wake up at night and I hear them. The rest, of course, is history.

So here we were in this train, nearly all the passengers of the Jewish faith, leaving Austria for various destinations out of Europe. We had a fright at Aachen—that's on the border—in the station in Germany when our coach and another one were disconnected. The main train went away and we were left there at the station. The Gestapo came onto these two coaches and while they asked questions and searched our belongings, the two coaches were taken back. We all thought that we were going to be taken all the way back. It was a ghastly terror. I cannot describe the looks on people's faces; the terror of impending death.

However, we were only being shunted to await the arrival of a train that would connect with these two coaches of ours. After what seemed an eternity, the Gestapo went away, and I think it must have been six to eight hours at Aachen before we were finally on our way to Belgium. More searches were carried out at the border and again on our way to Ostend.

So here we were at last at Ostend, weary, but even at my tender age, I felt the anticipation, seeing the expression and lively chatter of all concerned. The rail station was just yards from where the ship lay that was to take us to England, the land of the free.

I had in my short life only seen lakes and rivers. I had not been told about the vastness of the sea that we were about to sail on. However, I cannot remember very much about the crossing. The ship was either called the Peppin or Pinster, or some such similar name. I must have slept for most of the trip across the Channel. I remember all of us setting foot on English soil at Dover, or Dovercourt, Harwich; I am not exactly sure on that point.

It did not take long, however, for us to reach London by train. My sister and some people from a refugee committee met us, and we were taken in cars to a hostel somewhere, I think, in the East End. We—my father and I—slept in a large room on camp beds, where there were about sixteen or so other men and boys. The ladies and girls were in other parts of the hostel. We were there for about two weeks before we left for Scotland.

So having already covered our arrival in Scotland as well as memory allows and brings forth, as I think back to those times—a long, long time ago indeed—most vividly I can remember that nothing was ever explained to me, only that we had to go away from Vienna because there were bad people who, because we were Jewish, did not like us, and that they might, only 'might' hurt us.

I cannot remember how I took this in at all. Possibly at that age, it did not exactly register why, because we were what we were, people should want to harm us.

So at the station in Aberdeen—I can see it most clearly—there was a gentleman very smartly dressed. He knew exactly who we were. His name was Mr Roth. He had a lovely open motorcar and would have whisked us away without further delay, except for my backward glance at the old steam engine. I could have stayed there for as long as I would have been allowed, just looking at this fantastic, beautiful machine.

But we had to go on our way. I cannot remember exactly the distance or recollect the time factor. I know that within a short time, we were out of the city and into the countryside. There was a beautiful river most of the way, and finally we arrived at Heathcote House in Blairs, Aberdeenshire. This was an absolutely magnificent mansion. In its vast grounds was a huge garden in the front with woods and a farm—a large walled garden. It transpired, as my father finally told me—yes, one might ask how can I at that age remember these details now at seventy years of age but I assure you I can, most vividly—that he was going to work as a helper at the farm and the large walled garden, and that my mother was going to help in the kitchen.

I assumed, wrongly as it was going to turn out, that I would be going to the local school. How was I going to get on there, as I could not speak English? It all seemed very daunting and I was somewhat apprehensive. However, Mr Roth told me that many years before we arrived here, he too had to learn English, and it was rather easy. I found this to be of some comfort.

Next day—at what time of day, I cannot be sure of—a car arrived with two young boys, both of whom were older than I. The younger was about twelve and his brother about sixteen, I believe. The gentleman driving the car was, from my first impression, a very softly spoken man. Indeed he was a Christian minister of the Church of Scotland—to whom I and my family will forever be grateful—that is, to him, his family and the Church of Scotland.

My father and mother and Mr and Mrs Roth were all at the front of the house. My mother, I could see, was crying. She could not speak. My father however, took my hand and explained that this very kind gentleman, the Reverend Hadrian Stevens was going to take me to live with him and his mother and these two boys—also refugees— only for a very short time, as there was no school near Blairs, and it would have been very difficult for me to have to be taken to the nearest school, which was a long, long way away. It was indeed in Aberdeen. Where it was, I don't know, but Mr Stevens assured me that it would be great with the other boys and his mother, for whom I also have a special place in my heart, this dear elderly and blind lady. This moment too became a milestone in my life.

Of course, the fact that once more I was going off in a car seemed a great adventure at the time, and I recollect— yes I do, in every detail—the friendliness of these two boys. They were the sons of a Christian mother and a Jewish father, or perhaps it was the other way round, but of a mixed marriage. Mr Stevens, who spoke fluent German, asked me lots of questions, the type of questions that a 7½-year-old could answer. I realised somehow that here was a father-like man; I felt comfortable. I simply had no fear, nor did I have any apprehension, strange to say. Looking back, I am surprised at how much of what was going on at that time that I did understand. Perhaps it was the tension of the times that made my memories so vivid all these years later.

The journey did not take very long in this, another open car, but it did have a cover in case the weather got bad. The other boys chatted to me in German and tried to explain to me that when I met Mr Stevens' mother, I should say, "Good afternoon." Now try and say it slowly. We also could not speak English at the time when we first arrived here, but we were now getting on really well. I think that as we arrived at the house in Devana Gardens, Aberdeen, I could just about make, "Good afternoon." The 'good' bit was easy, as it was actually near the German.

There was a maid at the house called Betty, and later on as the days went by, I met her family; terrific people. They loved me, indeed they did. I felt so proud; I felt I was one of them.

I was taken downstairs in this big, lovely house, where the elderly lady mother of Mr Stevens lived in her own flat. Of course she was, as previously explained, blind. Mr Stevens said to his mother, "Well my dear, here is Walter Kress as I told you earlier. He is going to stay with us for just a little while." I can still picture that day as if I am there all over again.

This dear lady was sitting in a comfortable chair; she had a small table within her reach, upon which was a little brass bell with which she could call if she required anything. Also on the table was a cup of tea, some biscuits on a plate and a box of tissues. Here once more I felt that this was one big step in a great adventure.

"Come to me, Walter dearie," I can hear that dear lady's words to this day. "Come and sit here on my footstool." On which she rested her feet. So I sat down gently, without any fear or apprehension, on this footstool. I assumed that the lady was indeed very, very elderly. "Well Walter, Hadrian or the boys told you that I cannot see, but give me one of your hands. I would like to hold it." I remember that there was no hesitation on my part; I was in good care.

My parents had on many occasions instilled in me, although I already at that age felt that I had a mind of my own, that I must at all times show understanding, kindness and patience to people with any problems whatsoever; that I must not be rude or laugh at people who could not walk or talk properly, or blind people or people who act in strange ways, because if I did, then God would punish me terribly. This has stuck with me ever since.

So having hold of my hand, was it the left or was it the right? I cannot remember. I was sitting on the lady's left-hand side, so she put her hand, which I assume was her left one, on my head. She felt my face ever so gently, my shoulder and back, as she could not reach further. "My goodness," she said, "you are a wee fella, so you are. I think you're a bonnie boy. Now away upstairs and have a bath and something to eat. You must be a bit hungry by now, I'm thinking."

Betty the maid took me upstairs to the room I was to share with the younger of the other two boys. The elder had a small room of his own. "Now Walter," Betty said to me, "here is a towel. All your change of clothes is in the bathroom. I have filled the bath for you, but make sure yourself, will you, before you get in that it's not too hot or even cold, won't you?" I felt that Betty and I were going to get on really well. She had a younger sister, which as I stated before, I was eventually going to meet.

Before I go on I will relate another episode which happened while were still in Austria, when I was about the age of six. I believe it was when my sister and I went for a holiday in a castle near Vienna. It was for children up to the age of fifteen. In those days, when the Social Democrats were in government, the worker had good medical cover and the children, as mentioned, were sent on holidays, completely free. Yes, that's a real caring government for you.

We were taken for trips here and there, and so many things to do. The older kids were taken for a ride on ponies through the woods and the others would walk behind them. It was on one of these walks that I heard—and those words still haunt me today—two of the older boys on ponies say, "This is an ideal place where we'll bury them stinking Jews." I never told a soul, but it gave me—even at that age—a lot of food for thought.

People have said to me from time to time, "Haven't you any desire to go to Vienna after all these years?" If it is a female who has asked me, I restrain myself and say that I have not the slightest intention to go there, none whatsoever. However, if it is a fella out of earshot of a woman, I tell him in words what I cannot put on paper. It always makes me feel better.

After I had my quick bath and changed my clothes, I went downstairs, taking it all in. The rooms were big, or so they seemed to a tiny scrap of a boy like me. Nice furniture, old and heavy with ornate gilding and carvings. I had never seen anything like this in Vienna. Betty called up to me, "Walter, are you coming down? It's nearly teatime." It was about to be my first meal at that house.

I had just got downstairs when the front door opened and in came two rather big, but nicely dressed young men. "Hello, you must be the new boy," one of them said. The only bit of that I could understand was 'new', as it sounded like 'new' in German.

Betty said slowly to me, pointing to the two gentlemen, "Students, university, doctors." Of course I grasped what she was saying, for it was words that could have been German. I held out my right hand to them and they grasped it. Here were more friends. These two young men were lodging there while they were studying, and I spent many a minute with them, sitting in their study. They always seemed to be reading or writing, one whose name I simply cannot remember, strange to say, and the other one whose name was Bill Stuart or Stewart became a doctor in Aberdeen. In later years, many, many years on, I would come across regularly and see him, and he would always speak to me. The other gentleman went elsewhere after he too qualified as a doctor. I cannot remember exactly how many weeks, or months for that matter, I was with these lovely people. My parents came regularly and I went to Blairs about every two weeks on a Sunday.

The war was now on, however, and I remember distinctly having got off the bus on the lower Deeside road just by Blairs' little police station. I was walking up to Heathcote House with a lady and gentleman who had also got off the bus, and were going to that house also, I think, and I never got the facts, but there was what was then, to me at the time, a most horrendous explosion. The ground shook and my father came running down the lane to meet me. We never did find out what it was. I felt sure a plane full of bombs had crashed, and very close by at that.

Of course, I have forgotten to mention that a short distance away was Ferryhill School. I had for many a day— apart from being in a class with children of my age—English lessons with a teacher on my own. I had a little German-

English translation book and of course mixing with the other children, I soon picked up the language.

I was treated with the utmost kindness. I went also with the other children to assembly, where prayers were said. I did not feel any qualms, or even fears of any kind to be taking part in a Christian society. It was for me the start of becoming accepted, with a true feeling of belonging, and it did not take me long to feel that I was indeed a Scot. I pride myself on that, not only as I grew up and felt more and more a part of this race, but possibly because, like Jews from way back who have been persecuted through the ages by various oppressors as had the Scots been oppressed, mainly at the hands of the English. Yes, I know my history; I truly feel for my *ainfowk*. So it was no surprise that the Scots have this compassion for helping others who are oppressed. This was pointed out to me on various occasions. At school, I even came second in religion studies, got a certificate and was I proud at the time. My parents were also delighted. Of course, we did not give up our Jewish identity, but only told people the facts if asked.

My days at Reverend Stevens' home were very pleasant. I would sit on a little stool by the side of the dear mother of Mr Stevens and we would chatter about Vienna, my English progression, what friends I had made, was I happy with them, and so forth.

I soon made many, many friends from children of my own age upwards to adults. I was made most welcome everywhere. These people from all walks of life were my real friends.

I remember very distinctly, just up the road in a large beautiful house, there lived a lady and gentleman—I would say into their fifties. I cannot remember if they had children or perhaps they were grown up and living elsewhere. Their name was Macmillan. I always remember he wore his hair very smart and had a big hunter cap.  There were also two maids, with whom I became friendly, and they lived in a cottage not far away, near the railway line.  They too took me under their wing, and I often played with their children. It was just great; I simply thrived on it.  I think I amazed people by just how quickly I got the hang of the language, and did not find it difficult at all, especially as I had this little English translation book.

Time marches on, as it does, and now comes another milestone in my life.  The Reverend Stevens was going to move to another post some distance outside of Aberdeen, and unfortunately, us three boys were going to be placed with another family, but not the three of us with the same family.

# CHAPTER 2

There happened to be in Aberdeen a Jewish gentleman by the name of Bromberg, who owned the new cinema and the adjoining ballroom in Diamond Street. His secretary was a charming and mother-like figure—as far as I was concerned—dark, Jewish looking, but not Jewish I must point out. Her name was Ella Watt; this dear, dear lady is yet another true Christian in every meaning of the word, and in fact, another mother to me.

It turned out that Mr Bromberg, who had constant updates on my position, thought that Ella Watt's grandmother might be just the person to have me, although this elderly lady had two sons and a daughter; her daughter—to clarify the situation—was Mrs Watt, the mother of Ella Watt, this elderly lady, whose name was Andrews, was a widow. One of her sons, Clarence, was married. Her eldest son, James Andrews was away for weeks at a time as the skipper of a trawler. At the most, he would be home for about three days, and be off again to sea. We worried a lot about 'Uncle Jim', as the country of course was at war.

So the day came, I was eight or nine years of age, or fast coming up to that age, at this time I cannot remember clearly.

Everything was explained in detail to me, and of course I had met Ella Watt and Grandma Andrews, as she became affectionately known to me. Grandma Andrews lived near Devana Gardens, in Deemount Gardens, right across from where those lovely big railway engines were kept and looked after in their large engine houses. It really was a very big adventure to me.

Once again, I quickly took to dear Grandma Andrews; she was so kind. I was simply treated once more as family—her grandchild. The Family—the brothers of

Ella Watt and her sisters—was a big family indeed. In order of age (these may vary slightly I'm afraid), the eldest was Clarence (Clarry) Watt, a soldier; Harry Watt, I think he had some important work although not a serviceman; another brother whose name eludes me, he was a soldier as well; then there was Junior Watt, about four or five years older than myself. Great pals we became; he had some fantastic toys too!

The ladies of the Watt family were as follows: the aforementioned Grandma Andrews—unfortunately no longer with us—and Ella Watt, whose wedding I attended while still living at Grandma Andrews. Ella married the famous Scottish golfer Peter MacQueen. I wish I still had the beautiful putter made to his order with his name on the metal striking plate. Then there was Esther Watt and Dora Watt. I think Dora is still with us. Then there was Audrey Watt, who would be about seventy-six or so now. I loved her and she did likewise me, sweets, chocolates, money, hugs and cuddles; she was one of the 'toffs'. I missed Audrey last time I was recently in Aberdeen one mid-summer, as she was away somewhere.

These people and others, as they come into my life became so important to me, and my parents were without a doubt grateful for sure, they were more than grateful, but there is no other way that I can explain it.

Reminiscing like this has just reminded me that Grandma Andrews had a small dog, not sure what type; Rosie was her name. We became great friends. Also, the Watt family who lived in the same Deemount Gardens, four houses away had a Labrador dog called Jackie. He would be standing on the wide wall at the bottom of their front garden when we came home from school, wagging his tail, and would come down off the wall and play with us. It was great; things simply could not get any better.

Of course, I must mention the dreadful times, when the German bombers came and bombed various targets, but before I proceed, my memory has just clicked into an episode that took place while I was still living at Reverend Stevens' house, and must be recorded here while it is still so vivid.

The war had not long started, and late one morning I was in the house. It was, I think, a Saturday or maybe a school holiday, of that I am not sure. However, the sirens sounded and we all went down into the massive cellar. We boys were put into a large shelter-like steel-framed thing with a heavy steel top on it. It looked as if it was designed to stand the house collapsing around it. I think it was about ten feet long, four feet in width, and about five feet in height. So we had to lie down or crouch in it, and we felt quite secure, but of course, we did not know that directly above us, some spitfires—at a terrific height—were about to shoot down one of the first German bombers of the war.

After the all-clear sounded, we emerged and saw many, many of our neighbours in the street, picking things up, lots and lots of spent machine gun brass bullet shells from the spitfires. A huge cloud of black smoke was rising from a place near the Old Bridge of Dee, which I estimated was about a mile and a half away.

People were ecstatic, running up the road in the direction of the smoke, shouting, "They got him! He's down; he's crashed! We got him!" People got out their cars, motorbikes and bicycles and headed in the direction of the smoke and fire.

I cannot remember if I asked permission or not, I feel I did, and with kids, boys and girls of all ages, we ran in the direction of the crash. I cannot remember how long it took to get there. I do however remember most vividly police, fire brigade and army vehicles of all types arriving on the scene, and people, masses of people coming from all directions. The euphoria was ecstatic in the air about us.

We all gathered there, as near as we were allowed. I would estimate, thinking back all these years, we were about six-hundred yards from the crash scene. What had transpired, we were told by people in the nearby houses, was that the plane, now burning fiercely, had come over their houses literally feet above the roofs and took the top off a large tree. It appeared that the pilot had hoped it would crash land in a nearby field, but it clipped the corner of the new ice rink building which was there, and they were all killed. The wreckage was totally one mass of indescribable smoke and fire. Of course, none of us realised or even knew that the crew were dead, and I shouted to an army officer (cheeky little me!) that I could speak German. I did not half get some weird looks.

Then as luck would have it, I spotted Mr Bromberg evidently filming the scene. I called out to him and eventually he came over to where we were all being held back. I think he took me back home, but I am not too sure of that. But as I said, we were all very proud that day. I felt not the slightest hint of remorse or sorry for those Germans. I knew what war was, and also what we had had to endure at their hands in Vienna.

I did get a few spent bullets from a friend a few days later, and—being a boy—I think I swapped them for a dinky toy car.

Another vivid scenario comes to mind and looking back now I can see the funny side. Like all kids we just loved the Marx Brothers films. In one of those films, one of the brothers is in the army. He receives a letter from the Pentagon, and when he opens it, he exclaims, "Oi Gevalt, I'm a Major". Of course I understand Yiddish, so I laughed uncontrollably. Kids and adults looked at me and I cringed *floor please open up*. The fact is that I was the only person to understand this, as I was the only Jewish boy there. I left before the end.

So now having recorded these events in relation to the downing of the bomber, I will proceed with my stay at dear Grandma Andrews'. There came what at the time to me was a terrible shock, which took me some time to come to terms with, as my mother or those close to me did not or could not explain to me. They possibly felt that I could not grasp the situation and what had happened, as many moons later, when I got the facts, it was this.

Some very bright person in London in the government decided that all refugees, Jews, Christians, the lot, should be interred on the Isle of Man for the duration of the war, as a precaution against spies, fifth columnists and what have you. My father, a persecuted Jew who had been to hell in Dachau, was now a suspected spy. But this was war, and that was that. My mother was shattered, and now that I could grasp a good understanding of the language, which my mother did not seem to be able to do, we went regularly to a lawyer by the name of Downie Campbell, just off Bon Accord Street behind Jackson's Garage, where I would often stand outside and look in—I already then had the idea of becoming a motor mechanic. I could see clearly the hoists, the equipment and the men working. At times I even went just inside the entrance and stood on the left close to the wall. Nobody seemed to mind. There didn't seem to be too many cars coming in or out. Occasionally when a car was either slowly coming in or going out, I would move out of the way, then, move in just a foot or so into the entrance, which was very wide. The staff seemed not to mind; no one tried to tell me to go away.

I was as enthralled, as I was when I went to Mr Bromberg's new cinema in Diamond Street, directly opposite of which was another, smaller garage. The lift for lifting the cars up was just inside, clearly in full view, and I just loved standing there, watching the proceedings. Never, ever, was I told to go away, sometimes I would even get a smile from the engineers.

Grandma Andrews, Clarry, Uncle Jim and such great times. I cannot truly find the appropriate words to describe the true love and friendship, the various trips, presents unending that I received from the Watt family, the Bromberg family and not to forget to mention the few Scottish-born Jews in Aberdeen. In fact, there were so few that to conduct the usual Friday service, it required a 'minyum', possibly where the word minimum was derived from.

We required ten males, who had to be over thirteen years of age, as juniors such as I did not count until the age of thirteen and have had their Bar Mitzvah—the entrance to Jewish manhood. In fact, the secretary of our tiny little synagogue would go up to Union Street and try to find Jewish servicemen.

In making up the required minimum, minyum, of at least ten, sometimes we had success and got a few. But of course, these servicemen from Australia, Canada, France, South Africa and all the other overrun countries of Europe and other parts of the world were more interested in having a good time, rather than going to a proper meeting, although we gave them tea or coffee and cakes, etc.

So time, and time waits for no man, was passing and so I will continue. I must now relate further points as they come to mind; of course, these do not readily come in the order that they occurred but in the order that my mind has stored them.

Dear Uncle Clarence (Clarry) Andrews had a small fish processing business where he would buy the fish at the fish market where the fishing boats would land their catches, and a van or lorry would deliver them to his place of business, where ladies would fillet and ice the fish for despatch all over the place. I would often go there and watch.

Of course, I must mention that the wife of Clarry, Jean Andrews, treated me with the same care and love as she did with her own three children, Doreen, Jimmy and Claire. Of course, I lived with Grandma, but many times I was invited up to their flat. I played with the other children. To me, I can honestly say, and those who knew Jean Andrews can testify, that although she was to me Auntie Jean, she was more like another real mother to me. Dear Jean is still alive, and she resides in a lovely elderly people's residence in Kings Gate, Aberdeen.

When I was in Aberdeen in the summer (2000), Doreen told me that when I go to see her mother, I should not be surprised if she takes time to recognise me, or even if she does so at all. So I went to see Jean. I introduced myself as usual at the office and I was told that Jean was in the lounge, possibly having a little snooze. Well, I sat myself down on a chair just a few feet from her; one of the staff ever so gently woke Jean up. She immediately recognised me, "Oh Walter, hello," she said to the lady of the staff, "This is Walter."

I felt ten feet tall. Of course, I am not what one would call a restrained sort of individual. I have for people, as many times aforementioned, such as dear Auntie, more mother-like Jean Andrews, a love that time will never dilute. I will never forget, her love and kindness all those years ago, I gave her a big hug and kiss. The other residents watched. Of course, many of them already knew of the circumstances of our relationship.

When I later went round to see Doreen and Mike, her husband, and told them how her mother had reacted on waking and seeing me, they were delighted.

Of course, I am now going back from the time that I was still at Grandma Andrews' One day I had an incredible surprise, my father at last was back. I had written to him many times, as he did to me so we had kept in contact but I never expected anything like that to happen. He arrived completely by surprise with my mother at Deemount Gardens. Grandma had of course seen many photos of my parents and had usually seen my mother at least once a week when she came to see me.

So it was not long before my father asked the Roths at Blairs House if it was possible for him and my mother and I once again to become a family. My older sister was in London, in service with a Jewish family as a nanny, and was content there. I cannot remember exactly how much longer it was before we got the upstairs flat at a Jewish family house in Constitution Street, near the Sea Front and we were a real family again.

The war was still on, of course, and the bombers came and as we were close to the harbour, and also to the anti-aircraft guns, we got perhaps more than our fair share. Those days were sometimes very frightening to say the least. I recall one evening as we were going into the shelter, the guns going off, this bomber coming in very low, bullets going rat-a-tat all the time, bombs going off with the most deafening roar, and everything shook. We thought the world would end right then. And after the air-raid, people emerged from the shelters as if they were stepping from a bus.

Whilst my father was interred, I had led quite a reasonable sort of free life, not restricted in any way. But of course I knew right from wrong. I was to all intents polite, and I was not what one would describe as a tearaway. I felt that being with people who loved me and looked after me, I tried to believe it, to be grateful and not cause any aggravation or problems. Of course I played and ran around with the other kids. We would as kids climb over the wall where some railway workers had small allotments by the railway line, but never ever going near the rails. We helped ourselves to gooseberries, rhubarb and many other forbidden delights. Uncle Clarry by the way was a special constable. He was well over six feet tall, and one day two policemen caught us kids red-handed, so to speak. We had to give names and addresses, the few of us kids, all boys, some older, some younger. There was Junior Watt, myself, I think a boy called White and the other one I'm quite not sure of, all from the same Deemount Gardens. They took us all to the various parents' houses to ensure all the details we had given them were correct. So when it came to my turn, I pleaded with them not to take me to Grandma's, as I would probably be sent away from her. Of course, they asked me as we went to Grandma's house, as I had given Grandma's name, Andrews, how was it that my name was Kress. So I explained briefly that we were from Vienna, my mother was at Blairs House working at the Roth's, and that my father was interred in the Isle of Man. I think they discussed the situation between themselves. They were not in any way threatening or gruff with us. I think it was the fact of being so close to the railway line that was their real concern. I am however unable to recall exactly what the outcome was, whether they took me to Grandma's to explain the situation or not. One thing I am very sure of is that these two policemen were special constables, and they must of course have known uncle Clarry. Wow, did I get a rocket from him! He told me if I ever did anything like that again, I would have to go and live with someone else. I was in tears, I was in a dilemma. It was not nice of me, he said, to cause Grandma such worry and aggravation. He thought, he said, that I was such a nice boy, and not to go near the railway line again. It had the desired result, I can assure you.

Back now living with my parents. As said earlier, while my father was interred, I roamed freely. However, my father did not like me being with these he called, "not so nice street boys," but I definitely was not going to have that sort of a ban. After all, they were not hooligans or rough. I feel that my father just wanted me to be a nice Yiddish boy.

I will not deny the fact that my father—not so much my mother—was definitely from what might be termed as the very old school of thought. Possibly also the fact that he came from a rather old-fashioned Polish religious family had something to do with his out-dated beliefs. But, as I have stated, me having stayed with various Christian people and also having been in a school where I was the only one not of the Christian religion made my circumstances different. I was definitely assimilating and developing my character and personality in relation to my adoptive surroundings. In short, there was a rift between my father and I. Friction between us grew virtually daily. I was now about eleven years old and I definitely had a mind of my own. I was not simply going to give up my friends and it was about this time that these friends of mine were going to what was then a small seawater swimming bath by the beach. My mother—who I must say was on my side most of the time—thought—as virtually every week kids were falling into the sea or the harbour and drowning—that it would be a good idea if I learned how to swim.

Anyway, unknown to my parents, I had often gone to a slipway in Footdee, or to the locals it was called 'Fittie', to fish for small fish. In later years, this area of Aberdeen was going to figure in my life in a very big way.

We lived, I think, in Constitution Street until I was about thirteen years of age, and of course there came more problems, due to the Jewish boys at the age of thirteen having to have the religious ceremony known as Bar Mitzvah. In plain English, it is simply where one reads with the Rabbi some Hebrew text containing oaths of allegiance, as at thirteen I became, according to Jewish law, a man.

I cannot tell you how alien this all felt to me at the time, for subconsciously I was without a doubt becoming a *wee Scottie*, and what the hell was wrong with that? I was not going to be the nice little Yiddish boy that my father wanted, who was as stated before, just an ordinary hardworking baker at Messrs Mitchell & Muil Bakery.

So it came to pass a few months after I was thirteen that I finally became a man, but I was still mixing with other kids. My mother virtually kept a neutral position, often just asking me to be good and not to annoy my father. But I feel that she knew the way I was thinking and that I had a strong mind of my own. She had a mother's intuition.

About this time, however, I do not want to go into too much detail, as the children family of the people where we had the upstairs flat are still alive, no doubt. But without putting too finer point on it, I believe my father fell out with their parents.

Time passed and once again, luck was with us, as one of the aforementioned Watt brothers and his wife and daughter were moving out of a two roomed flat in the Hardgate, so my parents were glad of the opportunity to have it. We met the charming lady owner of the property, I remember clearly, at her nice house in Abergeldie Terrace. We had tea there and all the paperwork was signed and sealed. The lady said that I was a very nice boy, so that at least was a good start from my point of view.

Well of course, the time goes on again and we got on with life in our new surroundings. I mixed with all, and of course—I might be possibly repeating myself—but I seemed to get on with young and old alike.

Of course I immediately made friends with all the local kids there, but I never lost touch with my old friends in Devana or Deemount, as it was not far from Hardgate, but it was of course a totally different area. It had nice houses, quite well-off business people and nice children. They were my friends.

Now there comes a very memorable incident that must be recorded here; it simply must, as I feel that this was yet another step in the direction that fate was taking me. Some things, as I have said before, simply cannot be forgotten. One nice summer, in the late afternoon, I think it was during the school holidays, and of course there comes a time in a young person's life when *wow-o-wow, that's a very nice girl, oh yes, very nice.*

The girl back then is still alive today, married with children and grandchildren. I met the lady and her family and her brothers and sisters again, about two years ago, as they still go to the same church as they were attending all those years ago. Before I go on with my story it will help you if I say that I have never been 'backward in coming forward' as the saying goes.

On one of my visits back to Aberdeen, I went to that same church, for I felt that in all probability the family would still be attending there, so before I explain the next phase of this episode, I want to say that I will not divulge names in order to save any potential embarrassment. This is because at a certain part later on in this story, something was said to me at the time by the girl's father that stunned me. Yes, it had me in tears; I was so in love with that lovely girl.

So I am now—two years ago—standing at the open door of this church, there is a service going on; I estimated that there were less than fifty people there. A gentleman at the very back of the small congregation came to the door and asked me if I wished to come in, so I said, "Many, many years ago, the family (I named them) came regularly to worship here."

"Oh yes indeed, they are here today." The gentleman replied.

I actually now, believe it or not, hesitated to come in. Of course, going into a church was nothing new to me; I've done it all over the world in place that I have been to abroad and seen some beautiful houses of worship of various religions, for as they say in Scotland, *We are all Jock Tamson's Bairns*. That translated means 'we are all God's children'. Indeed, we are.

So, feeling rather hot, this fellow led me in and quietly took me to two ladies. They immediately recognised me, these two sisters. "Walter, it's you! Walter," the girl of my dreams all those years ago whispers, "come and sit here between us."

I was speechless. We just looked at each other. The lady's husband was in the front row, as he had, just before I arrived, given a sermon. I did not say anything at all because the service was in progress, but I am sure that all three of us were on some kind of a wavelength, as looks can often say more than the spoken word.

At the conclusion of the service I was introduced to her husband. The lady explained that I was from Devana Gardens all those years ago. We went out of the church and her sister asked me if I had been back to Aberdeen before.

I said, "Oh yes, many times since I left to live in London in 1954."

"So why did you not come to see us before?"

To that I had no answer. I was then invited by the lady's husband to come to their home the next day. The sister as I found out had never married, but I do not feel that I should delve into that. It was fantastic to have met them again after all those years. I will no doubt, by the grace of God, see them again one day.

So now I come to the end of this tale, but I must tell the part of how the girl's father, at the time, stunned me. You see, as I said, there comes a time when a lad looks at a girl and vice versa. I used to walk home with her. I could not take my eyes off her. Maybe it was just first love and all that.

I had no hesitation of walking with her right up to the door of the nice big house she lived in. Her mother spoke to me and smiled, "Well I see you've brought her home again. That's nice of you Walter." Of course, her mother knew my name, as I had lived there with Hadrian Stevens.

A few days later, I was still hanging around with this charming girl. I truly felt that this was it. I really did think so. "Walter," she said to me very hesitantly. I remember to this day that I thought she was going to say that she loved me, the way that girl looked at me. "Come in, my father wants to see you."

I could not think straight. This was my heart I felt I was about to give to this beautiful young girl. Yes, now that I have a lot of time to reflect, it all seems to come back so easily, in such detail too.

We walked up the few steps to the door. The girl's mother opened the door, "Come in, Walter, Mr [name withheld] wants to have a word with you."

"Hello, Walter, come in here. Sit yourself down. I just want to speak to you about my girlie." Her mother had taken her into the kitchen and closed the door.

"Well Walter, we have known you for a while. You're a nice lad, you are, and we see that you seem to spend a lot of time with our daughter. Well Walter, you're only a young lad, but it looks to me and my wife that you and my lassie seem to be together quite a bit. Well Walter, you see, it's like this. You no doubt know we are very religious Christians, and you are Jewish. Now Walter, you have to understand this. It's early days yet but we cannot let this friendship develop further. It does hurt us to say this, but that's how things are. We have spoken to our girl and she does really like you, but she has to understand the situation. Walter lad, you must know we like you but that is it."

So I got up and not with any malice, anger or feelings of sadness, or for that matter, the knowledge that that was that. The situation suddenly took on an air of surrealism. I don't think it was really me there that blurted out without hesitation, by some sort of inner power, possibly sheer desperation. "Jesus was a Jew."

Of course, I regretted saying that immediately. I felt that I should not have said it. But what else could a boy in love do? I left and yes, I cried, my heart was shattered.

Often as the days once more went on, I did see that girl, but of course we both knew the score, so to speak, even at our tender age.

I really do think when I look back, that I am sure that she was my first true love, but of course at that tender age, I suppose she was. But it did somehow affect me. Perhaps it was possibly a giant step in growing up. I must say that later in life, as I put on the years, I thought that as some sort of consolation, I suppose my father—not so much my mother—would have done the same as her father. The problems of religion, what can I say?

The mind again goes back to around the time of the end of this first saga. I have said that I often went and saw and played with kids that I had got to know over the years. So one summer, evening, I was off once again to the old haunts, but alas, it was I believe that the next day was a Jewish festival, so I was to be home by seven in the evening at the latest. And to give substance, so to speak, to the next developments, I have to admit that I already felt that if I were older, I would leave home. I simply could not accept my father's constant advice and restrictions, and we drifted further and further apart. We had some scenes, we certainly did, and as I went out that fateful late afternoon, I shouted out that I was never coming home, and took off to the old haunts.

One of my friends, who was a bit older than me—no names again, because of the present-day family—said when I told him that I was not going home again ever, that he would hide me in their shed.

I never gave a thought regarding tomorrow and so forth. It did occur to me that my mother would be extremely worried about me, and I would no doubt get a good beating from my father. So it must have been that the time was getting on, when my friend and some other kids were playing with glass marbles, that the oldest boy said in a hushed voice, "Here's your father coming." What the devil possessed me, I do not know to this day. Was it again some inner force? Was my mind now developing to take in a situation very rapidly and act on it? I took off. My father, I must state, was still quite a bit away from us kids, so I ran faster than I had ever done before, towards Devana. I did not look back. As I was running my mind was a complete blank. I just wanted to get away from my father; that was all I wanted to do and I would have run until my lungs burst if I had to. I came to a bend in the road, and with a quick backward glance, saw that my father was not there. Without hesitation, I ran into the front garden of one of the big houses there, and quickly ran round the back and down the stairs under the house to hide in the coal cellar. It was dark in there, and by now I was breathless and shaking with fear. I was also utterly exhausted and perhaps sobbing a bit.

After hardly getting down there, a young girl of about twelve or so, carrying a bucket for the coal, came walking down the steps. Of course, she heard and saw me. She dropped the bucket, screamed and ran back up the steps. My first thought was to get out of here immediately, but before I even moved, down comes her big brother and her mother, "Are you being chased by a man out here? He doesn't speak good English. He says he is your father, or is it a bad man after you? Now come on up and let's see the man." My father said that I was a bad boy, not a nice boy.

I assured the family that it was indeed my father, and we had problems. But this was not the end of the episode, oh no, but I will return to it later. Suffice to say for now that it is strange how fate and circumstances can come and play a part in one's life.

On once again to a time when I was older, I am now fourteen years of age. At that time and at that age, one would leave school, but could if one wanted try an exam to get into a college where the leaving age was sixteen, and where—if one was good enough—one could possibly go to university. This is all relevant to the events of above, as the next lines will explain.

The entrance exam to the grammar school I passed as a fee-paying pupil. I was older now, at fourteen and a bit wiser hopefully and the next two years of my life in education had been assured. My father and I seemed to drift further and further apart. I admit we nearly, very nearly came to blows, but as always, my mother was there to smooth things over. I am not ashamed to tell the truth.

I am now approaching sixteen years of age, and had just a few weeks to go before leaving grammar school. I must admit that those two years there had taught me a lot. I made a lot of friends, but I was not interested in going on to university. I wanted to be a Marine Engineer, so when I qualified I could go and see the world over.

Come the day therefore when during the art lesson, the gentleman teacher told us that shortly there would be a new art teacher coming to the class to take over, as he was retiring soon; all very relevant indeed.

There was a knock on the door of the classroom, and the teacher opened the door. This young lady came into the class (have you guessed?). Well, when our eyes met, for a moment I felt absolute terror, I was mortified. It was the young girl with the bucket of coal whom I had scared half to death in the coal cellar. Oh yes. The art teacher did mention her name, but I cannot actually remember it. She obviously recognised me. I could not look directly at her. I was in a dreadful state. The retiring teacher gave her a list of our names, and said he would leave us with the new teacher, but would see us all the next day to bid us farewell at assembly. The new lady teacher asked us to put our hands up when she called out our names to familiarise herself, so it came to my turn and I held up my hand, trying hard not to look directly at her. She of course must have realised how I felt. We both knew the score so it must have been equally painful for her.

When the bell rang for us to go to the next class for something other to study and be taught, I hung back, with the intention of asking the lady not to mention it to anyone. However, as we trooped out of the class, I hung back, made sure I was the last one, and before I could say anything, the lady smiled at me, put one hand on my shoulder and in a whisper, said, "We won't tell anyone, will we?"

Was I relieved! *What if she was going to tell the Rector or other teachers?'* I had initially thought, but all's well that ends well.

What a coincidence. I wonder if the lady is still with us. I think I will try and find out one day.

Yet again, things keep coming back to me. I forgot to mention that while I was still living with Grandma Andrews that my father, with the permission of the Roth's at Blairs House got a job at Mitchell and Mills Bakery. This unfortunately, was just before he was interred.

This job at the bakery meant of course an early start in the morning, and I think, although I am not too sure of the facts, that refugees were under some form of restriction as to their movements during the night, a kind of curfew, so he got lodgings in a guesthouse owned by a charming lady by the name of Macdonald, and assisted by her daughter,

Flora. There were many officers living there. High-ranking people they were. I used to go there of course to see my father, and would help to translate some of the words that my father could not understand when he was in conversation with these officers. They were also very kind to me, that I remember very well.

So I now, as it comes to mind, I must mention that Mr Bromberg gave me complimentary tickets for his new cinema. And I never ever forgot the kindness of chocolates and sweets and above all the love showered on me by Mr Bromberg. Besides him and people like Ella Watt—my mother thought the world of her, as she did all of these great, caring people that I had around me—I will never ever forget them.

So the maths teacher—to whom I am eternally grateful—(an understatement) got me a job in a small garage, but it was, to put it mildly, a dreadful place. Of course, I did realise, and especially in those days, that as a total beginner, I had to do some really awful jobs, and to top it all, I was not very big. Some of the older men, there was a mechanic and the foreman, could not believe that I was sixteen. They thought I was the usual fourteen-year-old school-leaver. There was also another apprentice of my age, but he had left school at fourteen.

Of course, they all knew that I was a product of the grammar school, and I must point out that in those days, all those years ago, the majority of the boys came from the elite of the town and myself with very few others from working class families attended or even got in, with the rare exception that one got a bursary. That is everything including the uniform paid for, but only if you passed the entrance exam with outstanding results. So there was a lot of spite and the usual snide comments about school for snobs and rich people. Well, I decided that enough, after only a short period, was enough.

Now approaching seventeen, I told my parents the situation. My father said that he would go and have a word with the owner. I impressed on him that no way did I wish him to do so. I had had enough at that place anyway. I wanted originally to be a Marine Engineer, but the maths teacher could not get me into one of those shipyards, as there were too many boys trying to become Marine Engineers, and I was not the 'crème de la crème.'

I therefore went to Jackson's Garage, where—as aforementioned—I had stood and watched many years ago. They were very nice people, and that garage was indeed something special and very modern. I did not hesitate to give them the truth as to why I had left the other garage. Unfortunately—although they did not directly say so—It appeared to me that it was only family of the owners or relations or close friends that seemed to get work there. I would have really liked to work there. It had that air of something about it. But nepotism ruled as it did in so many trades back then and there was simply no way in.

Next, I just went up the road to a place called Justice Mill Lane, where there was yet another very modern garage. The upstairs department was for cars, while the lower and rear part—which must have been the original older building—was for vans, wagons and coaches. The front of the building was used for people to park cars twenty-four hours a day.

I went to the front office, wearing my former grammar school jacket. Well, I felt that might just be a slight step to get on there. Another point which I felt might be in my favour was that a Jewish man that we knew (Ben Collins) kept a Hudson—a big American car there, and a Wolseley as well—as he was in big business and very wealthy indeed. So I thought why not mention this if and when I eventually get a time and date to come for an interview with the Managing Director. Wearing my jacket again two days later, one of the secretaries took me into his office.

"So why do you want to have a job here with us? I see you have already worked in a garage and that you felt that it did not suit you," he began. So of course I gave him all the facts, how they were treating me because of the grammar school and that my family knew Ben Collins, as we were of the Jewish faith. I did not hide the fact, nor did I hide the fact that we were refugees from Vienna, escaping from Hitler.

He was definitely impressed. "Well, you know young man," I remember he said, "I think we can fit you in. You seem keen, but you must also be aware that all lads start at the bottom, and some of the work is not very pleasant. So wait a few minutes." He then phoned the workshop for cars and a Mr Robson—who was the Senior Works Manager—came to the office where I was being interviewed.

The director said, "What do you think of this lad, George? He has worked at another garage for a few months, but has had, due to his years at the grammar, a problem of chastisement and bullying. He is very keen to be employed with us. What do you think? And by the way, he tells me that his family are friends of Ben Collins."

I am sure that, as the saying goes, it is not what you know, it's who you know, a kind of indirect nepotism.

Mr Robson said, "All right, you can start on Monday for a month's trial period. Now tell me, what wages were you getting there? Seventeen shillings a week, oh all right, we will pay you that, but remember; it's only a month's trial. By the way lad, are you attending evening classes?"

"Yes," I replied, "making good progress as well."

Mr Robson replied that very soon at this garage they were going to organise that the apprentices went once a week to the Technical College all day, but you must be ready to study hard.

So that was that. I could not wait for Monday. I re-read and studied all the work that I had done at every class. I also went to the library and looked at some books on motor vehicles. While at the library, I spoke to a young man who I assumed was around twenty years old. He was training to be a motor mechanic.

But he also, as we exchanged views on our work and where he worked and where I worked, told me something very interesting. It was that he wanted to be a Marine Engineer, but found that unless his father or uncle or other near relative worked in one of those shipyards, especially the engine shed, there was no hope of getting a job there. But as a motor mechanic apprentice, which at the time the apprenticeship lasted five years, on qualifying, you can get a diesel ships engineers conversion course in a Technical College.

I thought at the time that it was lucky that I met this lad. I may yet be a marine engineer after all. Now to use a phrase I have used before, as things come to me, this springs to mind, and I feel quite sure that my friend of yesteryear, who I must find if at all possible one day to meet up with, would not mind at all if I mention his name.

It was during the period of 1944 to 1946, while at the grammar school, that I met a lad who lived close by, who was also a pupil. His name was Ian Grozier, and we hit it off together. He was a likeminded sort of a fellow; no evil or anything of that nature. In fact, as far as I could judge, he had more up top than I had, and probably got a very good position when the time came.

Ian's aunt had a very small weekend cottage very near to Aberdeen, at a place called Cove Bay. It was a tiny, rock-strewn harbour with a breakwater that had many years before been destroyed in a severe winter gale. The seasonal boat that was kept afloat there was the Salmon Cobble. The other few little pleasure-fishing boats were pulled out on rollers just above the high watermark. Then there were these massive cliffs, where seagulls abounded in thousands. This led to terrible tragedies of children going for seagull's eggs high on the cliffs and falling, usually to their deaths.

Just by this little harbour, if one looked up, there was a slope, not exactly a cliff, but a steep, grassy slope. So, us boys being boys, bearing in mind that this was rather dangerous, we climbed up this slope, stopping occasionally to take in the view, which was really something. So onwards and upwards, it was as I said, not a cliff, not that steep, but steep enough for the inexperienced climber. Well, when Ian and I were nearly at the top, where it was fairly windy, we decided to go back down. Oh, but this was a different situation altogether, and we simply could not work out how we had climbed up there so relatively easily, yet found it nigh impossible to get back down.

We did not panic nor call for help, firstly because we felt that at this point we were all right. It was a long way off until evening. But there was not a soul below. There was a shut-up coastguard lookout, a small building not in use and not in our view. Even if there had been anyone there, they would not have seen us anyway.

We sat there discussing the situation, and of course we both realised that there would be hell to pay from his aunt and parents as well as mine. So Ian decided that he would go for the top, which upon reflection all those years ago, was roughly about thirty or so feet above us, possibly a bit more. He got nearly to the top and called out to me where I was still sitting on this slope that he felt the last bit was too steep and what was now looking serious, he felt that he could not get back down. So in desperation we decided to shout for help. It was no use whatsoever. *Should I try and get down*, I thought, *No, if I don't make it, Ian will probably fall*. We were in a real mess. Ian and I did not panic; that would have been fatal. I looked around and on the other side to where Ian was now apparently stuck, I decided to try and attempt what looked a slightly longer, but less steep route to the top. Well, I can honestly say that I have had some truly unbelievable lucky events—more to come in my story—but this was one of them. I very slowly—after calling out to Ian not to move—started picking my way up this other route and it looked better. However, I got within I would say about five or six feet from the top, and I could now clearly see the old coastguard lookout, but of course not a soul in it. I shouted, "Anyone up here? We're stuck!" Not a soul, nor had anyone appeared below who might have seen or heard us.

Now the very last bit was steeper. It was not vertical nor was it overhanging in any way, but it was, to say the least, very steep. So, very gingerly, ever so slowly, I felt and pulled the long grass. It held. I then sort of one at a time slowly moved my feet up, inch by inch, all the time calling out to Ian, "I'm all right, don't move. I'm nearly up." Well, of course in this situation it seems like an eternity, but I had no option. I think I knew that if I stopped, that I possibly would not altogether fall to the harbour, but would do myself some injury, and then we would with the approach of evening and night, be in a dreadful predicament.

So I finally—by Gods grace—made it to the grass on top. I yelled to Ian, "I'm up, don't move. I'm coming along on top to where you are stuck." I lay up there a few seconds, then. I got up, standing well back from the edge, as it was earth and grass and may be loose and break off. I ran along to where I thought Ian might be, calling out to reassure him all the time, looking round to see if there was anyone there. No one, not a single soul; it took only seconds to get to where Ian was stuck. I lay down and inched my way forward, digging my feet in, holding onto the grass until I got to the edge and looked over. There he was, holding on. "Ian, don't move. Are you able to hold on?"

"Yes, I'm all right, I can hold on," Ian replied.

"Be back in a few minutes." I ran off to where there were some cottages; still no one around. I thought, *Well, if I get someone, they will get the coastguard or fire brigade or police.* That was not an option that I relished. I grew hot and for a split second felt awful. Then suddenly the answer was there. As Ian was only about seven or eight feet down, I got hold of a clothesline and started to get it off the poles that it was fixed on. It was simply wound round. *Thank goodness,* I thought, *there are no knots in it.* And I didn't care if someone should see and ask what I was doing. I would simply tell them the situation, that the clothesline was all I needed, not the emergency services with all that would lead to!

Very quickly I raced back. "I am here, hang on. I'm here. I've got a rope, don't move. I'm just making it into four, as I don't know how strong it is singly."

When I had this rope in four lines and knotted, I edged down once again and shouted to Ian, "It's coming down slowly. Whatever you do, don't grab it and pull. There's plenty of length, so just hold it in one hand. Don't let go where you're holding the grass. I've got to move back from the edge. When I've got myself sat down, heels dug in and braced myself, I'll tell you to wind the rope round your wrists. Don't let go the other hand until you can safely grasp the grass, as you come up. Don't worry if you slip, but don't let go of the rope, whatever happens."

So slowly but surely, he came up. "That was close," he said, "I'm not half glad that you managed this without getting the fire brigade or the police on to us!"

We sat there, not a soul anywhere to be seen. We counted ourselves very lucky. After a few minutes, I rolled up the rope, left it as it was. We trooped off to where I had taken it from, looked round to see if anyone was about, threw it down and we tore off, and thought about how the owners of the rope must have wondered how that rope got into the state that it was in.

When we got back to Ian's aunt's cottage, she was horrified, "What have you boys been up to?  Look at yourselves, your clothes! What's happened to you? Did you fall in the water?" She put her hands on Ian's clothes, "You didn't, did you? You are damp, but not wet." We explained that we had larked around in some long wet grass. "Anyway, get those clothes off and get washed.  Your teas have been waiting for you." That was that. I wonder if Ian ever told his aunt the truth. I never told my parents. What would have been the good of that?  My father without a doubt—and I daresay on that occasion, he would have been justified—would have taken the belt to me, so I didn't let on. What the head doesn't know, the heart can not grieve.

That cove was a terrible place.  In later life, as this life of mine unfolds, I came in a small boat in the summer with chaps that I got to know, as we sat in that beautiful little harbour, eating our sandwiches.  I looked up to that slope and told my friends what had happened not so many years before. They were in total disbelief, upon looking up at the top, that we made it.

Of course, I forgot to mention that I had been in the Scouts. I loved every minute of it, but somehow or another, I am now relating the time when I had left school and was an apprentice at the second garage.  I was always—when time allowed—able to have a go at fly fishing with a Greenheart trout rod and all the bits and pieces and big waders, so I could stand in the water in the River Dee. As usual, this led to more heartbreak with my mother, and my father would regularly come and see what I was up to. Somehow or another, at that time, girls did not come into my life. Maybe subconsciously I still felt for my first love. Also, I had seen too many boys and girls of my age get themselves into very serious trouble.  I even knew of a boy, who went to Ferryhill school with me before I went to the grammar school, who, it transpired, got the blame from a girl who got pregnant, it was not his fault, but that's a different story and one for someone else to tell.

# CHAPTER 3

By this time I was spending a lot of time down at the harbour and especially 'Fittie', where the River Dee ran into the sea, that's how the name of that place, a fishing village in bygone days was called Footdee. So one day when I was down in Footdee, just by the Sea Cadets place, and they were all standing there, I was enthralled. They were certainly a smart lot. After one of the senior lads called out the names of those present, he came out of the gate and said to me, "You look interested. Do you fancy joining?"

I told him I had not long left the Scouts, that I needed time to study for my work, which was my first priority. But of course by joining the Cadets it would give me access to the motorboat they had amongst others. A boat the Navy used to train sailors, the art of sailing, known as a whaler, and four other types of boats with outriggers on each side. These terrific little boats were the same type, not the actual, but same type as had been used by the Marines in the cockleshell heroes' attacks during the war.

I did not ask my parents, I simply told them that I was joining the Cadets. Of course, my father with his philosophy did not think I should join, as "The other boys would probably be a rough lot," and all the strife I had had to put up with all surfaced once more, "And then of course you'll want to go into the Navy?" They are nothing as far as he could see but a bunch of a rough lot and so on and so forth. He couldn't see that his tirade only strengthened my resolve to follow through my decision, so I damned well joined. Of course being a mechanic apprentice, I was immediately introduced to a lad of my age, an apprentice marine engineer who had been in the Cadets a few months before me. He assisted the officer in charge of the engine on the launch. I became the second assistant. It was great. I wasn't half a smart chap.

This lad was Kenny Ross. We became very close

friends for life. He came, like me, from a working class family. He had brothers and sisters. His father was Chief Engineer on a steam trawler. They lived in a council flat in Torry. We had by then—I forgot to mention—moved into a fantastic brand new council flat in Kincorth, right by the River Dee, where I used to fish. Torry and Kincorth are housing estates in Aberdeen.

Kenny, by the way had dark hair just like me. His family could not get over the likeness between us, as we also had very similar names, Kress and Ross.

As I said, we were inseparable, Kenny and I. I was now just over seventeen years of age, passed my driving test and occasionally for doing work on someone's car, especially Uncle Clarry, he would let me borrow his Hillman car. I thought I was in utopia, I thought I was 'Archie' as the saying goes in Aberdeen. So Kenny and I and two or three of his sisters would go a few miles out of Aberdeen to see their Uncle Jim and aunt whose name eludes me. They had a small holding and their uncle was a foreman in what was known as a fish processing place. These people always treated me as family, as did Kenny's family. They were wonderful, warm hearted people. I told Kenny and his family that I was of the Jewish faith, but it never entered my mind at the time to tell them where I had come from. They no doubt thought that as I spoke as they did, with that distinct Aberdonian accent, that I was a Scot.

His family consisted of Steven, the eldest and an engineer on a ship, away for months on end to the other side of the world. Then there was George; anyone could see as the term implies by the cut of his jib that he was the typical material that starts from the lower deck to become a commander in the Royal Navy in no time at all. I liked George and was he smart! I felt proud just to know him. Then there was the eldest sister, Christina, then a bit younger Betty, then Mina then the youngest, Margaret.

Well, I practically lived there half the time. Kenny,

many years later, told me that his father would gladly have let me marry one of the younger girls if I had shown any interest. But, I say again, these people to me were my family, as the others I had lived with before that time, and the thought of romance never entered my head for that very reason.

Well, of course, down at the Cadets, after the session was over, Kenny and I would go along to where these little boats were moored. These were simply for a bit of recreation and fishing, not boats used solely for commercial purposes.

We got to know the chaps who owned these boats, "Engineers, are you, lads? You are more than welcome here." Those old boats were owned by working class fellows, just like us. Not proper boat engines, as these were simply not affordable, so they all had adapted motorcar engines and we were made most welcome of course to go with them.

I will say no more about the rows, trials and tribulations with my father except to say that daily I got more and more towards leaving home. If only I could, if only. He simply did not like the idea of me mixing with this type—here you can assume that my adult comments once again nearly led to blows. I was more determined than ever to do just what I wanted to. After all, these chaps, older of course than Kenny and me, and wiser to boot, they were who I listened to and they were not rough types. They were married with young children. I got to know their families in time. They were working class and my father judged them wrongly by what he thought rather than by what he knew.

There were no yachts to speak of in those days, but one chap moored this tiny yacht that he had built, as that was his line of work actually on the River Dee, but only in the summer. When he sailed, he towed this tiny one-man dinghy. It was a picture. Of course, we regularly spoke to him when we went out and again as he was and coming back to his moorings. We Cadets were learning to sail in the harbour on this fabulous novel training whaler, it really was the beginning of my love for sailing boats. This was truly nature's way of skimming across effortlessly on the water. Aberdeen harbour being big, we had a whale of a time.

Two of these older chaps, who had a boat half share each, by the name of Andy Riddle, a foreman pattern maker at Wilson's Engine Makers and Jack Stevens, a railway engine driver, were the chaps that we usually went out fishing with. One day, as we Cadets came back, having sailed the whaler up and down the harbour, Andy and Jack, who were sitting in their boat about to go home, said that they had been watching us and they would like to have a sail. Although their little boat did have a small mast end sail, it did not sail well. So we explained the position to the Commanding Officer—an actual Naval Captain—called Reid. He said that he certainly wouldn't mind, but it was of course strictly not to be discussed with anyone, as after all it was for the use of Cadets only.

My two friends soon got the hang of handling this boat. It was a flyer. On board were myself, Kenny, the Commanding Officer and a cadet Chief Petty Officer, whose name at the moment eludes me. We had a terrific sail that day.

Kenny was not that interested in going fishing, so he did not come out as much as I did. There was another officer who had been a lieutenant in the Navy for twelve years. Unfortunately, he thought he was still in the Navy and treated us Cadets as if we were sailors. He ran us around until we were just about all in, critical of the least bit of one's uniform was not clean or properly pressed. I didn't think so at the time, but his discipline paid dividends for me later on in life.

I remember one day in particular. I had problems with the chain on my bike on the way to a Cadet meeting. I had oil on my trousers, hands filthy. As one outcome of the dressing down I got, I informed the C.O. that I was leaving. The next week I handed in my uniform. The C.O. tried to persuade me to stay. I told him that perhaps the other officer might be anti-Semitic, and anyway, I had friends with boats and that was that. "Oh no," he said, "I don't believe that."

My pal Kenny was, on the strength of my leaving, also going to leave, but they persuaded him to stay, as there was only the senior engineer and now only Kenny left. He was immediately promoted from able seaman to senior leading seaman.

Kenny and I were as always going around together, and about a year after I left, he said that he simply was not interested since I went, and he left too. It just was not the same after I went. But how could it be, we were a team?

Now I am approaching eighteen, I was deferred from National Service until I had completed my apprenticeship at twenty-one. Some of the other young lads at the garage, who had not regularly attended evening classes, without proper excuse, had to go and join up at eighteen.

Around this time I noticed one of the small boats where the others were moored behind a large dry dock seemed to be getting lower and lower in the water. We knew that this boat was called the NADA, which I found out was Spanish for the word 'nothing'. It was owned by three chaps and we knew them all, but it transpired that as we kept bailing it out week after week, the engine was just about finished. They had trouble with their wives over spending money on the boat, and as winter came on, the boat was only an outline full of water, only stopped from sinking by the mooring lines on the front and back. So one day, Andy told me he had seen one of the owners, and that they would just forget about the boat. It was causing too many problems. In fact, they never used it as much as others who had boats there.

My dear friends Andy and Jack said, "Go on make them an offer. We'll help you get her up the slip and sorted out. You can probably fix the engine or get another old engine from somewhere."

For the princely sum of six pounds, she was mine, all properly signed and dated by the owners and witnessed by my friends.

In early April that year, we pumped out as much as we could and towed her with my friend's boat to the slipway at high tide. She was an ex-trawler's lifeboat, extremely well built—of wood—of course as they were in those days. She was about twenty years old. Slowly we manoeuvred her into position and with blocks and tackle it took at least forty feet or so. We finally got her up on the top of the slip and then clear of the slipway. The slip was 40 feet.

There she lay; there was no fear in those days of vandals or thieves. Then it was a different world. I took the engine gearbox, shafting and propeller off, as well as any parts such as rudder, fuel tank, etc. There was no battery or lights because the engine had what in those days for the ignition most engines had a unit known as a magneto. As the engine turned, this was like a miniature power station that developed its own spark for the plugs. If you got a shock off this magneto, you did not know what hit you, especially if you had wet and cold hands.

I had, over the years, developed a very deep respect for the sea. I never challenged its moods. I read as many stories and information as I could on boats, ships, weather, survival and all associated things to do with seamanship.

I got all the parts I had removed from the boat to my shed at home in the garden. We turned the boat upside down to let it drain and dry out, as the stern on the front of the boat and the supporting wood behind the stem had broken and had to be replaced, which was no problem, as Andy was going to make the new stem and the apron. However, there was a slight problem, due to the fact that we needed electricity for the drill and other tools. As luck would have it another friend who had a boat (Jim Leaper) knew the caretaker of a tiny religious group's assembly place there in Footdee. This hall had the upstairs part in use, while below was just like a small garage or large storage room with electricity points. I am not sure why this building was so designed. It may have even been a fisherman's house upstairs, with the lower part used for his equipment.

Well, the fee was really what we could afford to give for their funds more or less. It was very fair indeed. The only hard and fast rule was that we were not to work there while the bible class was in session or on a Sunday. Which was understandable, that was indeed very fair. I cannot remember the amount that I offered them, but whatever it was, it was accepted. They too were charming people, ready to help. One would say true Christians.

Again, time pushes on. The beautiful stern and support apron that my 'friend indeed' Andy had made was now fitted to my boat with the assistance of Jack Stevens. The Austin Seven engine however, took a considerable time to rebuild. New parts—due to lack of money—were impossible to purchase, so anything that needed to be replaced either came from a friend or from a scrap yard. Jack Stevens, who had a similar engine in his boat, helped me modify the gearbox like the one in his boat, so that it would drive the propeller in reverse at the same fast speed as it went ahead. And as any sailor will tell you, that is a handy modification to have.

I have forgotten to mention that Andy Riddle only asked me to pay for the wood he had used, not for his time or the screws and nails that were used. I say again, what a blessing to have friends like these.

I also think that during these last years of the Cadet days to approaching nineteen, I had no thoughts of getting to know the opposite sex. I know some people thought that it was odd but I suppose they were entitled to their thoughts. I used to go to a fabulous jazz venue known as the Argosy at Bucksburn. Could they play jazz, and how! it was great, just great! Of course, there were some good-looking girls there. I would be conceited if I said that they did not appeal to me. I danced and jived with umpteen of them, but that was all. No 'see you home' or anything like that; definitely not, and why? Was it due to the events of my first love that had such a traumatic ending? Ask me another.

I must admit, in Footdee during the Cadet days and for a couple of years on, I regularly tried to chat up one young girl of about my age. I knew her name, as I knew her brother, but I do not wish to name names for the sake of their families. The harbourmaster's son at the time, whom I also knew well, seemed very interested in this girl too, so I made no secret of the fact that I liked her. This lad was way above me in lifestyle and the clothes he wore, but that did not deter me. I also learned from her brother that she was a seriously devout Christian. In fact, I also knew the hall that she attended. It seems that fate always had a devout religious girl in the offering.

I once waited outside that hall; I am not ashamed to admit it. When she came out, I said, "Hello [name withheld], can I see you home?" She never replied and went to the bus stop to await a bus. I got on the same bus, but she steadfastly refused to talk. Of course, I did not say anything more. I did not want a scene on the bus; I just wanted her to know that I was interested in getting to know her a little better. Actually, I wanted her to be my girlfriend but I couldn't just get straight to it could I? And just to clarify another point may I say in all honestly yes, on my dear mother's life, that my feelings towards this girl were genuine even though she was no oil painting, no hourglass figure, or glamour girl either. But who can define the chemistry on these matters? There are volumes; there are songs. It's just nature, simple as that, man looking for a mate.

It was not—as seems to be the thing these days—a matter of any port in a storm or an easy, quick hop into bed and bingo! Absolutely not! And for those who think otherwise, all I can say is beware of the consequences because there are many.


The girl got off the bus as I did at the terminus. After she got off I walked with her more. I said, "I'm truly fond of you. I mean that sincerely." I think she blushed, looked down and quickened her pace to her house, which was about a minute away.

Once again, a father comes into the saga. He was just coming round the corner near her house, as clear in every detail as yesterday, not over half a century ago, but it was, time does fly. He was a working man, big, sombre-looking. She then ran up to him. I hung back and was tempted to turn around and run, but I stopped and awaited the outcome. Her father beckoned to me, so we approached each other. *Here we go again*, flashed into my mind.

"My daughter does not want you following her about. I know you are friendly with my son; that's all right with me. [His son was not a Cadet] But I don't want to hear that you are chasing her. She is a very shy girl."

So I suppose that was the answer. I did as suggested. It did not bother me or give me any feelings of rejection. At the end of the day, had it worked out, the begging question of the cause of heartaches and wars the world over, religion, without a doubt would have been the insurmountable stumbling block, as with my father's attitude.

Of course, time can be a great healer. I jump forward a few years again, as things come back to me, and I feel certain that had we not moved to London in 1954, I would have tried to find my first love, assuming of course that she was still single.

My memories of the days of that boat and me will be with me always in virtually every detail. I, with Andy and Jack Stevens' help, built a small cabin on front, as the boat was completely open, and I did not fancy taking a big sea without some sort of protection up front, as most little boats had.

Finally, the day came, all complete except for the engine, for it was the norm, after a wooden boat had been out of the water for some time, to let the wood take up its shape, and any possibility of very minute opening of the seams will show up while ashore.

The boat however seemed dry. Then again with my friends' help, we got the motor into the boat and I set about getting all into shape. This engine had no battery or starter motor. As mentioned earlier, it had a magneto and starting handle.

There comes now a true story of fate and unbelievable coincidence. It simply defies belief, but the person referred to may still be alive, and records in Aberdeen may also be available, so to commence.

I was trying to start the engine. It was a bit tight, due to the way that it was fitted. It was not possible to turn the handle round and round like in a car. It was only possible by half a turn. There was no other way than that. It was hard and hot work trying to get that engine to start. The incident I am about to relate took place on the second day of trying to start the engine. In the dry dock next to where these little boats were moored was a big dredger which was being worked on. It was a Saturday, but it was common for the work to be done at weekends, it was even being done on the Sunday, as that dry dock was a busy place. The dredger was the Annie W Lewis; her crew were not on holiday. No, they were there doing work on her. The time was about five in the afternoon. They all come off the gangway; some had bicycles, others went to the bus. I had noticed that on the first day a well-built chap had leaned his bike against the railing and was watching me try to start the engine. He never spoke, just stood there looking. Next day, Sunday, I was aboard again trying to start the engine, and it nearly started, but just did not want to. Off come the workmen at five o'clock again, about four of them. All had bikes, and they propped them up against the railings and watched me trying to start the engine.

The chap who had been watching me the day before called down to me, "Yer havin' a bit of trouble are ye, no? I'll come doon an' gie ye a hand."

"Oh thanks," I said.

So down the steel ladder he comes, the boat fairly heels as he steps on it. He was like a bear, heavy and well-built. He got hold of the handle and in about ten or twelve attempts, the engine started. I remember that for a few seconds the smoke belched out of the exhaust. His friends on the jetty cheered.

"Thanks mister," I said, "Here's half a crown." I only had two shillings and eight pence altogether on me, as I had come on my bike. Things were tough in those days.

"Oh that's a' right. I dinno need that."

I replied, "If you get a motorbike or perhaps a car one day, I'll look after it for you."

His work mates shouted down laughing, "A motorbike or a car? [who had a car in those far off days?] Man, he can just about afford his bike!"

"Well, I might be able to do you a favour one day." Afterward, indeed it was soon to turn out, they laughed and laughed about the favour.

Time marches on. I saw the dredgers crew often, until she was back in the water about a week or so later. I was, as time and weather permitted, down on that boat of mine doing the necessary work. I was getting there. It was a few weeks later on; the engine was working well. I found that the gauze seawater filter was getting clogged up. This I dismantled, because it was important that the engine did not seize up for lack of cooling water.

It was all in bits, when suddenly there was a loud splash in the water; most distinct it was. The dredger—which I could not see as she was on the other side of this big, high dry dock—she blew her horn on and on in the nearby shipyard. Some workers were shouting, "Man in the water!"

I thought, *Hell, I'm going round there. Never mind no water. Well, if it ruins the engine, so be it. I'm going.*

I quickly let go of the lines, motored flat out and came round the side of the dry dock in seconds. There, near the stationery dredger was a man in the water, swimming. Roughly—less I imagine, than a full minute later—I was at his side. I stopped the now red-hot engine. The paint was smoking on it. I leaned over and grabbed him by his water-sodden jacket. "I'll hold onto you, don't worry." I could see the motorboat, which was used to moor and release moorings when boats came into the harbour, with two men in it was fast approaching. The weight of this chap with his sea boots and water-sodden clothes made it impossible for me to pull him aboard. In fact, my boat, a good three and a bit feet out of the water when level, was down to about ten inches, the way she was leaning over.

Yes, you probably guessed; it was my helper to start the engine. I held on, reassuring him that it was okay. "I won't let you go. Help is on the way."

"God man, I never thought yer favour'd come like this."

It took the two boatmen and me with a bit of a struggle, I can remember, to get him into their boat. "I'll come along later and see ye," he gasped.

This is what had happened. This chap was the man who got into the small rowing boat to moor the dredger between two large mooring buoys on the other side of the dry dock. He had tied the little boat as usual to the buoy and got onto it. As he was securing the heavy lines he was jerked off the buoy without a hope of saving himself from falling into the harbour.

I said to the other rescuers as they were just about to take him to the quay, "Come back and give me a tow back, will you? I can't run this engine. I've come out here without water connected."

"Well, it might be a bit of time. We'll have to let a couple of boats off," they replied.

Anyway, I had these two sweeps, very big heavy oars. I did not relish the thought of being stuck where I was, in case a ship came in or out. So very slowly, I got the boat back to my moorings. I felt really proud. *Just wait 'til I see his laughing work mates. I'll make them eat humble pie, I will.*

Days later, he came round on his bike. "Thanks lad, ye were good. Whatever happened to yer motor? Is it aright?"

I told him that I had renewed the oil and everything was all right so far.

"My boss will probably come to see ye. Cheerio."

His boss never did come, or perhaps he came when I wasn't there, but in any event I never saw him. When I relate this tale to people, they are simply astounded. It seems to some a tall story, but it is true. There might be records at the harbourmaster's office.

I eventually took my boat across to moor with other small boats in Old Torry, as it saved me cycling round the vast area of the harbour, and Torry was on the same side as my house.

My pal Kenny would sometimes come out with me, although I was mainly on my own. I had a life belt, antiquated old thing it was. Then as an addition to my safety equipment, years ago while on a visit to London, I went to Gamages and bought for the then princely sum of five pounds and ten shillings an ex-RAF fighter pilot's one-man dinghy.

Kenny and I had played with that at the beach on a warm day with a long rope attached. It also had paddles that fitted onto each hand like a big flat glove. This was now my lifeboat. I never went far, only just out of the harbour, round by the lighthouse, sometimes perhaps a bit further on towards Cove Bay. That was as far as it was required to do some fishing. If during the autumn or early spring, weather permitting, there were big cod to be caught, I gave them to friends and, I remember, to our doctor, a really marvellous man, he was an ex-army Colonel in the Medical Corps.

I did on some occasions catch over a weekend a box and a half of cod. I knew the McBay people who had a fish curing business near where I kept the boat. I would phone them at their home—that had been pre-arranged—and before I went to work on Monday, their lorry would meet me at the jetty in Old Torry and take the fish. Next day, I would be paid the top price that cod were fetching at the fish market.

Going back briefly to the time that I was a Cadet. Yes, I really took it all in as a matter of fact. After finishing my apprenticeship, I was definitely going to join the Navy for my stint of National Service, as a Sea Cadet and engineer and what have you I thought I would have a great chance of being accepted. I was politely told that there were no vacancies for the Navy, and even had there been, they would only take those whose fathers, brothers, uncles, etc had been in the Navy. The interviewing officer then asked me why I was volunteering and why—if I had served my apprenticeship—when I had opportunities as an engineer and motor mechanic.

I pointed out that I felt as if Britain had given me sanctuary and I was really keen to go. Pity I never got into the Navy, as later on—much later—I ended up in the REME as a NCO, and furthermore, had I got into the Navy and done as well, I would without a doubt have signed on for at least six or eight years.

Another point worth mentioning, which I hoped might have got me into the Navy was that I had been, as Kenny the month before, Cadet of the month. The two of us were sent to Chatham Naval Base for two weeks' training from engineering to big ship instruction. We lived on board the new destroyer, The Vigo.

His Majesty the King came to Chatham Naval Base. Eighteen Cadets, including the two of us, were presented to His Majesty and were complimented on our turnout. Dig that, I say.

It is now March 1951. I feel it is time to sell NADA, my beloved old boat, but I must relate some further happenings in the year before, 1950. It was early autumn. I come down to the boat one Sunday morning, grey sky, quite windy even in the harbour. The sea was a bit choppy. There was not a soul to be seen there. I did see that one of the boats was not there, so I thought, *Well, if he can go out so can I.* Now, the engines on all these boats had a straight through exhaust, no silencers, as these would have got very hot. So when you got going, it was very noisy; it just roared…

sounded great!

The roundhouse watchtower and harbour control evidently called me on their loud hailer, but I did not hear them. I got down to the entrance between the North Pier and the South Breakwater. It was rough there, as I cleared the shelter of the Breakwater. Immediately when I got into the rough water, what with the wind there, it would have been I reckoned a disaster to turn there and go back. I would have been rolled over for sure. So keeping what is known as head on to the sea, I kept chugging on a bit more into deeper water. The worst it seems was what is known as the bar, the bit when you leave the river and enter the sea.

No, frightened I was not. That would have been fatal. Apprehensive, indeed I was. Who wouldn't be? So within a few minutes of getting clear of the breakwater, I already had my lifejacket on and the one-man yellow dinghy at the ready. I waited for a sizeable trough and quickly got the boat round before the next wave came. I didn't half surf back, the waves pushing the flat end of the boat, a totally different sensation from battling and banging into a sea. I began to feel that it was quite an accomplishment, as once I was in between the two piers, things were much calmer. The roundhouse flashed their searchlights and I heard them call me to come over. So from my side of the river, that is the Torry side, I went over to the Footdee side, where the roundhouse was situated.

"Did you not hear us when you went out? What the hell do you think you were doing?" they asked me when I arrived there, none too pleased.

I shouted up to them—having slowed down to just a tick over speed and not driving the propeller—I called out that I thought the other boat, which I think was either the Panther or the Vine, was out and if he was, so could I.

"My God lad, you were lucky! He's gone up the river. Did ye not hear us shout on the hailer? We have even got the lifeboat lads on standby."

I didn't know what to say. Thank God that they did not come with the lifeboat, as the chaps in the roundhouse had been watching me all the time. I am sure that if they had sent the lifeboat, which would have taken three to five minutes, I might have survived if I had got into the dinghy, always a big *if*. I never told my parents. My father would have got somebody to beach the boat up river and set fire to it, that's for sure.

Back to 1951, a month had gone and it was now April. I had put the word around and advertised in the paper to sell my boat, but I was not having much success, so I drained off all the cooling water and prepared to leave Kenny in charge of the boat for two years.

It was about this time, one day while I was fixing extra mooring ropes on the boat that a man came by regarding my advert. I was asking fifty pounds for that lovely old boat. I coupled up the water, etc and we went round the harbour. He liked her and paid forty-five pounds cash for the lot, fishing gear, lifejacket and my dandy little dinghy. He thought—like me—that that dinghy was really something.

It was sad to part with the NADA. But who knows, she might have been destroyed in the winters while I away. Forty-five pounds in 1951 was a fair sum of money. I banked it. I also had to get my parents to sign a form from the War Office that they were indeed my next of kin. More tears from my mother!

My pal Kenny however would have had only a few months to look after the boat if I had not sold her, for he either had to join up or go to sea in the Merchant Navy. He did toy with the idea of going into the Navy, but changed his mind. And furthermore, I recall a few years later, and it was in the Aberdeen Papers—I had gone to London—due to some mix up, two military police arrested Kenny as a deserter, but in four hours all was sorted.

Comes now the sixth of May 1951, a cold day it was in Aberdeen. It is truly amazing how these things put away at the back of one's mind can suddenly surface, and with such detail. I was ready to go to Honiton, Devon to the Training Battalion of the Royal Electric and Mechanical Engineers branch of the Army for a six-week period of learning—In the first instance—how to be a soldier. I had, as it was bitter cold that day in Aberdeen, all my heavy winter underwear on, thick shirt, pullover, jacket, heavy old coat, woolly hat, gloves, the lot. My parents and I went by bus to the station to get the ten past seven train to London Kings Cross. We were rather early. My mother was tearful, so I told my father to go and take mother home. There was some time to spare before the departure of the train, so as the engine arrived and was being coupled up to the carriages, I walked down to the front of the train. The engine, of course, immediately brought back the memory of the very first day that we arrived in my beloved Aberdeen.

Next morning, my sister who lived in London met me, and by tube we went to Waterloo station to get on the train to Honiton. I arrived there at about two in the afternoon, with many other lads. There were about six big army trucks with canvas covers waiting for us, but was it hot there in Devon! I was cooking with all my underclothes on, so I took my coat, great heavy thing, and my jacket and pullover off as well. It was actually eighty-one degrees, and it got hotter as the days progressed. I thought we were on the Equator!

To say that this was yet another big milestone is putting it mildly. The NCOs, especially Corporal Reid, was he smart; he did nothing but scream commands. On the other hand, there was Sergeant Dale, a big powerful, no-nonsense chap. These were regular soldiers, the age of the Corporal was 20 and the Sergeant was 22. Sergeant Dale was also very smartly dressed, a reasonable chap he was. No bullying; you could even hold a conversation with him.

Well, they did knock us into shape, or should I say worked us from morn 'til evening. Six weeks of this and was it hot! I had never known heat like that in Aberdeen. Halfway through our training, as we were good lads, they told us they had organised coaches to take us to Torquay for the day. We went swimming and there was great camaraderie, a real adventure. The training was at times very tough, especially as I was a smallish sort of fellow.

Despite my size one day the Corporal decided that I should carry the Bren gun halfway up Giddisham Hill at the rear of the camp where it was mainly dense forest. We were going to ambush or try to evade each other in Platoons, as well as carrying this heavy machine gun. We did it up this one in seven; I think it was at the double.

I say again it was hot, very hot. It was while we were at the top of this hill, where the view was out of this world, that Sergeant Dale, while we had our lunch break, did some amazing displays with a rifle, at times even with a fixed bayonet on the rifle. He also pointed out the large mansion that the author Agatha Christie owned. Then of course the Corporal started his usual screaming and we reverted to being soldiers.

One day, coming back in a lorry to the camp, there was this very pretty young lady walking to the married quarters. As we passed her, we shouted and whistled at her. The Corporal and Sergeant had gone back in a different vehicle.

After tea, however, there being no let-up whatsoever in activities, the Corporal and the Sergeant arrived to commence more training. "My wife," said the Sergeant, "tells me you lot, as you were the only truck there at the time, whistled and shouted at her. That's not on, do you understand? I've got a good mind to give you all extra duties."

No one batted an eyelid. We cringed, all of us,

about thirty lads, but then Walter Kress, being Walter, said ever so slowly, and in a very low voice (it was not really me; it was some form of inner force), "Sergeant Dale, permission to speak."

"Yes, Kress, what is it?"

"Well Sergeant Dale, we did not, of course, realise that it was your wife. I'm sure had we known, we would not have shouted and whistled at her. Anyway, she is a very beautiful lady, and I offer my apologies."

"Well Kress, that's nice of you to speak out," the Sergeant said, "and do you other lot think the same about my wife?"

So the ice was truly broken.

At the end of our six-week training, we that had arrived as young lads, some of course eighteen years of age, others like me were twenty-one, had worked hard. We all came to the conclusion that the Corporal with his constant screaming at us was what he was. Sergeant Dale was a different Army man altogether. He of course knew I was Jewish, because of the different lads' church attendance.

I got the chance one day just before the end of our six-week stint to talk to Sergeant Dale and I got around to telling him that the powers that be gave me the choice as to my previous Austrian Nationality, to either decline National Service, or to do it. It was my choice.

He was definitely impressed with what he learned. He thought for a moment, "You know, Kress, you are a quiet sort of chap. I can tell character, but with a Scottish accent, I'd never have guessed where you originated from. I think you'd make good here in this training camp. I'd recommend you for Lance Corporal, how about that, Walter Kress?"

"Thank you Sergeant Dale." One always had to address a senior in that way, "I would like to move on to Taunton." [Where we—irrespective of our previous civil

qualifications—had a three-month course on all types of
Army Vehicles.]

"By the way, tomorrow morning after muster and
roll call, the Colonel wants to see you. I don't know what
it's about, but maybe he has seen your report and wants to
promote you, so don't forget."

At nine o'clock in the morning, this was one day
before the end of the six weeks, smart and tidy, I thought
the worst. Had someone at home died, or maybe a bad
accident?

"Ah, hello Kress," the Colonel said. A fine figure of
a man, he was, absolutely charming. Well, he was a Colonel
after all. "Do sit down young man," he said after I had
stood to attention and saluted, "Would you like a cigarette?"

"I'm not a smoker, sir," I replied.

"Fancy a lemonade? Can't give you alcohol Kress,
not in barracks. Well Kress, it's a bit of a tricky subject. It's
not, I must say, anything that comes, shall we say, from my
end here. It's simply this. I have been informed by the War
Office that, as you no doubt know, one of the top boffins,
generals, etc, that as you hail originally from Austria, this is
rather a bit of a ridiculous question as far as I'm concerned.
Would you sign the Official Secrets Act? As an engineer,
you will in due course handle some very 'hush hush'
equipment. That's all Kress. You do understand, and it's
not down to me, but I don't think you would let us down
anyway. And by the way Kress, why did you decide to join
up when you had the choice not to?"

"Well sir, I had, as you probably know, been a Sea
Cadet, and I feel that it was my duty in gratitude for this
country taking us in, sir."

"You know," he said, "chaps like you ought to sign
on for a few years. Well, you have got two years to think
about that. Just sign here and good luck in the future."

I stood up to attention, saluted and went.

71

So I went to the gym, where Sergeant Dale told me to report to after seeing the Colonel. "What was that about Kress?" he asked.

"It was just a simple formality to sign the Official Secrets Act, as I would at some time or other be seeing and possibly working on top secret equipment."

"Strange that. He hasn't asked some of the others. He never told me what it was all about. Looks like you could be specially selected one way or another."

On the final day, having been up until about midnight, we were to have the passing-out parade. That was really something else. It was yet another lovely Devon summer day. We assembled on the parade ground, the large regimental band of the REME played our regiment's own tune, which went as follows, "I want to be near you; you're the one, the one for me. That's so very plain for all of us to see…" So forth and so on, and then I think it goes, "I'll see you in the morning and see you then at night."

What a day it was. Not only was the Colonel on the platform, there was also a General. This General told us, whether he did to all at the various passing-out parades, that we were smarter than the marines or the regiment of guards. "Yes indeed, you can all be proud of yourselves, and I may add all the officers and men who trained you." We had a terrific farewell party.

Next day, we went home on leave. I wasn't half proud strutting around for at least three days in my uniform. I was a different man.

I went to see Andy Riddle and Jack Stevens. Kenny was still at home, as he hadn't gone off to sea yet, and Jim Leaper, who had a little shop in Footdee. I went to the Sea Cadets place just for the hell of it. I was a proud soldier. I went to the grammar school, the Town & County Garage where I served my apprenticeship and saw most of my other boating friends. I went to Friday evening service at the Synagogue in my uniform. All the Andrews and Watt families, and of course I forgot to mention Kenny's family thought I was the top, and they genuinely meant it.

And yes, I made a point of hanging about outside the church where the sisters of my first love worshipped. I can still remember that day. Not only were they there, also their brother whom I played with way back in Devana Gardens was there. I did not see the then boyfriend, nor was any mention made as to whether any of them had married. These people were the most genuine that God put on this Earth. They told me that I looked stunning. The girl that broke my heart (well, nearly so) gave me a hug. Her eyes said much, much more than any words. For a second, we were in love again. I felt that all that slog and hard training was being repaid.

I went to visit all I knew. I cannot put the appropriate words to my feelings. Oh, and my parents— over the moon, they were. I went to my father's work, Mitchell & Muil Bakery. I had never seen my father full of such joy. All the people there, I can tell you, I see it as just today as if the scene is unfolding all over again right here before my eyes.. I felt ten feet tall, I did, all due to the wonderful welcome that I got.

The week's leave went by very quickly and then I went to Taunton in Somerset for the three-month's course. A peculiar thing—It nearly always turns out that I mixed with older people, as Andy and Jack were and most of the other boaters—and now in Taunton where there were army as well as civilian instructors.

There I met lads already weeks on in their studies from Aberdeen, including one of the other apprentices from where I had worked, John Tindall.

I then met a Sergeant instructor, dear chap. He was

Irish and was twenty-six back then. Of course, it did not have the strict discipline of the former training camp. We just mixed with the Corporals and Sergeants instructors, but not with the officers.

There of course come back memories of a few things that took place there at Taunton. I would not have missed this place for anything. One of the chaps who had signed on for three years was in our billet. He had a Panther motorcycle. Well, what has the chocolate cake my mother sent me got to do with a motorbike? And no, I cannot remember his name, but he was from Yorkshire, Cleckheaton I believe.

Upon opening my parcel one day, he was sitting on his bed next to mine. "Oh," he said, "What you got then?" So I showed him the cake. "Smells good," he said. So that the others did not hear, he asked, "Give us a taste."

I said, "Okay," and cut him out a bit and put it on his metal plate. We had to take our own plates, knives and forks to meals.

"I've never had the likes of this before," he said.

"Tell you what, let's have the bike for a little bit round the square, then I'll give you more cake later," I offered.

"It's a deal. Come on out now if you want," he agreed.

This Panther motorbike had a big sloping engine. I drove around gingerly, great fun it was. So I gave him another bit of cake later, and he was delighted.

This has stuck forever in my mind; it's a real howler. I can see it all today still. Every billet had about twenty sleeping in it. At the entrance, however, was a small room where a regular soldier (that is, one who is not National two-year Service) and either a lance or full corporal, just to keep us in check, that's all. We had a smashing Royal Marine lance corporal. After he got paid on payday he went on the town with other NCOs.

He usually arrived back a bit merry, singing and swaying about, not offensive, at all hours of the night. So all of us being, as one might say, ready for any capers, we decided to remove the bulb from his only light, then each of us as required produced a part of uniform. This we made up into a dummy. It looked fantastic, so we fixed it above his door on the little room. We laughed 'til we ached, we did. I can see it all still.

So comes the time when our corp arrives. We should have been asleep, but we simply had to wait to see the outcome of this thing. I am surprised he did not hear some of us trying to hold back our giggles. He put his hand to switch on the non-existent bulb, at the same time pushing open the door. The dummy then fell on him and he took off! I think that in the state he was in, he must have thought a bloke had ambushed him. "I'll [bad, very bad word] kill the lot of yer, so God help me! I will kill you [bad word]!"

We were all convulsing with laughter, then he too he saw the funny side. "God, you lot didn't half give me a funny turn! Who the hell thought this one out?"

We said that we all put our heads together and came up with this lot.

Next, the officer of the watch, no doubt hearing the rumpus up at the guard house (he was a Scot in the camp's regimental police), big sergeant (forgot his name), storms in with his great big Alsatian, and a big dog he was. No one ever dared touch this dog. "What's all the hilarity here then? It's well past lights-out."

"Corporal fell over when he came in, Sergeant," one lad piped up.

"Yes, I fell over. My bulb packed up and I fell over." All's well that ends well.

Next from the mind's store, we all had to do night

guard duty, firstly after tea at least four times during the three months there. Of course, you had to present yourself at the guard room looking like you just passed out, smart as the guards regiment.

The Scottish sergeant, dog in check as always, would inspect the six of us, look behind the ears, everywhere; check if you had your pay book on you, that sort of pedantic thing. He was really on the ball. He then detailed who was going to do the different times. It meant that two of us went walking round the perimeter carrying pickaxe handles. I would have liked to carry a gun; the place at night, set deep in the woods, was eerie. The civilian instructors told us of past traumas of yore.

My guard duty partner for the night and I, the sergeant said, were going to do the 8.30 to 10.30pm. It was now mid-August, nice weather, so when it came to our turn to walk around the perimeter, we picked up the wooden axe handles and sauntered off. I as said earlier, none of us were too keen especially when night came on. There were rumours of bloodbaths in the early years of England's history and what have you.

We dutifully did the rounds, as the wily sergeant would suddenly pop up to ensure we were not sitting down or swinging the lead, so to speak. As the two of us approached the area where the commanding officer had this big house situated in the woods, it was just starting to get dark. As we came up a narrow path, we saw a big man in a raincoat walking on the road towards the house in front of us. He had not heard or seen us, as the path we had come upon was wet and leaf-strewn.

"Looks like the old man," I said to the other lad.

"I think you're right," he replied.

"Well," I said, "we are going to challenge him."

"You can't do that. It's the Colonel!"

"Yes, but if we don't challenge him, we will get a rocket. That's what we are here for. He could well be testing us."

Before my companion could reply, I called out, "Halt, who are you and what are you doing in this area?"

The man turned round. "Surely you know me. I'm the commanding officer."

So we promptly saluted, although he was in civilian clothing. "Yes sir," I said. The other did not speak. "Sir, I do recognise you, but have you any identification, as we might not have recognised you sir."

"Well I do appreciate your actions. Here are my credentials." To say that we were chuffed is an understatement.

"Thank you sir." We promptly stood to attention and saluted.

"Well when I get home, I shall tell my family that we can all sleep soundly tonight, as we've got some great fellows out there watching."

When we had done our stint and got back to the guard house, the sergeant plus dog were about to go off duty, but he was waiting for us to arrive. "I've had the CO on the phone. He is absolutely cock-a-hoop about you two lads challenging him. I think Kress and [name not sure] are to be at his office in the morning. Well done lads. God forbid if you hadn't challenged him. I think there would have been hell to pay. I'm sure of that."

Come the morning, we explained to the civilian instructor what had transpired the night previous. He too felt that we had done a great job, as all the civvy instructors were ex-army or other services.

When we got to the Colonel's office, the RSM (Regimental Sergeant Major) was there. He must have been in the Army since the year dot. He was tall with a moustache with dramatic up-turned bits at the ends. He looked just like an RAF type.

"Ah, last night's guard boys, are you not? CO's expecting you both."

We promptly came to attention and saluted.

Wow and wow! He shook our hands. We both felt ten feet tall. "Sit down please."

Cigarettes were offered. "Thank you sir," we both piped up, "we don't smoke sir." (Always say sir).

"Well then, how would you two, considering last night's most efficient work, on completion of the course here, like to be immediately promoted to full corporal in the Regimental Police here?"

I was stunned. Neither of us replied immediately. The CO could see that we were totally surprised, "Go away and have a think about it lads."

We stood up, saluted and went off.

The guard sergeant told us it was an appointment not to be dismissed lightly. "You'll make sergeant in six months' time. I'll see to that boys; you bet I will."

To coin a phrase once more, the mind truly boggles. "Are you going for it?" said my buddy.

"To be honest, I don't think I will. It's a good looking sort of thing, but I want to get out and about; see different places."

Came the time to tell the RSM that we really wanted to go on (all our pals had told us that we were daft not to grab this great chance), at the end of the three months. The CO in the big hall the day before we left to go to different REME workshops inspected us and bade us farewell. As we were about to get on the trucks to go to the station, the guard sergeant plus dog, of course, was at the gate. He spotted us. "Pity you lads are only National Service. You've certainly got what it takes. I feel you're both going to do well in the future. Cheerio then."

"Thanks Sarge, cheerio."

Naturally, the instructors and our Royal Marine corporal all were at the gate seeing us off. It was yet another great sunny, memorable day in my life. I say again, and as time in the Army went on, that I would not have missed it for anything. It certainly broadened my mind. I also turned from being a lad into being a man.

The next stop was the barracks at Arborfield near Reading. From there I regularly went to see my sister, who was living in Wembley. Then, while I was at Arborfield—which was just a transit camp—from where one was sent to a workshop anywhere in the world.

The RSM was, in my opinion and those of the other chaps also, a man with a big chip on his shoulder. It was just like being at the training camp. There, the RSM (not our sergeant) was a terror.

Days went by and we saw for the first time, and heard for the first time, a very low-flying plane. It was going to Farnborough, the De Havilland Comet; that was astounding.

After about two weeks there, on parade one morning, the RSM on his inspection of us lot was taking his time more slowly. He had, as usual, a corporal with him, with a clipboard to write things down. I could see the corporal writing names down, not many. Then I came face-to-face with the said RSM. I simply froze.

He stood there looking me up and down. "Name lad."

"Kress W, sir," I said in true training camp style.

"Unusual name. Spreckensie Deutsh?" I could have, but talk about knocking the wind out of your sails, people will not believe it.

"Ya sir," I said. I could see the others looking at me out of the corner of their eyes, of course, not daring to move in any way.

"Corporal, put Kress for the office." I was going to be, until posted, the runner, message boy. It is truly amazing that a person on the parade ground, and out and about in the camp, can strike such fear into us lads.

I duly, after the muster, immediately reported to the RSM's office. "Ah Kress, come in. I must say you're one of the smartest turned out." His attitude was totally different. He was not the grim fellow we all knew. "You see, Kress…pull up a chair."

"Thank you sir."

"I've been in the Army a hell of a long time, all over the place, been in Germany for a long time. Tell me, as I haven't yet got all the information from records at Taunton."

I simply gave him all of the facts. It took time however, as people were coming and going. Then the officer in the office behind called the RSM in and so forth it went.

# CHAPTER 4

"I think you'll fit in nicely here; so off now to lunch.
I'll see your corporal and tell him from now until further
notice your duties are here."

"Thank you Sir." I replied, no salute, as he is not a
full officer, known as a non-commissioned officer (NCO).

After lunch, I duly reported, got rid of rubbish in
bins, tidied things up, went and got the afternoon tea and
cakes for the office personnel. I was happy to be a general
dog's body. One of the other sergeants asked me if I could
possibly once a week—he asked me not told me—if it was
ok with the RSM (Regimental sergeant major) whom he was
to ask first, to tidy up his room in the sergeants' quarters, as
yes, believe it or not, the RSM inspected those as well. I
even got a paid a few shillings. I even ironed his uniform.
Once again, I was friendly with a senior NCO. Not only
was I then excused ridiculous things as painting, cutting
grass, marches for miles in all weather, charmed life, some I
daresay would use the phrase—which has never offended
me—'luck of the Jews.' And to top it all, this sergeant who
was away most weekends made arrangements at the
sergeant's mess that I would come to the back door there
for his lunches and evening dinners, take them away to his
room and eat them there. The food of course was much
better than our squaddies stuff.

We are now approaching a fateful and yet another
most unbelievable story of coincidence. One late afternoon
while preparing to call it a day at the office, the RSM said to
me, "Be here sharp at eight Kress, will you? We have about
150 coming in. You will have to get some of them settled
in."

Duly I arrived at the office at ten to eight the
following morning and the RSM was already at the door,

"Hello Kress. The new ones will be here very shortly. Here's your list of forty. There are corporals and sergeants amongst them. Don't let them push you around in any way. You are acting as my deputy."

I say once more, wow oh wow.

Outside this office was an area the size of two tennis courts. I think it might have been the original square. The trucks arrived and they all jumped out. Well, never mind the proverbial feather to knock me over. I just stood there for a split second, a sergeant had his back to me and he was having his kit bag and case passed down to him.

"Sergeant Dale!" I yelled out.

He turned round. "Good God Kress!" he put his gear down and came up to me, "My goodness!" holding out his hand and shaking mine. The others looked on; I can see them still, this sergeant shaking my hand. "Of course you're in transit like the rest of us. I see you've got an important job. You should be a lance corporal by now I feel. See you around."

He got his gear and turned to go on his way. He was not on my list to handle, so I called out to the others in my detail, "Who's got Sergeant Dale please."

One of the others on the detail, a member of the staff there, a lance corporal called out, "This side, Sergeant Dale."

I picked up his case, to assist, and between the truck and the corporal, he whispered to me, "Keep on the right side of the RSM here. He can be evil." That was nice of Sergeant Dale.

I did not see a lot of him, but about three days later, he was getting into a truck being posted somewhere. "Good luck Kress," he said as I waved to him. He said it within earshot of quite a few personnel as he got onto the truck. "You're going to get to the top, I'm sure."

"I hope so, thanks to you." I could see, tough as he was, he was taken aback.

What recruit, I wonder, especially National Service, the majority of whom were not interested, did not tow the line, waiting only for their release date, had ever expressed any feelings towards a sergeant or other NCO in a training camp. I would have loved to meet Sergeant Dale again. Who knows, one day...who knows?

I had been posted—lucky me—to Scotland to a REME workshop in the heart of the most beautiful highlands at Grantown on Spey, with its famous salmon and trout river, not to mention its world famous whiskies. We soldiers got a free permit to fish once a week, but I never caught a fish. However, a civilian who worked at the camp was the local super catcher. I have seen salmon that he caught and they were big ones.

Grantown on Spey was about 84 miles from Aberdeen. I often got the opportunity to take a motorbike or staff car or truck, armoured car, etc to Aberdeen units or Army cadet units, and also to pick some up to take back for repair. This is all of interest of course...well, I think so anyway.

It was a very small unit, serving the north of Scotland. As usual there were many civilians working there, the majority ex-Army and Infantry at that. They told us of their experiences in the war and told us that the only fighting we were going to see was to get first into the NAAFI canteen when it opened. But once more, they were all a marvellous crowd. A Mr Clark, who was manager in the workshop where I was employed, gave us all his knowledge and help when required. His son, who also worked there, organised for us such things as occasional use of the snooker hall. I also learned to dance, thanks to his organising these things. Also, as it comes to mind, there was a small hotel—there were quite a few hotels, as it was a very popular resort, people came from the four corners of the Earth for fishing, golf, and walking the hills. This small hotel situated opposite the war memorial gave us soldiers a fantastic meal of choices of either meat and soup to start, then puddings or ice cream, and tea—as many cups as you like.

No, I have not mentioned before, I do and have eaten bacon for years, since the Reverend Stevens days, and I am not ashamed to admit it. I am my own man.

So at this hotel, we could get bacon, three rashers, two eggs, bread—as much as we could put away—tea, even cake, all for two and sixpence. As time went on, I got to be a full corporal and I offered to pay a bit more, but they totally refused to hear of it. Once more I had been fortunate enough to have met people of the right kind, no doubt whatsoever about that.

There was however a staff sergeant there that is a rank above sergeant and below RSM. He had three stripes plus a crown. The lads and I thought that he had the crown on his head, if you get my meaning. No names here— family, present-day descendants and all that. The less said the better. How I got my first and then second stripes was not down to him, be assured. The CO was a fatherly figure, a Major L A Warn, the adjutant was a Captain Crowther; a stickler for discipline. He lived in a caravan at the camp. The CO lived with his family down town. I got my first stripe when I passed the Army's first class certificate of education. Oh yes, we were taught general knowledge stuff, as if we were at university in those days. The second stripe I got after passing my final exam in my trade and became vehicle mechanic class one (VM1). I was told at a later date by a civilian—whose name I will not disclose—that by rights I should have gone for the sergeant's mess, with that qualification. Also, a fellow whose name I do not know nor would I disclose anyway, a civilian, but one who had been a rank in the infantry and had been in action, had seen it all in all its firsthand horrors. He was, I assume at that time in late 1952, about 65 years of age, possibly more. He was allowed to come and socialise at the sergeant's mess as he pleased. Nice chap he was, always when I was on guard duty, being an NCO I stayed all night in the guardroom, only going to check the perimeter patrol occasionally. One evening as he was leaving to go home, he came in. I was there alone, as the others of the guard had gone to fetch the food for us all for the night.

"I'll tell ye somethin' corp, but don't you tell anybody at all, by fit 'ave heard up there, ye should have been sergeant by now. Aye, that's the truth. Cheerio."

That, believe it or not, never troubled me. I now had about six months or so to go before discharge. The staff sergeants service time was at an end and he was being discharged. We NCOs all contributed to a small gift. I did my share of that. I cannot remember exactly what it was, but I think it was a smart leather case containing quality writing equipment and pens, etc. All eight of us NCOs of course went and saw him onto the train and that was that.

Talking about his leaving reminds me of an incident concerning the staff sergeant and Captain Crowther. The captain had his food and socialised with the sergeants and staff sergeants at their mess. A few weeks however—and remember we were a small camp—before the sergeant left, it was late at night, the corporal on the guard house and two guards came shouting something hysterical. We had no ammunition but grabbed our rifles and bayonets. All hell had broken loose at the sergeant's mess.

When we got there, only thirty yards or so, the staff sergeant and Captain Crowther were rolling on the ground, knocking the hell out of each other. We did not know that the captain had boxed for the regiment years ago, and what a beating he gave that staff sergeant. "Sir please, Staffie. Do stop! God, you'll get a court martial," I called out to the amazement of those unable or unwilling to intervene.

Finally, Sergeant Leask, the only National Service sergeant there, he was the regimental policeman at our camp, although off-duty, arrived on the scene seconds after us and separated the two. The staff sergeant had definitely come off worst. His face was in a real mess. The peculiar thing was that the other sergeants did not come to his aid during the fight or after, which made us think that Staffie was to blame for the whole incident. We never found out.

Captain Crowther went off to his caravan, so being a full corporal with quite a bit of authority, I and two other corporals got Staffie back to his room at the sergeants' quarters. We got him stripped to the waist. "Thanks lads, oh steady, oh hell." He was in a mess, the worst was his face. One of the other corporals, a regular, close to Staffie, as he was a regular soldier, not a National Service like us others, said, "Staffie, I'm taking you to the little cottage hospital. Look at your face! Let's go."

"God no, never!" he said, "There'll be a bloody court martial for sure. Ok, Kress and Thomson, you can go. Thanks lads."

Next day all was calm. I assume Captain Crowther told Major Warn. We were not asked any questions and that was that. That evening, that is the evening after the trouble, we were in our [six man to every billet] when Captain Crowther came into our billet. We stood up to attention. "Carry on chaps; it's a social call, thanks for your attendance it's just a small private matter." Then turning to me he said, "I've come in to ask you corporal, as you seem to press your uniform very well, can you press my tunic? I've cleaned it up. Be careful with my pips. That's captain's rank, three pips on each shoulder lapel."

"Certainly sir," I replied, "I'll do it now." So he gave me his tunic and I heated the iron. We had a collapsible table in the middle of the room, which we all used to iron our uniforms. When I had finished doing it, being what I was, I thought, as did the others in the billet that I should try it on. I did, and looked in the mirror inside the door of my locker. "Suits you matey! Go to the other billets and give 'em a laugh, Kressy. Go on!"

It was now dark, about 10.00pm or so. I had just gone to the next billet, went straight in. "Stand by your beds. What a bloody shambles! What the hell is this dust on the window ledge? You lot are on jankers [punishment duties] tomorrow morning.

"Walter," their corporal said to me, "how the hell did you come by that? Must say it suits you; you Scots git!" He was English, by the way. It was all said in good spirit of course. I wouldn't have given a damn if any privates had taken the Mickey. I was just like all of us here, just one of the lads, even as a full two-stripe corporal. I never harassed or threw rank at them, no way.

"I'd better take this off and get back to our billet." They all laughed as I went out the door.

I was about six feet or so from the door of my billet, jacket still on but not buttoned up, when who should come out of our washroom across from the billet but Captain Crowther. He always used our washroom, because as I mentioned he lived in a caravan. It had electricity, but nothing else. "And where have you been, masquerading as an officer, corporal? And improperly dressed! [not buttoned up] That's two charges," he smiled, "Get it off and bloody quick. How far have you actually been?"

I said, "Just to the next billet sir. They all had a good laugh sir. I told them their billet was a shambles sir, and that there was dust on the window ledge. Corp said that there'd be hell to pay f I was caught out by you sir."

Fortunately he saw the funny side of it. "Oh well, I suppose it got a few laughs, Kress."

"It did sir, it did."

Never a dull moment, never; just about two months before this, once again I had weekend leave. I left

Grantown on Spey very early in the morning with a staff car to deliver in Aberdeen by midday. I was there by 10.00am at the barracks to deliver it, but before I went home I had to go to a nearby TA centre where they had an armoured car with problems. The officer to whom I got the form for delivery signed gave me a lift to the TA centre. The vehicle's exhaust was burst; it roared like a spitfire. Also, it was built in Canada and had an automatic gearbox. I had never driven one. The noise was not so bad at slow speeds, but if you started to motor, what a din!

I told the chap in charge at the TA centre that I had authority to take it back to Grantown for repair. Yes, that was all in order. I signed the documents and took my copy in case I was stopped by the police or military police.

When I got home, having driven the beast slowly because of the noise, my mother said that my father was in the City Hospital for chest problems, taken in the night before, only for observation. Was it the truth or not? So driving this beast, I drove to the hospital less than ten minutes away.

The City Hospital was not big. As I approached the entrance very slowly, I crept up to the open gates wide enough to let me stop there without blocking it should an ambulance arrive. The chap in the gatehouse came out and I explained that I had come to see my father and the situation as to why I had this beast in my possession. I asked if I could possibly park it by his gatehouse.

"Take it down slowly to building four," I think it was he said, "That's ok, go slow through." There was lots of room by that building so I gingerly crept up to it. This was a hospital that I was in so I was conscious of the noise.

It did not sound too bad, and hey presto, where I stopped there in a bed, propped up, was my father. He recognised me. I jumped out, shut the door, went in and introduced myself to the sister. "Ye needn't tell us yer name soldier. Yer father's been telling us that ye might be commin' hame this weekend, and whatever have ye gotten out there? Dis every corporal hae een a thae?" [Does every corporal have one of those?]

"Not really," I said. I knew she was taking the Mickey. "I've just got it to take it to Grantown for repair. And the man at the gate said drive in slowly because the exhaust is broken. I did offer to leave it by his place there, but he said to take it in."

It turned out that my father had chest pains and a temperature. It was a marvellous place. I could see that the nurses were impressed with me, this foreign lad, here a corporal, great stuff. I saw the young duty doctor. He had just done National Service, as an officer of course; we were on the same wavelength immediately.

I left my father in good hands, said goodbye to all, got into the beast and very slowly backed away and turned it round, and then slowly drove to the gate, said cheerio to the attendant and went home to my mother. I assured her that he was all right. They were looking after him well.

On Sunday, I left the armoured car by the house and took my mother by bus of course to see my father. She was reassured that all was in order, and as my father had had this problem before, it appeared that the problem was lifelong flour dust as a baker.

I decided to take this beast to Grantown about 5.00 in the afternoon. When I got out of town, I didn't half go. It went like a train, the automatic gearbox. Well, that was what I reckoned was the eighth wonder of the world. It was terrific!

When I arrived at Grantown on Spey and waited for the guard to open the gate, the duty corporal came out to sign me in. "I heard you at the bridge three miles away. We all thought that a plane was coming down, we really did."

"Yes, I was doing 80 just before I slowed down by the bridge."

The next weekend, I was on guard duty on the Sunday. My father had been discharged on the Wednesday, and all was well.

Until I was at the finish of my stint in the Army, I regularly took vehicles up and down to Aberdeen. One of the privates (here again I cannot reveal names) who came to our unit six months before I was dismissed, his father and family had a garage in Aberdeen.

Strange, I thought, very strange, when I saw on the daily orders and duties roster that he was going to an extremely cushy number, as a mechanic to look after the TA unit at the university. Very nice, I wonder how the hell he got this.

When I finally got dismissed, and even before that, I saw my friend in Aberdeen. To say that he had landed a cushy little number was a gross understatement. He told me the unbelievable, that he was allowed by the university chap who was ex-Army and kept the vehicles clean and the garage tidy, etc, to come in civilian clothes. I was astounded, no comment. I think this was a case of not what, but who you know. No duties of any kind.

Yes, it was dismissal day. I had still to do TA service once a month, I think it was for two years or so. Some facts stand out clearly, others not so. I had to attend the TA usually on a Friday evening, plus I had to do fourteen days annual camp.

I went to see my boss where I had worked. They knew how I had made good in the army, as I always went to see my work mates. In fact, I forgot to mention on one of my visits, about four months before dismissal, when I went to see my mates, the foreman Horace Law—a smart ex-marine—said to me, "Walter, you'll never guess who is working here."

Well—to use the proverbial, knock me down with a feather—It was Harry Watt, from the Watt family of course. "I know how you did it," he had been a soldier in the last year of the war, "I bet you'd crawl under the belly of a snake without disturbing it. That's how you got them stripes, Walter."

Out of the six apprentices, only one, by the name of Simpson (can't remember the first name) got one stripe, lance corporal.

Old William, a former mechanic of yesteryear was in charge of the department where the tools, metal and nuts and bolts and all equipment was kept, said to me when I started work back there, "I always knew there'd be no holdin' you back, whatever."

I have it in writing on my discharge papers, Major Warn—whether everyone gets the same I don't know—but I have it to this day. It states that I have first class, thorough and able in every way, as a soldier and engineer, and that I should do well (he feels) in civilian life. He was right, I did do some wonderful things in civilian life; I have even been on a cruise ship through the Panama Canal and to Aloha, Hawaii.

My parents then decided that we should move to London to be near my sister. I, however, to be honest, was not all that keen. I was, am, and will always be an Aberdonian. Personally, as I was now 23 years old (this is my view of the situation) I think they still had at the back of their minds a nice Jewish girl for me. That's all to be written down some way on from here, but written down it will be. I also feel that they thought, but never said so, that I might fall for one of Kenny's sisters, so let's go now.

However, I immediately of course went to see the boaters down at Old Torry dock. I had kept in touch regularly when on leave. One chap in particular, Peter Garioch, who had a son of 26 years, had a small boat just like mine. Doreen, she was. Peter said to me that his son was moving away, and so would I like to be his shipmate and also could I do something with the engine, labour only. He would pay for the bits. Peter had a good job. He too was in a pattern shop at a shipyard. He knew Andy Riddle.

Andy, however, had packed up boats because of his wife. Jack Stevens had sold his boat and got hold of a real little fishing yawl—the real thing—with a proper marine engine. He had tried fishing for a living, but it had not paid. He was offered the job of driving the pilot boat and accepted; so he sold his lovely yawl. If only I had had time to organise three or four of us, we would have bought her, who had in 1953 sold for £240. She was worth every penny. She was sold very quickly and went away.

They do not build boats like that these days. It would cost, I reckon, at least £25,000 today—that is providing you could find that kind of a boat builder.

So Peter and I got on well. During the winter of 1953, I did some work on the engine in his shed in Torry, just down the road from Kenny Ross's family. I did not get much boating in come spring 1954, when we put the motor back in. It was just like my boat, an Austin 7 old car engine.

One thing clearly stands out in my mind. We, that is, my family, were just weeks away from leaving Aberdeen. My sister had found a flat to exchange for someone who wanted to come to live in Aberdeen. If I had seen that flat in North London, I would have told my sister in naval language what she could do with that place. But that's another story to come.

I had left my job, and got myself a tatty old 1932 model Austin 7. I fixed it up within what my cash at hand would allow, and it went reasonably well.

So on one of the last trips out with Peter in late April, we set off at five am, which was still a bit cold, but the cod were there. We just could not go wrong. We hauled them in. We had about a good two boxes full. Peter thought, "It's just gone eleven. Fish market stops at one on a Saturday. Let's make it."

We were lucky, it took us three quarters of an hour to get there, and lo and behold Clarry, the son of Grandma Andrews, was buying his usual supply to put by for Monday. All the business was nearly concluded, and the market staff looked busy boxing all the rubbish. We had arrived in time. Not that it would have mattered, as the auctioneer who takes a small commission called out, "Now lads, this boat has just come in. Wee fish caught this morning. They was up early so they have to get a good price. Quick now, it's near finishin' time."

Clarry was also bidding and told me later that he kept upping the offer. We were delighted when he got the fish. Of course, he had paid well over the top, good old Clarry. Peter wasn't half pleased about that. I think we got 36 shillings, less use of the fish market and the auctioneer's commission. The total we got was, I think, around 31 shillings. We were made. Peter insisted that I got half of the 31 shillings. We were rich that day.

Peter Garioch had been, as I said, a foreman. Also, he was a first class, much sought after trumpet player. I had a few lessons on his trumpet, but I just could not grasp learning music, which brings me, believe it or not, way back to Vienna, indeed so.

Probably a few months before we left Vienna, my mother took me for my first, and due to circumstances, my last music lesson. I was about seven and a half years old— and once again most clearly—I can recall the lady teacher.

She did not show me any sheet music or explain the various notes either. She just told me to watch. I was put on the seat that the teacher normally sits on at the piano. She stood behind and very slowly played a few bars of the very famous Blue Danube Waltz. She did this for about three or so minutes, then she took my right hand and with the finger next to the thumb, with the others slightly turned away, still standing behind me of course, guided my finger and we did the same few bars.

As I have said, that was the only lesson I ever had. I can still without hesitation play the same few bars that the lady taught me. People are in total disbelief that at the age of seventy, with just one short piano lesson, the memory has not faded.

The furniture lorry came early in the morning on moving day. Pickfords, it was. We soon had everything on board. I had hoped that my little Austin car would fit in, but it simply would not do so. The lorry left for London mid-afternoon. I took my parents to the station in my car, as they were going on the overnight train. Friends came to see them off, and as usual, there were tears all round. Now with just a few hours to go before I left, I tried to sell the car. Pity that I did not find a buyer, as the following horror story will explain.

The last night before I left Aberdeen was a most heart-rending business. I managed to see most of my friends. I was, to say the least, totally choked. The restless night at Kenny's family home, where I hardly slept all night, stands to reason really. At five am I was up and in that old car and started away.

The utter horror of the journey to London would, to recall it all, take reams and reams of paper. About forty-five miles per hour was its lot. Also, to top it all—and this finally made me ill—oil fumes came into the car, and open windows only gave slight relief.

I had, before I got to the border, two punctures. This was due to the wheels, which had spokes. The insides of the tyres of course had inner tubes. These tubes were being chewed by the spokes, and it required new tubes each time. Even though I got the fitter to wind some tape round the inner rim, it made no difference.

As I was delayed time-wise, I stayed in a lorry drivers' hostel. I should have gone to a private hostel or guesthouse, as the noise of the comings and goings from four am made sleep impossible. Therefore, by four-thirty am I was on my way again. To make a very long story short, I had another three punctures before reaching my sister's flat in Belsize Park, London at about ten o'clock that night—completely shattered.

In Grantham, I desperately tried to sell the car to all and sundry for four pounds, more than enough for the train fare to London. In a nutshell, I was totally clapped out and I was slowly being poisoned by the fumes. I had previously only used the car for short journeys in Aberdeen; never a trip like this, or anything like it. A round trip to Kenny's uncle of fourteen miles was it.

I even asked a policeman. He offered to take it off my hands, but I did explain as I had had to buy five inner tubes and he changed his mind. I had about twelve shillings and needed money for the train to London. So I had no choice but to proceed—thankfully with no more punctures.

There comes now the recounting of yet another trauma. Ok, life is not a bowl of roses but I seemed to be bouncing from one disaster to another.

My mother and father and I had left it up to my older sister to get us a flat. She eventually found a retired couple who originated from Aberdeen and were living in North Finchley, London. They clearly wanted to return home. I let my sister handle the entire exchange, our flat for theirs. The London flat was privately owned, and the Aberdeen council and the landlord of the London flat both agreed to the exchange.

I never thought that I should go to London to look

at this flat. I left it, trusting my sister's judgement. The day after arriving at my sister's flat, my parents had stayed with a friend of my sister's and her husband, as they only had the tiniest flat that I had ever seen.

I do not recall whether we went by car or by taxi to North Finchley, but my sister had the keys and we went in. They must have heard me explode some distance away, as a lady next door opened her upstairs window. I was swearing unreservedly in my Aberdonian accent. This lady was without a doubt a snob of the first calibre, "What dreadful language you are using! It's absolutely terrible!"

I had left the front door open, as I forgot to close it behind me, due to the scene I encountered. May I say that had my sister been a brother, I would have knocked the living daylights out of him! My parents were speechless. This dreadful place—remembering our big lovely place in Aberdeen—had all the linoleum on the floors in tatters; the wiring, which was condemned that very day, and the electricity cut-off, was laid in a thin, illegal course on top of a wooden surround, known as a picture rail. The gas stove was ghastly; then the gas was cut off. They told us it was lucky that the previous people had not had an explosion. In the front room, the damp was halfway up the outside wall, the place smelt musty. In a proverbial nutshell, after I regained a bit of composure, my sister kept insisting that it would be much better when it was all 'fixed up.' Fixed up! It should have been condemned and torn down!

"How the bloody hell, you stupid woman, could you let us in for something like this? I am going back and you can look after mother and father, damn you." Yes, I said all those things.

More trauma was yet to come.

My sister took my mother and father back to her place, but I completely refused. Her husband, who had kept out of the goings on, said to me, "You were lucky that we got a place at all, Walter. It's not easy, and this flat will soon be in shape. We did it for you, and especially for your parents. Come on over to our place."

I was adamant that I was finished with my sister. I was considering the trauma of motoring to London that I still had some strength left. "No, I'm not going back with you, and I'm not staying in this bloody hole. The people that lived here must have been complete and utter morons, the rubbish they left behind; oh Lord, what a mess!"

I had of course before and during National Service, passed through London and I knew that we had a distant cousin Oscar and his wife Ruth who lived there. I did not want to bother them, as they had just had a stillborn baby, and naturally were in turmoil over that. There was also a friend of my sister's and her husband, but no names here, as they did not want my sister to know that they had put me up.

However, the next day I went to that cursed place, my mind truly in such turmoil, as I had not experienced anything like this, not even during the bad weather sea river entrance that I spoke about. My father arrived shortly after. I told him there and then, but of course he knew the score, that I was not living there. I had never, ever used such bad language in front of my parents, but I came close to it that day.

"I have to tell you that yesterday's scene has affected Mama. She is not at all well." And as the days wore on, my mother, it seemed, had had a breakdown with it all. It would take me hours writing it all down. We had dreadful scenes daily. The only reason that I did not return to Aberdeen there and then was the developments with my mother. Of course, I got all the blame. She was taken— after being seen by various specialists—to a psychiatric hospital for observation at Kings Cross. And to top it all, with my near poisoning car fumes, it was just about as much as I could take. I simply could not think straight anymore.

No, I could not leave my parents, especially my mother. I was her number one. The landlord got things sorted out as days went by. He too was aghast, and frankly he was worried about the wiring and the gas. After a few days then, my father and I moved in. It was a horrible existence. My father did his very best. I had lost all interest. Next thing, I went down really bad. It was the damp, the smell, everything together. I developed glandular fever and ended up in Finchley Memorial Hospital. I was, to tell the truth, not only physically ill, but mentally exhausted.

My mother was still at Kings Cross Hospital. Of course, my sister and her husband and my father came to see me in hospital. I did not have the energy to restart the row, and I did not want to cause a scene in a hospital. I was too clapped out anyway. This episode definitely was the thin end of the wedge in the breakdown of my health.

When I came out of hospital, they—the hospital authorities—had made arrangements for me to go to Deal in Kent to a convalescent home. I, who was reasonably tough with boats and heavy mechanical work, was going to a convalescent home. *My God,* I thought, *what a bloody state of affairs.*

My utmost concern, I hasten to add, was not for myself, but for my mother. So naturally, before I set off for Deal, I had an appointment at the hospital at Kings Cross, where my mother was. The specialist had all the facts, the lot. "I can understand how you felt about the place you were going to live in. That, however, is not what set off your mother's problems." She was now very subdued.

I was mortified. Things could not get worse.

"It all stems from the fact, you will not be surprised, that subconsciously your mother has kept the trauma of Austria bottled up inside of her. She has never shown outward signs, but we humans do keep things like that close, very close within us, and it's not wise, definitely not." He tells me the obvious; don't I know it, and some.

He went on; he certainly knew his job, this specialist. I had confidence in him. To say that the hospital here was only really a place where people with suspected mental problems were diagnosed  and either got better and were discharged; but unfortunately in my mother's case, she would have to be transferred to Nappsbury at London Colney. It was a mental home. The specialist went on to explain that there was a possibility that she might never fully recover. Once more, I simply could have, without a lie, had the ground open up and swallow me.  I was totally devastated. This fellow could see my reaction, as I could not speak. I simply could not. My mind was a complete blank. It was simply an unbelievable nightmare. Of course, we were all totally taken aback. My sister did not put any blame on me, nor did I start pointing any fingers either. My father now told us that for years, he suspected that my mother had harboured her problems, and had on many occasions confided in him that she was deeply troubled that I might have been sent to Korea. This all adds up when one looks at the scenario. Hindsight is often very cruel.

I decided that I certainly could not go back to Aberdeen now or possibly ever. My father said to me as I was getting on the train to go to Deal, "When you get back, your sister wants to make it up to you. Walter, please listen for your mother's sake."

Finally the train started, and hearing people talk, I realised that there were a few going to the convalescent home in Deal. The carriage I was in was the type that had a door at every separate compartment. Shortly after the train left the station, Waterloo or Victoria—I am not sure—I became aware that a rather well spoken lady of about forty or older was looking at me. I had a newspaper with me, and every time I turned the page or took a sweet from a bag I had in my pocket, I found that the lady was looking at me. She was definitely looking at me. I asked her, "Would you like to have the paper?"

"Oh thank you," she said extremely politely, "I think I can detect a Scottish accent, oh definitely. I think it's a lovely dialect."

I was rather taken by surprise. "Yes, I'm from Aberdeen."

"Ah, that's the granite city, isn't it?"

"Yes," I replied, "Would you like one of my sweets?"

"Please," she said, "Thank you, Callard and Bowsers, I like them."

She took a sweet and began to read the paper, but even then she was still looking at me.

I began to wonder why she was looking at me straight in the eyes. I began to feel slightly uncomfortable. I do not know why, possibly as I was still slightly unwell from the traumas of the past weeks. Had she been more my age, I would probably have looked straight back at her and right in the eyes. That's the first contact, is it not so?

At every stop, I expected this lady to be getting off, but no. Just before the train reached Deal however, she was looking at a piece of paper which she accidentally dropped. I reached down and as I picked it up, I saw it was the same as the instructions that I had received from Deal. A bus would meet us and take us to the home. I gave it back to the lady, and I just happened to see the name of the convalescent home when I picked it up. "I'm actually going there as well." I said.

In that case, with that ever present straight in the eyes look, I must confess I began to think *Hello, hello. Well maybe, or is she just like that, possibly even a bit eccentric.* I never thought of myself as many fellows do, that they were the cat's whiskers or the answer to a maiden's prayer, oh never. But as this lady—probably old enough to be my mother—

was nearly always sitting opposite me at mealtimes in the lounges, sure enough she would find me, and she was knowledgeable on a great many subjects. A fellow who was at the meal table near me, I assume he was about sixty, said to me very quietly one day, "If you don't mind me saying so, young man, I think you've got it made with that woman, by the way we noticed that she always seems to be hanging around near you, and a good-looking thing she is at that. You've got it made."

Well, I will confess that I had never gone all the way with a woman, or young woman, ridiculous as it sounds, but it's true. Cynics may laugh or even think how odd, twenty-four years old, was in the Army, you know what soldiers are like. But I knew older chaps who had not had the pleasure. It was nothing to be ashamed of.

I think it was about the fourth day at the home, at breakfast, the manageress suggested as it was a nice day, that any of us reasonably fit should go for a short walk along the seafront. "Scottie," the lady said to me, "I'm going with another lady. Come with us. We would like you to come with us." Those come-hither eyes were once again on me.

Well, I was twenty-four and definitely a real hot-blooded male. Here was something that I was reasonably sure was going to be it. I was no macho sort of a young man, but to coin a phrase the penny had suddenly dropped.

So the lady and another lady that she had made friends with, who was much older it appeared, were waiting at the entrance. Some of the others had already gone. I think not more than about a dozen of us went for that walk. The three of us ambled off slowly. We were none of us that fit to be able to step out lively. We had gone about ten minutes from the home when the older lady said that she had a minor problem and that she was going to go back. "See you later then. Take care," the lady of the eyes said to her. "Let's go down the steps there and sit down by one of the boats pulled up on the shingle, just for a little while.

What do you think, Scottie?" she said to me.

"Seems a good idea to me," I replied. We got down to the little fishing boat—there were quite a few boats there. We sat ourselves down between two of the boats.

"Nice here," she said to me, "out of that rather cool breeze." There was not a soul there.

My heart was going some. I thought, *It's time now, right now. I'm going to make a move to get her reaction.* I had never attempted this ever, not ever. But a split second before my move, the lady came closer to me, those beautiful eyes came closer. It was definitely going to be the come-on, we both realised this.

It could not have been more than about six seconds or so since we sat down. "Scottie, you're younger than I am, but I really fancy you and I think you feel the same way, don't you?"

This was definitely it. But before I could reply that I felt the same, she said, "Scottie, the down below problem that I had fixed isn't ready yet. But Scottie, it will be soon, or we would do it here now." We hugged each other.

I never even knew her name, nor did it matter. We each knew the score and some. "Dear lady, you can believe it or not, but I've never done it. No, never. And that's no lie. I had a strict upbringing."

She replied, "I never did it 'til I got married at twenty-nine. Can you believe it? We are indeed a right pair." A few seconds of hugging and kissing ensued—very nice.

I felt ten feet tall. I think that not having given it any thought when we set off from the home I was not at all sure where this was going to end. I had never thought of going to a chemist for the necessary Boy Scouts motto. Anyway, we were in daylight, absurd to think such a thing. "Are you divorced or perhaps widowed?" I asked her.

"Oh no, I'm still married, but Scottie, that does not matter at all. My husband is very much older than me.

There are problems, many amongst them, the first that he has a lady friend." She could not speak further; she was choked. I was in a feet-not-touching-the-ground situation. "Oh Scottie, don't be put off. I've been honest with you. I don't care or want to know if you've got a lady friend or even if you're a married man."

"No," I said, "believe it or believe it not, I have had two disappointments many, many years ago. The first one when I was but a boy; she was my first love, the girl truly loved me, as I loved her." I hesitated then thought, *yes, I'll tell her all*. I was about to continue, "You see, dear lady…"

But she was all over me and a long kiss followed.

I continued, "You see, the girl was from a very devout Christian family, and I am a Jew."

"Really?"

"Yes, I am what I am, and I don't keep it a secret, especially in this lovely situation. Her father politely told me that the relationship must stop. We were of completely different religions. It just could not develop. He said, 'It has broken my daughter's heart, it really has, but that's it. Cheerio.'"

The lady, oh dearest lady, never told me her religious faith. I thought it was time to stand up in case some of the others were near or worse, saw us in this situation. However, the lady—I found out her name that day—said, "Let's go down a little further to the other boats." This took us further away from the promenade.

I said, "Let's walk a little that way, where the promenade and the road ends; by those boats and fishermen's huts." It didn't take long. We trotted off across the gravel. "Don't hold my hand in case someone sees us," I said.

"I can always say," she smiled, "that I was a bit unsteady, and had asked you to help me."

There was not a soul there by the sheds and boats.

We sat down again. "We will have to get back for lunch soon."

"No hurry," she replied, "Oh Scottie." It got better and better. We both of us had arrived at this most beautiful point that a man and woman can share. "I'm so sorry that I can't right now."

"Well, I didn't come prepared to be invited to have intercourse, dearest lady." I must say my heart was going some, it was. I was in paradise, heaven; call it what you will, I was in another world.

"You would not have needed any such thing if my problems that have been fixed below, I can assure you Scottie, if only I was six weeks further on, if only." We were totally on the same irresistible wavelength. Oh joy. "Tell me, Scottie, you don't have any problems, do you, in that department? I would not think for one moment that you had. A young man of twenty-four, and a virgin as well, oh Scottie."

All I can say is that I could not—nor could the lady—keep our hands off each other as lovers almost in full flight. What can I say? It's the most natural thing in the world to touch. "We have got to move. It's just about lunchtime."

"All right then, pity we have to go back already, it really is." the lady said.

"On occasions such as this, time really does fly," I said, "We must keep this low-key at the home, otherwise you never know, tongues will wag."

"Oh Scottie, I realise that." On the way back I had to tell the lovely lady not to try to hold my hand. "I've completely gone on you Scottie. We are going to do wonderful, wonderful things Scottie, just you wait and soon, very soon."

I am sure that had the lady said these words to a fellow who couldn't contain himself, she would have been seduced at the boats with dreadful consequences with her problems. Mind you, I had to keep control of myself, but who wouldn't in this situation.

It was just as we were getting back to the house that the other lady who had gone back, but had evidently come out again to look for us, came into sight, "Hello, which way did you go? I thought I'd find you just a little bit along the prom."

"We went the other way, as we thought the view may have been better. Where the promenade ends there is a path that leads to the boats there on the shingle, and it was worth that short walk just for the view."

*Not half it was, not only to see, but to touch.*

We got in for lunch just as the bell was ringing. We both went to our individual toilets to wash before lunch.

That evening, there was a trio of musicians in the dining room, where the tables and chairs had been moved to the side. The music, of course, considering the state of most of the people there, was gentle, a sort of Victor Sylvester. No swinging Jazz or Bop.

The lady, I couldn't refer to her as just a woman, for a lady she was indeed. I really thought at times as to what she saw in me, fascination or desperation, or love at first sight. That brings to mind a song about something, fools rush in, where angels fear to tread.

But something about wise men never do, so how are they to know? So let this fool rush in. I am no fool, but wasn't I just ready to rush in, and some!

After dinner, as we were going to the lounge for tea or coffee, the lady asked me if I danced. I replied, "Well, I wouldn't get medals, but I can get by." I was rather good, I must admit.

"See you there then," she said. Without fail, I assure you her looks again said it all. This is no female looking for a quick fix. I am convinced of that. My mind was now in overdrive thinking, *God, perhaps with my non-existent experience, have I in my utter excitement thrown away all caution or reason? Hell no, I'm going to go all the way!*

At eight o'clock, we met for the dance in the dining room. Few of us danced; some were elderly, and others simply owing to their problems could not do so.

The mistake I made was to dance virtually all the time, except when the lady asked me to ask her friend that we went out walking with for a dance. She was rather stiff in her movements, due of course to her problems. The lady and I did some of the tunes rather close to each other, and yes, we mistakenly did some real smooching. That was to have some quite serious repercussions.

# CHAPTER 5

So at nine-thirty the dancing was over. People either went to the lounge or to bed. We played it as cool as we could. I wanted, and told the lady that I would love to take her outside somewhere more intimate. Impossible of course, but if only we had a room for each person, and how the situation was small dormitories with six males in each and upstairs the ladies had similar. However, it was not difficult to say goodnight that evening. We had to really keep ourselves in check. What a day this has been, I could hardly sleep. In fact, just before I went to bed, the chap who thought I was onto a good thing said, "I saw you going out with the lady and another lady, how are you doing then?"

"She is quite pleasant, very upper class, beyond me. She's old enough to be my mother," I said and that was that.

Next morning, after breakfast, the manageress beckoned me as I was walking out of the dining hall. "Oh Mr Kress, can you come into my office for a moment please?" Once inside she opened up. "Mr Kress, I'll come straight to the point. I saw you and Mrs... canoodling when you were dancing, as did some of my staff. Is there something going on between you and Mrs..? Are you aware, or perhaps not, that the lady is married, you are twenty-four and she is forty-six?"

"Oh, I think there's a bit of a misunderstanding here."

"Not really," she replied, "You have been virtually inseparable. It hasn't escaped our attention." There was a knock at the door, "Just a minute, will you please." A member of staff brought the lady into the office.

I was not going to let the lady be trapped so I tipped her off just enough for her to grasp what was heading her way. "Hello, they seem to think as we were so friendly last night—"

"Mr Kress, if you don't mind, I will ask the questions," The manageress insisted.

"This is ridiculous," I said, "So we danced and OK, we canoodled a bit. Make what you will out of it. Really, with all due respect to Mrs..., she is old enough to be my mother, that's for sure. Yes, I think Mrs...and I are just comforting each other. I do not know of her background, nor is it any of my business, but let me assure you, if you knew what I have been through the last few months, you'd need a bit of canoodling, and furthermore, we did not do it hidden away somewhere, but on a dance floor. What a lot of fuddy-duddies you've got here. Old maids—are they jealous?"

"That's enough Mr Kress. You can prepare to be sent home...Disgraceful behaviour! Mrs.., what have you to say?"

"I think Mr Kress is a very nice young man. I have found him to be educated. He is quite knowledgeable and pleasant to be here with. Most of the others, I can understand of course, wish to be left to their own thoughts due to what they have recently had to endure, no doubt. As I have, as well as Mr Kress. I must say that you are being most unfair to have him sent away. I really do."

The manageress hesitated for a few seconds. "Alright, I'll have to see about this later." That was that. And later that day, the manageress told me, "Well, we may have misjudged yours and Mrs...'s behaviour. We haven't ever seen anything like it here. Anyway, you are adults. You can stay."

The lady and I therefore made sure that we did not give further impressions of our close association. The staff that had watched our antics were not at all pleased with my comments about them. Well, we could not simply say that we were indeed very close, or divulge the truth that we had actually touched each other.

Should I be ashamed of all of this? Never! As I have said, we were both adults, knowing exactly what we were doing, and I even told the lady when we finally parted that if she was not married, divorced or a widow, that I truly felt that I would love to keep up our close relationship. She was indeed a lady in the true sense of the word.

"Scottie, I do love you in the truest sense of the word, I really do. My life for a time now has been totally without love or affection. By what you have told me about yourself, and I believe it, you too have had more than your share of grief and disappointments."

"I do believe in fate," I said. It all adds up.

So the bus arrived to take us to the railway station. As we sat next to each other, we dared not to look eye-to-eye, as some of the other people were also there. *So what, let them stare,* I thought.

She pressed a small piece of paper into my hand. It was her telephone number. "Only phone on Saturday evening; our number is fortunately similar to a car hire service, so if my husband's home, I will say that this is not the car hire company; we are fed up with getting their calls."

We parted on arrival in London; no close encounters, no sad farewells, for all we knew, her husband might be waiting here for her.

I forgot to mention that during this time I should have of course been attending the required Territorial Army attendance, but the hospital had notified the authorities of my illness and further convalescence, so I did not have to attend, at least not until I was fit.

When I got back to London, I of course had to go to our flat of nightmare memories. I have not the slightest doubt that my illness was brought on partially as a result of that dreadful place.

I had all sorts of things on my mind. I must get a job soon; my state of funds was £216 in the bank—well, a fair amount in 1954, I suppose. I could not really come down to earth. Every time I tried, I ended up most of the time thinking of that lady. Oh yes, it was only going to be a matter of time before we got it together, of that I was certain.

I would be a liar if I said that I had never read things about sex or heard of the explicit exploits of others, although never ever was this sort of thing spoken of, believe it or not, not even by my boating buddies. Yes, we swore a bit at times, but we never spoke about sex. Of course, they often asked me how my love life was or had I found a lassie yet, but that was just playful ribbing. They knew how I felt about boats, and as I said before quite a few thought I was a very odd young fellow indeed. Some I am sure even felt that I was gay—no girls.

However, I simply for the moment had to put the idea of meeting up with the lady out of my mind, but that was simply not at all possible.

While I was away, the various problems with the flat had, to my surprise, been fixed. My father again I say, and especially the situation with my mother, had made me make the decision to stay, and of course, need I say, so had that lady.

I had gone the next day to Henlys at Henlys Corner, Temple Fortune, and I got a job immediately as a mechanic, of course. I pointed out that I had however just come back from convalescence and could not start work until discharged by the hospital and the doctor.

My father then said to me that he had agreed with my sister and her husband to lend them some money, and I would be invited also to contribute, to a house they were going to buy in Golders Green.

"Are you telling me that I should live with them after this damned episode? Papa, you must realise how I feel."

"Do it for your mother's sake then," he replied.

Yes, he had hit a nerve, indeed he had. "Alright, but I'm not keen, and furthermore, I'm not giving them every penny I've got, and I hope that you don't either."

"I might not want to stay with them for any length of time, and I forgot to tell you, you're going to be an uncle soon and I'm going to be a grandfather!"

"Oh well, okay, anything to get out of here." I cannot recall the exact sum of money involved from my father and myself.

The house, I believe was about £3,000. One could also in those far-off days buy a Rolls Royce for that same figure!

Then came the day that I had discussions with my sister—I hasten to add that she was a social climber. She was way above her station. This stemmed from the fact that she had arrived in London before us, and was older than me and she had lived with wealthy, very wealthy foster parents. It later transpired that my sister became nanny to her foster parents other children and of course, the trappings of wealth and stature were an idea that she could not let go. Of course, I could not care less. Her husband was a violinist in one of the big orchestras.

At last, about two months after coming to London, or perhaps a bit more than that, we moved to Golders Green. Where we lived was not far from Hampstead Heath.

On vacating that rotten flat, the landlord tried to get us to pay fifty percent of the price that it had cost him; I think it was just over two hundred pounds. I told my father that we were not giving him a penny, and the landlord threatened legal action. When we told him to go ahead and we would get a statement or get the court to get a statement from previous tenants, the builders, gas people, plus the electricity company. That was the end of the landlord's threats. The court, I feel, would have thrown the case out.

I was not at all happy, but now with hardly any money to my name, how could I improve my situation anyway? Only the continuous thoughts that I would soon meet up with the lady really kept me from getting depressed, as after a serious illness this can often happen.

Late one Saturday evening, I phoned the lady from a phone box. I tried, just in case someone else might be there with the lady—her husband or friends—to speak in a somewhat broken English style, regarding hiring a car.

"No, I'm afraid this is not that company. You have the wrong number." That was that for the moment anyway.

I went to work eventually at the garage after being discharged from hospital. I was even told, as I appeared to be a smart and clean sort of a chap, that there would be a vacancy in the car sales department, and they felt I might well fit in there.

Now I also had to start my TA attendances. The venue was in Camden Town. Of course, I was only a corporal at the time. The first time I turned up there—yes, I was still proud in that uniform—the CO who was in uniform said that he had not seen such a smart turn-out for some time. "We don't require you to turn out here quite so smart. In fact, you'll see most of the chaps, except the officers, come here in civvies just to put their time in. There's not much to do here. We go to the bar, have a few short lectures and go home. That's it, very easy here."

Here now I must confess that as some things come back so clear, some others do not. I cannot remember if it was once a fortnight or once a month that I attended the TA. Anyway from then on I went in civvies. I had however not been going there for more than about four or five meetings when the CO asked me if I wanted to move to a unit at Kingsbury as they were short of NCOs.

"Well sir, if it's all right with you, I think I would give it a try sir."

"Well Corporal Kress, if you don't like it there, you're most welcome to return to us here. You have, in the short time that you've been attending here, impressed the lads. They are not all ex-REME, and they like your explanations when you have lectured them. So you'll be most welcome back here, and good luck. I don't know why a chap like you didn't make the Army a career. I daresay you would have got a commission. Goodbye Corporal."

He shook my hand and that was that.

I of course turned up at Kingsbury. It was an all REME unit. Just as I had at Camden Town, hair cut short, smart as they make 'em—I was proud of how far I had got and what I had done in the Army. It did me a power of good, and I met some great people at the time. It definitely was character-building.

"Come in," said the CO, a captain ex-REME. I saluted smartly. He did salute in return, after a style it was, no smartness to it. "So you're the chappie from Camden via Aberdeen. Been there years ago; nice place when the sun shines. You know what I mean, usually cool and damp to say the least.

"We here, except the privates, as we have to keep some form of order, do relax military ways a bit, hence corporal upwards to ranks such as myself are on first name terms here, but not if we go on exercises or some high ranker comes out of the blue unannounced to inspect us. In about twenty minutes, at muster and roll call you will meet the whole bunch.

I have your records to hand of course. You certainly have

had some experiences in your lifetime. I particularly like the volunteering for the services, but most of the lads here would not have gone in if they had such a choice. Now, before we go any further, cigarette, drink?"

"Yes please, just a small one." Lucky day, he had some Drambuie, a smooth liquor that I very occasionally had, usually as a miniature. "I don't smoke sir."

"Ah, I forgot. No sir, here. My name's Edward Taylor. Here Walter is what you'd call in Scotland just a wee nip. That's the term, I remember it well."

Come the muster and roll call, some of course were in civvies, but not the NCOs or the officers. There were about thirty privates, four lance corporals, myself and three other full corporals, one sergeant and an ex-Army sergeant major who had been in the Army for many years, including boys' service. He was not married, and the TA I feel was his only interest. We got on well that evening. And I forgot to mention the lieutenant. I cannot remember his name; he was National Service but got a commission as he had a university degree. It was a short meeting that evening, then after business, we all went into the bar. The sergeant major—a chap called Fred—who had been in REME of course, but in engineering, was not the regimental type at all, and I doubt if he ever had been that type. Anyway he approached me one day in a cheerful manner and said, "Corp mate, the captain wants to see you for a minute. Come with me pal."

I followed him and he knocked on the open door. "Come on in Fred, and new lad. This may take you by surprise I think, but earlier on I had a word with Fred, our sergeant major here and we need another sergeant. Well, if you want it, it's yours. We would certainly like you to accept it."

"Thank you. I'll take it," I replied without hesitation.

"Here are the stripes. Have them on at the next

meeting. So Fred, we've got us a good lad, I'm sure of that."

So I am a sergeant. Well, it's TA but that matters not. How I would love to meet up with some of my Army pals, especially Sergeant Dale of the training unit. Perhaps the MOD or War Office or REME association might know if he is still around? In later chapters I will by then be able to say if I have been successful.

My thoughts now turn once again to that dear lady. It must be time now, with my burning desire that keeps me awake. How soon, I ask myself, is it going to be the big day? So I phoned the lady, and it's my lucky day.

"Hello, yes I was expecting and hoping that you'd ring this evening. Only hubby thinks that I have got more cheerful and seem to be full of new life. I assured him that it's probably due to the fact that I'm getting over my operation, plus the convalescence has done me a power of good, and some Scottie." She went on to ask, "Have you, and be honest, now that we have parted, given this any more thought? Are you still of the same feeling?"

I replied that this question cannot be discussed on the phone. One never knows who may be listening.

"Scottie, all right, ring in two week's time at ten pm, I am just waiting to see you, and very soon. Bye."

Frustration is putting it mildly, and more was to come, for when eventually I rang on the allotted day and time, her husband answered the phone, and putting on a European accent, I enquired if I could have a car.

"No sir, afraid this is not the car-hire office," and he put the phone down...disaster!

My new job at the garage kept me busy but my thoughts were never far from the lady. The work was not general garage work for the public, it was only preparing cars that had been bought or part exchanged to be re-sold. The workshop was under the showroom. It had strip lights, and was semi-dark there. No ventilation as such and there would be many a row, when the others ran engines, and especially moved them which filled the place with fumes. It was like fog—dreadful.

But fate, as always, was just around the corner. I had stared to do a little private work at people's homes, either in the evenings or at weekends. There then came into my life one of these meetings with a person that was yet another big milestone in my life.

Of course, living in Golders Green, it was a district where the majority of the residents were Jewish. I happened to be walking down the road—North End Road, Golders Green—one evening on a Saturday, when outside a block of flats, a youngish chap had the bonnet of a Jaguar up. There was water dripping from underneath. This episode was the start of my becoming a one-man self-employed mechanic.

I stopped and asked if he had a problem.

"Do you know anything about cars?"

"Indeed," I assured him, "I'm a mechanic."

"I haven't seen you round here before. Do you live locally?"

"Yes, up the road with my sister, Mrs..."

"Well, well," he replied, "You're the brother that's come to live here from Scotland. What a stroke of luck for me. Could you just have a quick look? I really would appreciate it. But don't get your clothes dirty."

It was a simple problem. I took my jacket off and rolled up my sleeves. It was a simple matter of locating a fine leak on a water hose. Some tape was the solution; it had the desired effect. I did point out to the chap who introduced himself as Mr Shutzman that it was temporary and would require a new hose as soon as possible.

"Would it be possible for you to come on Monday early evening and fit a new one? I'll get it on Monday and

116

you can fit it, if that's all right with you."

I agreed, always ready to earn a few extra bits of cash.

Also, I carried my tools in an old leather bag. I did not have a car then, only an old bike that came with us to London.

Word soon spread, and also more luck came my way. Bobby Shutzman was a partner in what then was all the rage, a coffee bar nearby in Temple Fortune. Also, at the rear was a bakery, small but efficient. He was producing delicious pastries for the coffee bar, The Madelaine, it was called.

He was also on the point of expanding the pastries business to other coffee bars, restaurants and even to private residents when they held a function. As I said, the pastries were absolutely great. You see, I loved these and chocolates, in preference to alcohol, believe that of a soldier if you can!

Then Mr Shutzman and his partner asked me if I was interested, say three evenings per week, to wash dishes and tidy the kitchen, etc.

"Yes," I said without hesitation. After all, why not, it was more money, and many prominent people have worked in kitchens in their lifetime. I was not, shall we say, thinking that this is not a job for a qualified mechanic. Not only that, but I got pastries. I got a meal before starting at seven pm until midnight and hot chocolate etc throughout the evening, what a bonus! There was a full-time Scottish woman, Peggy, in the kitchen. We immediately got on well. When I told her that I was from Vienna, she replied that that was the same place the owners came from.

"They dinna spik English proper, and I woudna hev thought the way you spik Aberdenian that ye was from Austria, never."

So with me working there some evenings, Peggy got

some time off. That woman had had a hard life, divorced from a drunkard of a husband, the lot; she had seen the hard edge of life.

A crunch came one day at my sister's. My mother was showing signs of improvement, and the home suggested that we should take her home for short periods to see the reaction. There was now a baby girl in our family. How could we bring Mama home? There's simply no room.

Well, this was my chance to get the hell away from there. Yes, facts are facts. There had been dreadful scenes in this house. She condemned, and you may find it hard to believe my father for being what he was, plus of course that I should have gone on to university and made something better of myself.

I was also very friendly at the garage where I worked with the son of an African chief. He was the washer and greaser and had originally come to study, but for some reason he got a job as a film extra quite regularly, plus the work in the garage. His name was Frank Jaja. He was married to an Irish girl and had new babies—twin boys.

Also like me, he was a jazz fan in a big way. At lunchtimes and other times, we would walk the short distance to his flat and listen to some great jazz.

I told my sister about Frank and his great collection of music, but I am not putting into writing what that bitch of a sister of mine said. Being Jewish, I was mortified by her remarks, amongst which were that this association was not helping me in any way. She did not seem to know that we are all God's kids. Am I looking for association to help me climb the social ladder? Not bloody likely. I can take or leave people as they are, and they me. What has the colour of a man's skin or his choice of his religion got to do with friendship?

Anyway, her attitude only served to strengthen my resolve. "Ok, Mama's coming home, you've got this house; I'm moving out. That'll make room."

"That's the least you can do," she replied, so that was it.

I got a nice room in Windemere Avenue, at a Jewish lady's house. She had come from Germany. Only breakfast was served but that was no problem. I could always go round the back of The Madelaine. Very soon after I moved from my sister's house, my mother went to stay there, and it did the trick, especially now that she was a grandmother. The truth was never told as to why I moved out, only that it made it easier, as the house was not that big, and my mother thankfully seemed to grasp and understand the situation.

One evening at the Madelaine, doing my kitchen stint, Bobby Shutzman asked me if I would like a morning job, driving a small van to deliver pastries in the West End he was starting. He had already got a small Austin 8 van and also here was the opportunity not to be missed. It meant that I could now do my work afternoons, and also one of my customers who was recommended by Mr Shutzman and lived in the same block of flats, went to business at seven-thirty am and came back late, he agreed to let me use the garage he kept his car in, but only during the day, of course. Things were getting better and better all the time. I had of course by now left work at the garage. In those days, the traffic downtown was nothing in comparison to the present day and driving in London was still enjoyable.

Here follows more incredible luck. Yes, things were coming my way. At the flats there regularly came this very pleasant chap. Much later, he told me that he was half Jewish. He washed and valeted cars, and he also did odd-jobbing. He was a hard worker, Fred Harris. We hit it off from the start. 'Jockie', he called me.

He had connections everywhere, Hampstead Garden Suburb, where a good percentage of the residents were not only Jewish, but very wealthy to boot. Amongst the people he knew were some very famous names, the late Mr Peter Sellers, Spike Milligan and Val Doonican. The work was such that working at my trade in the afternoons and some evenings—I was getting to the point, even working some weekends—that I regretfully had to give up the pastry deliveries. It was a bit much to do this, plus of course the evening kitchen work. Bobby Shutzman and his partner, and Peggy and the waitresses were delighted for me.

I was even—through connections—building up in the motor trade and began to sell the odd new or used car. I dealt honestly and true with people, irrespective of their wealth, their situation in life or whatever their position and work they had. Cars were my business, not to look at what business my customers were in.

Mr Peter Sellers sent me on a two-week course to the London Service Centre of Rolls Royce and Bently cars, at Hythe Road in Willesden, London. Near the end of this fabulous two-week course, the instructor took four of us at a time out to drive an old Rolls Royce. That whetted my appetite to own a Rolls or Bentley one day. It felt absolutely as if it was on a silent cushion of air, what a car!

Peter Sellers at the time was living in Oakleigh Park, North London. He bought a fabulous mansion at Chipperfield, north of Watford. This place had at one time been owned by the car magnate, Lord Rootes, of Rootes car group.

Mr Sellers even told me one day soon after we met that his father would like to meet me, by then I was regularly looking after his car, and so it went on. I remember one day he said to me, "Walter, I'm thinking of buying a helicopter. I would pay for you to have training."

I was completely astounded.  I thanked him for the offer, but I told him that this required something I honestly felt was beyond me.  He was impressed with my honesty.  In the end he gave up on the idea because as it turned out he was about to go to America.  There were two occasions just before he went to America that really did, what one would say, make my day.  Very near Henlys Corner there was a Salt Beef Bar, and I regularly had a sandwich there.  Peter Sellers would often come in there too.  One evening I was sitting there having a sandwich when in walks Peter Sellers, "Hello Walter."  Hand outstretched, here I was shaking hands with The Peter Sellers—wow, oh wowee.

The owner said to Peter, "You don't know this chap, do you?"

"He's the only Jewish Scotsman that I know of." Laughter all round.

The week after, at lunchtime I was parked—I had a small old brown van now with all my equipment in it outside the Madelaine—to pop round the back for a plate of soup and a bit of cheesecake.  I had just got out of my van when on the other side of the road a Rolls Royce PS199 pulled in and parked up.  The driver was of course Peter Sellers. "Hello Walter," he said as he came across the road, hand outstretched.  My hands were absolutely filthy from work and I was going to wash them at the Madelaine's outside tap.

At first I held out my hand, then realised the state they were in.  I gradually withdrew my hand ever so slowly. "I'm afraid I've not got clean hands."

And once more, I use unbelievable as the only way to recall the next move.  Peter Sellers quickly grasped my filthy hand and also put his other hand on top of that.  The world looked on.  I was over the moon, believe me, I was, Peter Sellers shaking my dirty hand—what a man.  I also got free tickets to the Camden Theatre to see the Goon Show being recorded.  The antics before, during and after the show were in the can, so to speak.  It was something I will remember forever; absolutely spontaneous and hilarious. Peter Sellers went to America and I never saw him again. That does sadden me. We have seen and heard lots about Peter Sellers; to me he was, to use a Jewish term, A-Mensh—a real human being.

Ah now I am afraid once more, upon further reflection, I should have put pen to paper a few pages ago, but things come back from time to time, but not always in order. These are of course very important, as they were again to change my mind.

The lady's letter duly arrived. She feared that her husband may have even had her watched, so for the present we could not meet up. I rang on a few occasions but always got the 'this is not the car hire company' line. TA attendance also had to be done. Then the day came that all from the rank of lance corporal to the officers were to hold a party for us. My friend, the sergeant major brought his charming mother along. As I said, he was not married. Now, that very evening—as the party started at seven-thirty and was going on until eleven pm—made things awkward for me. I being into jazz, had read in the paper that the Big Bands of those days, one of which was Jack Parnell and his band, were appearing at Barnet Drill Hall. So I made my excuses and left, "Well friends, I have to meet a pal of mine, I've remembered, at a jazz do at Barnet Drill Hall. Please excuse me, won't you? I really have to go. Thanks and see you next week." I left just before eight-thirty and got to the Drill Hall by nine. It was in full swing. This was a great band and the place was packed. This was normal, as jazz was the thing and this was one of the great Big Bands of the day on the British Big Band circuit. Is it fate or what is it? Ask me another. Well, a chap has to dance and jive a bit at these sessions, does one not? There were two girls in particular amongst a big crowd of people. And no, I was not looking for the same experience that I had at Deal, not at all.   However, one of the girls seemed a bit different, a bit classy, I thought, well spoken, hourglass figure, nice perfume, nice dress. Yes, she was to become my wife in due course, but not without its traumatic events, especially my sister's sadistic comments about a 'shikse,'—a dreadful Jewish remark not only about the girl being from another religion, but more in the meaning of a tart. My language here I cannot print; my father too had had enough of her nonsense and soon after left her and got a room, as I had done.

Before continuing with my story of the meeting at the Drill Hall dance, I should mention that I did go on an occasional Sunday evening to a synagogue hall, where there was a dance, either to records or a small group of musicians. I cannot say exactly how it was there because things were rather odd; I went to several different ones, only it just was not for me. Was it my rough Scottish accent? Was it my workman's hands? Was it me? Was it them? I do admit that I felt totally out of place amongst my own people. Every one of those young men and girls were extremely well-dressed, and some of the young men and even very young men smoked cigars, wore flashy watches and jewellery. I was very much the odd man out, absolutely. I did go out with a few girls from time to time, a good evening down the West End, take the girls home. I was, to coin a phrase, by Monday nearly skint. What it simply boiled down to was this—I was and am what I am. You cannot make a silk purse out of a sow's ear. These girls were looking for a budding student, a doctor, accountant, businessman and what have you. The fellows of course, who were well-off, most had nice cars, I noticed, and were looking for wealthy girls. You cannot kid me; I knew what it was all about. I came to the conclusion that the idea of marrying within the faith was out.

Back to the evening at the Barnet Drill Hall (a TA centre, of course). Near the end of the evening the girl described before asked me where I lived. I told her in Finchley, near Henlys Corner. She also asked if I was living on my own or with my family, or were they in Scotland. My memory of this point of my life seems a bit misty to say the least. Was I living the last days at my sister's or was I in Windemere Avenue? Anyway, that's beside the point. I asked the girl where she lived. She told me it was at Turnpike Lane. I had never heard of it, and asked where it was.

"By road, to explain, you would come from Henlys Corner along the North Circular Road, if you know that."

"I do," I said.

"Then at the big Express Motors, turn right, come to Wood Green, turn right and it's just about a few minutes from there," she explained.

"Could I see you and your friend home?" I asked her.

The girl told me many weeks that she thought I was a nice, not the ordinary sort of *looking for it*, fellow. All three of us got on a bus, and quickly we were at the Oakwood Underground Station. I had never been here either. The girl's friend said goodbye, as she was getting a bus to Enfield. We got on the tube and sat down. I remember it was really full.

This nice girl had been brought up in Wiltshire, in a working class family. Then to my surprise, she gently took hold of my right had with her left, the way we were sitting. "Have you got a girlfriend or a serious relationship?" she asked.

"No, I have not. I definitely would not have given you a false impression. I would not be seeing you home, and I mean it."

She just looked at me, never letting go of my hand, nor did she speak. This again I must say, was not going to be a lady in Deal, intent on one thing only, but who could

124

have blamed that lady, if not me, there would have been someone else along the line, that lady in Deal was lonely and in need of the warmth and love that she didn't get from her husband.

Soon we were at Turnpike Lane. It was a very working class area, but it is not the area where you live, but what ticks inside your body, nor is that the beauty on the outside, but when a person has both they are indeed special.

It was by now very late. I thought that when we got to Turnpike Lane that we were well on the way to Southend. Of course, this was not the case at all; it just seemed a long way from Barnet; London is big. We said goodnight and I set off for home; it took me some time to get back to where I was living. It was well after one in the morning.

I had made a date for the next day, Sunday. Avice—by now I knew her name—was living with a sister and her husband in a downstairs flat of a big house. She was a librarian at a Boots Chemists. Nice young lady, well-mannered, of good education and background. It was not *head-over-heels*, I can say, but it was a slow, steady development.

We eventually got engaged, and my mother absolutely admired my girlfriend; religion was never even mentioned by my mother, nor by my father, I hasten to add. After all is said and done, I was a full adult.

Walter with one of his early Guardians,
a lady whom he called "Grandma".

The passport photograph of Walter's mother.

Walter aged about 9 years

Walter as a Sea Cadet Cup winner. This photo was
taken in 1946 when Walter was aged 16.

**1947 A weekend aboard a Royal Navy minesweeper.
Walter is in the second row on the far left.**

Walter on a friend's fishing boat; aged about 18.

# THE TOWN & COUNTY MOTOR GARAGE L<sup>TD</sup>

Wolseley, Riley, M.G. and Morris Commercial Distributors.
19 JUSTICE MILL LANE

*Telephone*
NUMBER 22388.

## ABERDEEN

*Telegrams*
MOTOR. ABERDEEN

24th. April, 1951.

TO WHOM IT MAY CONCERN.

This is to certify that Walter Kress has completed an
apprenticeship of Five years as a Motor Mechanic on the 24th.
April, 1951.

During that time he has been employed on Maintenance and
Overhaul of Private and Commercial Vehicles, and shows good promise
of becoming a first class Motor Mechanic.

He is conversant with the use of Portable Machines in connection
with his trade.

He is interested in his trade, having attended Evening Classes,
and we have found him a very hard worker, honest, temperate in his
habits, a good time-keeper and very obliging.

We have no hesitation in recommending him to anyone requiring
the services of a good conscientious Motor Mechanic.

*G. M. Robson*

SERVICE MANAGER.

Walter's qualification papers to say that he has served a
full apprenticeship. This document would also serve as
a job and character reference.

Walter aged between 18-19 on his first boat. It was an ex-trawler's lifeboat and was his pride and joy. Unfortunately the picture quality is poor. In the background is old Torry which still stands on the banks of the Dee estuary.

Photo of "Friendly Freddy" the dolphin taken by Walter at Amble, Northumberland about 16 years ago.

**Walter doing National service 1951-53 aged 21-23**

Walter taking a well-earned rest during his REME
duties.

**A small yacht which Walter kept at Maldon River Blackwater, Essex from 1971 until1978.**

Time goes on. The passion that had burned inside me for the lady at Deal had come to an end. There were no goodbyes, nor explanations, in a way they were not necessary, it was left to burn out until it was just a sweet memory.

Work was always there, and Fred Harris always got me more work, especially for Jewish people. They had never heard of a Jewish fellow getting his hands dirty, lying under cars to make a living.

Avice and I went to Wiltshire to meet her family. I repeat once more the fact that I assimilated into the Scottish (British) way of life. I am still what is known as a Yom-Kippur Jew—born as one and I will die as one. That is, I go to a reform synagogue on the High Holy Days, and the service is half in Hebrew, half in English, easy to follow, but in the more stricter ones it is all in Hebrew and most of it cannot be understood by the likes of me. It was the celebration of the Exodus from Egypt, when we eat unleavened bread, known as Matzos. It's like a big cream cracker. So remembering this event, I took some Matzos to my girlfriend's home. They thought it was rather good of me to remember my history.

The family consisted of the sister living in London, then an older sister, a younger sister and two brothers. They were down-to-earth working class typical country people. One brother was also ex-National Service.

Avice's father worked at a titled lady's estate. It transpired that evidently when we left after the weekend to return to London Avice told me that her father had told the family that he did not want any comment about Jews. "If Avice likes the lad, then it's ok by me and mother."

That has, contrary to the know-alls, turned out well. Oh yes, just like all marriages, there were ups and downs, one of which comes unfortunately to mind was the forgiving nature of my wife to my sister. Well it left a bitter taste in my mouth, but I never have or ever will say to my wife that she can or cannot say or do what she feels is right.

I believe that a person can express what they wish to, but I just could not see it considering my sister's dreadful outbursts. My wife says that as a Christian she feels that she should forgive my sister and has for many years been in contact with her, of course letting me know that she was in touch. Well, as I have said, I am not going to lose sleep over it. And it is not going to affect our marital status in any way whatsoever. I have got a real winner in my wife. She is in a political organisation, WI, freemasonry, here there and nigh everywhere, a true brick to say the least.

We have two boys, who although at very young ages went to Hebrew Sunday school, of course with a Christian mother, could not become Jewish. This concerned us not a bit, either from my point of view or my wife's or parents. We had already decided that when they grew up, they could decide for themselves which faith to follow. The trouble with religion is the undeniable fact that it is the cause of most strife and wars. Just look at history, look at Europe even today, ethnic cleansing and all its unbelievable horrors.

Both of our sons have married into Christian families and they have both been lucky to have found young ladies in the mould of their mother. By that I mean educated and cultured. One is a teacher with degrees of course, and the other one now with two children was head pastry chef at the Caprice Restaurant and the Ritz Hotel; say no more.

There was a period in my life however that I feel I must also put to paper. I think it was about 1964 or possibly a few years on, when due to being over-ambitious, working all the hours that were there to be worked, I had the misfortune of going down, and seriously so, with a then little-known disease that even some in the medical profession today do not acknowledge. It was ME or yuppie disease, with reference to over-ambitious people. In a nutshell, only those that have had it know the true despair of this illness. Books have been written about it. Claire Francis, the yachtswoman, had a terrible ordeal with it. Especially when you have two young children, a mortgage, insurance, health schemes, and all the associated items of running a home, it can cause serious depression and more. The symptoms are quite dreadful. Very often, one perspires, lacking completely of energy, no interest in food, very hot all the time, loss of weight, shivers and shakes, bad sleep, nightmares due no doubt to the medication that I had to take, some of it I suspect.

My wife had a part-time job in the mornings only at the Standard Telephone Company locally.

I attempted several times to restart my business, but it caved in every time. I tell no lies, nor do I exaggerate when I say that I felt that I was approaching the end of the road. In utter desperation and as a last resort—one can imagine the effect this was having on my family—I went to the Homeopathic Hospital. I also at that time heard of a Mr Sidney Rose Neil, a Naturopath in the West End. Yes, it was expensive, but I was—as was my wife—absolutely desperate.

This gentleman explained to me that the nightmares were caused by the medication and some of the drugs could kill a horse. I eventually had a week's treatment at his Tyringham Clinic, at Aston Clinton. It was a long uphill journey back, but I still felt that I was not the man I was way back.

Being a one-man business, when I eventually got back—within reason—on my feet, all my clients had stood by me, yes indeed. Of course, they had to go elsewhere in the meantime, but I had made arrangements with a connection in the trade. I cannot remember exactly when I got back to the work. It was years, on and off. As we were low in finances, I got a tribunal at Haringey Town Hall to see if I could get some financial aid. Two men and a lady, with the evidence I provided, listened and discussed the problem of my claim. "Well, you have a van and a car, so we therefore suggest you sell the car. Also sell your house and under the circumstances, we will recommend that you get a council flat."

"All right, I'll sell the car, but I don't want a council flat, thank you."

"In that case, we certainly cannot help you."

In the next cubicle I heard a man shouting that one hundred pounds a week, with three young children and rent was simply not enough. And that was about thirty-five years ago. But you should have seen the beautiful white convertible Mercedes he got into and drove off in. Even then I imagine that it must have been worth in the region of six thousand pounds. So even back then, there were those who would quite knowingly try to milk the system.

With my health problems, it was decided that I should go abroad occasionally. I could not afford to go on an all-inclusive type of holiday, therefore I got cheap flights and with a small English-Spanish book of travellers translations, went off to Spain and the Balearic Islands from time to time. I soon got a fair grasp of the Spanish language, enough to get by on. I found some very reasonably priced hostels or guesthouses, off the beaten track so to speak, places like Benidorm—which back then was a tiny village—Malaga and Barcelona. Benidorm has been ruined for me, once visited, never again. In my time I have found some fantastic places to stay, miles from swinging Benidorm and anyone looking for the real Spanish holiday can still find it, if you are prepared to look.

These short holidays really helped to build me up. I even took a day trip from a port near Gibraltar only eleven miles across to Tunisia.

Having started life in Vienna, which was of course on the River Danube, there were steamers, small boats, all kinds, motor and sailboats. I confess that a natural wind-powered silent and smooth sailboat was indeed the introduction to my ever-increasing desire to be in boats, sail in particular, plus of course the previously mentioned boat of my uncle's in Budapest. All my experiences of my Sea Cadet and small fishing boat time in Aberdeen came back to me and once again I could feel the old pull of the sea.

Family matters came first after all; therefore boats were put at the back of my mind, but I knew in my heart that it would not be for long.

How can I put this next episode in my life, fate perhaps? Or as one would say, just one of those things? I am once more in the year 1969. Very clearly I do remember, on my first of two trips to Benidorm, I was as usual on my own. It was always my wife who decided it was time for me to have a break. I was at Gatwick Airport waiting to board this small jet (ABAC-1-11) when I spotted a fellow and his wife. Classy indeed they were and obviously very wealthy. He was reading Motorboat magazine. Are you ahead of me yet?

I don't remember how we initially got talking but due to various situations and developments in our friendship that derived from that first meeting—I cannot divulge names—for the family's sake I cannot do so. Anyway, we became friends. R and his wife M were real down-to-earth people, like me from a working class family, but they had a very successful business. They were flush, very much so. They were the nicest people one could wish to meet up with, and that's not just the type you meet on holiday, putting on the style. They did not have to do that, they were genuine, so to continue. His most lovely wife was a fair bit younger than he was, a charming woman with an air of real of class. As we filed out to get on the plane to Alicante, I said to the fellow who was my age or thereabouts, "I see you're looking at a boat magazine. Are you into boats?"

"Yes I am, got a trailable 18 foot speedboat that I tow down to the Hamble and run around there. I go to the Isle of Wight, great fun."

"I bet it is," I replied, "My love of boats started at the age of four." I gave him the facts, all of them, from the Danube to Aberdeen. We got on the plane, "Well, well, seats next to each other." he said. I would not like the reader to think that I was talking to this chap because of his obvious wealth because that was not the case. My interest in the first instance was in his clear connection with boats; the fact that our common interest lead to a great friendship was a bonus. We soon discovered that we were all going to the Roseleda a small two-star hotel in Benidorm. In those days as I said, it had not got mega-sized.

These two people were to become to my wife and I and our children the nearest we got to family, since I left those great friends of mine in Aberdeen so many years earlier, and of course, my wife's family is included.

R and M came regularly to Spain. This time they were very seriously looking for a Villa. In those days, you could and eventually they did find one on a high hill overlooking Calpe, known as the miniature rock of Gibraltar. It was indeed a similar rock formation, but much smaller, price £12,000.

As we talked about boats, etc, I explained that my holiday was part of getting fit and back to health, as I had ME, etc. These two people decided that I needed cheering up. I was too young to laze around and swim a little, go out

140

on a pleasure boat trip, take it easy. Oh no, no. They hired a car. We met an American who was also convalescing, he was just getting over a second and worse hip operation and he was also immediately taken under the wings of R and M, and off we went to see properties, vineyards, restaurants. Would they take money for our share of things? Not likely, it was embarrassing.

We simply had a great time. R and I spent most of the time talking boats. Now it dawns on me that R must have been older than me, for he was in the last two years of the war in the Navy, as his father had been also. On one occasion, R had towed his speedboat all the way from England with a friend, years before down to these parts, but never again. Towing a boat that size all that way and back was really hard work.

One evening we went to a small bar—a Spanish one—I hasten to add. I did not come here to go to a British, German, Dutch, Norwegian, etc pub; I wanted and got the culture of Spain. The bar owner and his wife and family ran this small but typical place, Spanish as could be. They danced the Flamenco in true style, not the stuff that passes off as Flamenco today in some places. There was the usual beer served here, and of course Spanish wines. We had an evening that I will never forget. There were not many people there; it was indeed small. I think there were about twenty people at most, and some drifted away until by eleven o'clock, about to close for the night, there were only myself and R & M, as the American guy was not well. We had definitely enjoyed ourselves. We danced at times; deep down I have a feeling for Flamenco. Just as we all got up, I got to the little bar first and insisted on paying. However, the owner asked if we would like to stay, as some friends of theirs were coming for a while, not any more of the public, and they thought that as we had enjoyed ourselves, that we might like to stay on for a while. M whispered to me, "No, let's go. They'll probably take us for a small fortune."

"Oh M," I said very quietly, "I don't think that these people are that sort." I just felt that they were genuine. Possibly some were of gypsy blood, but in Spain being a gypsy is not looked on with distain like it often is in other parts of Europe. I am sure I have got some of that quality in my blood too. Anyway, I managed to talk her round. So we stayed and had, to put it mildly, a ball. These later guests too were the most genuine people that God had put on this earth, as well as their friends and family. We got food, not that we were hungry. We sang, we drank, we laughed, we danced, and we were honoured to be part of the family…a very rare experience.

The hours went by and about one in the morning when everyone was going I could see that M was still a bit apprehensive. She had no need to be, these people did not even want to charge us the bill that we originally were going to pay? But I managed to press money into the hand of the owner. There were hugs, kisses. We had arrived, appreciated people's efforts, gave them applause, felt for them, danced, spoke to them as best one could; language was no barrier here. M, usually with a bag full of money, insisted on giving the lady dancer and the family who had been at the bar a few hundred pesetas. They refused, but M insisted. She was deeply touched, hugs again. What a night!

I can say that years later, on my own in Almenecar again, I wandered up town to where the streets were rough, no concrete or tarmac roads, deep working class, kids, dogs, rubbish, broken old cars, a few small café-like places. One in particular had a lovely smell coming from it. Many people, all Spanish of course, families with kids, couple of dogs. I love the real Spain. You can keep your four and five-star hotels. It was now nine o'clock, and I continued in and said good evening in Spanish. I was politely told by one of the sons of the owner to sit where you please. To cut a long story short the musicians arrived soon after and another great night followed…what a night it was too! The people congregating there, singing, dancing, and I got into the thick of it. Yes, it was another ball. It was great. Spanish guitars played by gypsies, or people of that origin, is something else. At midnight people were still coming in. It was the cheapest evening I had had in years. Handshakes all round with absolutely everybody there.

Back now to Benidorm and my growing friendship with my new friends. With R and M and sometimes including the American fellow, we went to markets here and there. Amongst those places was beautiful Guadalest, what a place. In Javea, we saw the big house where Edmundo Ros lived full-time in retirement. We went to Denia and umpteen other fantastic places.

R and M were staying one week more than I was, so we bade farewell, promising to get in touch soon. I thought no more of it however. These lovely, genuine people were—to put it honestly—beyond my station, living in a fabulous townhouse in the countryside.

When I got home, I told Avice about these people I had met and the time we had enjoyed together and to my great surprise and delight, on their return to England, they got in touch with us. Avice and I plus the boys were invited to their home. Wow, I say again, what a place. Talk about the Ritz, it had nothing on their place. We met R's mother and spinster sister and we had yet another ball. They loved our kids. I was absolutely in a different world, and I can only say again, what fine people.

R told me that he fiddled about as a hobby with his car, and one problem had him puzzled, so I got my old van, which by the way in protest to the then government's levy on the increase of the self-employed stamp, I painted all over my van 'Self-employed Refuse to Pay the New Levy.' R thought it was great, as did his wife, "Good for you, Walter. Well done. We admire your actions."

I soon found and fixed the problem that had baffled my friend. They offered to give me £50 for coming out to them, but I refused totally, reminding them that this was but a tiny amount of gratitude for the time we had in Spain.

"You're a real good chap," M said to me.

"And you're the tops," I said, "You are indeed, and I mean it from the heart."

Avice and I, sometimes with the boys and sometimes only R and I, towed the boat to the Hamble. I liked it, but sailing boats were my love. Then R sold the speedboat and bought a twin screw diesel motor cruiser, 38 feet long, and a few years old. She must have cost about £28,000 at least, and he kept her in a marina on the Thames. We regularly went down the Thames and up the Medway, right up until we could go no further…great trips. However, M never came on long trips, which was a real shame.

Sad to relate, but things were not well with R and M, as we found out from the sister of R. Sad yes, but not my problem, I will not pry into other people's business. R it turns out turned a blind eye to M's behaviour, I gathered. Ask me another. That's life for some, I suppose.

There is now a rather hurtful little episode that my wife told me about. Of course, I should have given one of her sisters a kick in the shin or something of that kind. This sister and her husband, not saying which sister, met R and M at a party for our twenty-fifth wedding anniversary at our house. Believe it or not, but this sister of my wife told my wife that she could not see what these people (R and M),

144

obviously wealthy and way above our station, could possibly see in me. And yes, she told my wife that she should watch it, because of this lovely 'raver' as she put it. She implied that M could be trouble and maybe it could be you know what. Well, it bloody well was not. I should have gone for the jugular. What a bloody insult, or was it envy? It was only my wife's wisdom that prevailed.

# CHAPTER 6

In 1971, at the height of winter, January it was, I had seen an advert in a Yachting Magazine of a small river cum short coastal small sailing boat with a small engine inboard, not hung on the back, but in the boat itself. The owner was fed up with time-wasters saying they were interested and not turning up, so when I turned up, the boat was on a trailer in mid-January, foul weather; we struck a deal and she was mine. A friend with a Land Rover towed it to another friend's house, later on we took it to a farm he knew of just outside London, where it stayed for the winter. I went to Maldon in Essex and got cheap moorings and a mud berth, where you could only get the boat off and on at high tide, hence the cheapness of the moorings. At some times with tides being very low, you could not get away at all.

Avice did not like it at all, especially as the weather in 1971 was horrible. Snow in early May, it really was awful. On the day the jet crashed on take-off at Heathrow and made headline news we were down the river Blackwater, all four of us, the boys clipped on, etc, and life jackets, of course. A squall hit all the boats and a split second before it hit us I let go of the sheet (rope) holding the main sail, but even with that released, she lay over quite a fair amount. The kids thought it was great fun, but Avice was not at all impressed.

I spent most of the time on my own, and eventually with a friend at times. R came sailing, but was unwell with the movement, which I thought was strange, as he had been a sailor.

Around that time I decided to join RNLI, shoreline member, continuing by standing order from the bank. I also became a member of the Cruising Association, with their headquarters at Ivory House at St Katherine's Dock by the Tower of London. I met some very interesting boating people there; more on that later on.

At the height of summer in settled weather, my youngest son Andrew went boating with me, as my other son Simon was not that keen, and also I felt that in an emergency I could cope with only one child and by myself, two could be a problem. Often Avice and Simon would come to the waters on the Naze backwaters Marina by car and stay while we puttered round the quiet backwaters there and did a bit of swimming. To this very day, I have still got the inflatable dinghy that we towed as our lifeboat.

I always had an idea that one day I would like to sail some distance, but my little boat was no use for that sort of seafaring. So, after having had a great deal of pleasure from that little boat, I had decided that at the end of the season in 1976 I would sell her. But in August of that year, I had planned to sail alone along some of the beautiful Suffolk Rivers that I knew of. I had read all the books on navigating to East Anglia from the Sea. I could not wait; what a place of tranquillity it appeared to be. Do you know that when I got there eventually in the first week of August, I wrote in my log book when I got to Iken, up the River Alde, miles above Aldeburgh, that here indeed was utopia, as far as I was concerned it was anyway, a more tranquil place would be difficult to find.

David and Joan Hays book of East Anglia from the Sea had truly in every minute detail with feeling said it all. I was following their journey every bit of the way; perhaps their spirits were with me. Then—as I always did—I studied the weather and listened to land forecasts, plus of course the every important shipping forecast. So it looked as if in about two days' time, the weather was going to change, so when the tide was right, I left Iken, that most idyllic and beautiful I had ever seen. It was four am and I not only had the sails up, but also the engine running at half speed.

Of course, it is of great advantage to work the tides, and I got back to Maldon from leaving the River Alde, where it enters the sea in under eight hours, arriving in Maldon just as the tide was to run against me. That was a distance of 36 miles, and just as well, as true to their forecast, the wind got up next day, as well as the promised rain. I then returned home.

Now I will relate a situation that I could well have done without, but afterwards, in hindsight, I should not have gone to a new customer's house to work on their car. I should have brought the car back to my place, but I was rather busy at the time, so it was not unusual for me to work at a customer's house or flat as I carried all my equipment in my small van. So it was that I went to a house in Golders Green, just to the rear of flats known as Riverside Drive. The car that I was going to check the brakes on was a Mini located in the owner's garage. There was however, a steep slope down to the road. I set the handbrake fully on, but as it was later proven, the cables were rusted and seized. So although the handbrake was pulled up, it was not operating the rear brakes. They were proven to be completely free. I was just starting to loosen the front wheels when the car began to move. I tried to push an axle stand under the left front wheel, but it was not sufficient and the car moved over it. The car was now starting to go down the slope while I was walking backwards pushing against the front of the car to slow it down. Of course, my van was right in line, but that was of no consequence. I was more concerned with the damage that was about to take place on the car. Despite my frantic efforts I was caught with my left foot between the car and the very solid, unyielding metal of the rear body panel of my van. My foot swelled up instantly to the size of a small ball. The horrible searing sensation from my feet crept slowly to my face. In fact, at that moment I thought I might even die. The lady of the house had heard the crash and came rushing out. I just lay there in total agony. The ambulance arrived very quickly and took me off to Edgware General Hospital. The hospital staff immediately got to work on me. I believe it was an operation that took two and a half hours, as I had broken the bones going to all the toes. When my wife arrived, they told her in confidence that if I had been over sixty years of age, they would have taken my foot off, as this was a very complicated operation.

Another point I remember in this trauma is that as I was coming to, there stood near me a young lady, all in white. In the after anaesthetic state that I was in, I truly believed for a fleeting second or two that I was in Heaven. I did tell her later that I truly felt that I arrived there. It seems that the mind can be strangely affected at that stage of consciousness.

Yet more on this saga; just before I went under the anaesthetic, I phoned a mechanic friend and told him of the situation I warned him about the handbrake and he said that he would take care of it. He took the car on a trailer to Finchley where he had his workshop.
The car owner came to see me. He was not the least bit worried about his car, but extremely worried about me. Also, my dentist at the time was a client of mine, and had recommended the people with the Mini. He had his wife came to see me, as did many friends and customers.

I now relate some very vivid memories of my stay in hospital. I had a room of my own and here is what I would say was a bit of a scenario, quite ridiculous. After a few days, I was taken in a wheelchair with my foot in plaster— heavily covered in plastic so that it would not get wet—to the washroom. I was not going to have a bath or a shower, but to stand up, supported by a male nurse, while a nurse gave me a wash all over. Of course, I was nude—It was a hospital—then the female nurse stood back and said, "You've been sunbathing in the nude, haven't you? Oh yes, look at him," she said to the male nurse; he agreed.

"Well," I said, "I have a little boat, and when I'm in a quiet creek or river and it's a nice day, hey presto, tanned all over."

Then there now comes to mind what I can only refer to as the saga of the two differing matrons. As I stated, I had a room of my own for a while. In the morning, I would draw the curtains and stand at the washbasin and slowly give myself a wash as best I could, without clothes on of course. In storms a matron, "Open these curtains! We have to see that you are all right and haven't fallen over." I explained, although of course she could see that I had no clothes on, "Doesn't matter, just leave these curtains open." she said.

So next morning, curtains open, I am at the washbasin and in storms a different matron. "You cannot stand naked washing, for goodness sake!" said the very angry matron, "Close the curtains!"

Before she could say any more, I shouted, "You'd better go and see the matron who was here yesterday morning and had a real go at me saying that I must not close the curtains, which I had done, because if I fall over...I just will not bother to wash all over, and that's it!"

The other patients all had a good laugh over that.

Then there was a trainee nurse—a rather good-looking lass from South America. Her native language was Spanish. I had only then a very limited grasp of the Spanish tongue, but I eventually worked it out and told this young lady that she was indeed, a 'Rosa del sol,'—a rose of the sun. When my wife and children came to see me, this nurse said, "Your husband speaks quite a bit of Spanish."

My kids thought that was hilarious. "Dad doesn't speak hardly any," they told her.

"Oh I can understand your father," she replied.

Now please do not get the 'aye, aye' idea now that I relate the fact that this charming young nurse came to see me often, not in uniform, but in her time-off duty. She cheered me up to no end, and was even sitting by my bed when my wife and kids arrived. "Special attention I see you're getting, lucky fellow," my wife said. Of course my wife did not mind. She thought that it was very nice of this young lady to give some of her time to me. It was as simple as that.

Time moved on and I was moved from my single room to the main ward and I had a few snide remarks from some of the other patients, but that did not worry me in the least. They can say and think what the hell they like. I find and have found with my experience of life that if you reach out to people and not adopt this 'foreigners' attitude, they will reciprocate, as indeed this young lady from South America had…it's as simple as that.

After the removal of the plaster cast, I was bandaged up and a smaller, lighter plaster was fitted and I went home. Of course, I had to go back and forth to hospital and I was sent to my local hospital after about three months to continue treatment and physiotherapy etc, as it was a fair journey from Palmers Green to Edgware. Luckily, I had an automatic transmission car, so the left foot did not come into the scenario.

My mechanic friend, Dick Baker and his son refused payment from me, as the owner of the car had paid for the work and the repairs to the damaged front of the car.

I remember that my wife and kids and I went to Maldon to see how things were with the boat. John Tassier, the owner of the mooring, who lived in a flat above his chandlery, kept an eye on the boat for me, as we had phoned and told him of the situation.

It took nearly six months in total to get back on my

feet, but of course I took it easy. No big jobs for a considerable time ahead. My dear departed mother-in-law said that I should look on the bright side, as this accident was probably fated to be, so as not perhaps to have an even far worse accident. Who knows, indeed?

It was now 1977 and I felt the time had come to sell the boat, as being a member of the Cruising Association, there were always boat owners looking for crew members and—wishing to go much further than my small boat was capable of—I put my boat up for sale. I point out that the Cruising Association was not about cruising on cruise ships, but simply yachts people—not racing—but simply cruising, nice and gentle.

Having been in boats from the age of four, I had a good grasp of, and above all, a great respect for the ways of the sea. I had a call from what I can honestly say was a real gentleman, a retired headmaster, justice of the peace, coastguard reservist, a Mr Clarke Lewis. He had a motor sailer 36—which is a boat with a big engine as well as sails; heavy and wide, she was. So I was invited to come to Bradwell Marina in Essex. When I arrived there was also a young lady there who was helping to get the boat ready to sail shortly. From the very start, I detected negative vibes. She was sullen and hardly spoke. She simply said, "Hear you've done a fair bit of sailing these parts."

I was polite despite the fact that I had picked up her feelings of negativity towards me and I acknowledged her comment. Mr Clarke Lewis and I discussed various things and he decided that he would let me know when he was going sailing again, as I had only come for an interview anyway and not a trial sail that day. Two weeks later, I went for a weekend trial trip to Walton on the Naze backwaters. I have always felt and even been told by various people whom I have crewed for that a motor engineer such as myself was a very handy person to have on board. At that time, I did not have any papers regarding such proof that I was indeed up to my claims. I have heard of and seen for myself some that claim they know it all, but when it comes to the crunch, it's a different story. That is why there are so many tragedies with yachts and boats in general.

I cannot remember the exact amount of time that I was with this boat, but we went to France, Holland, through those beautiful canals, as far as the German islands. I was not at all happy to be on German soil, but had to go or not go at all. My wife sometimes came, leaving the boys with relatives. She even came by plane and joined us in Holland. It was all a good experience.

However, things were not to last and—due mainly to the sullen woman who often behaved like she was the skipper—shortly after the following incident I decided to go to pastures new.

I had arranged to meet up with the boat at Ramsgate, as we were going to Calais for a boat get-together. It was a great weekend, but, we sailed with two members short of a full crew. There were usually four or five including the owner, and of course the young woman. She had an extremely big chip on her shoulder. Did she ever smile? No, not even when we had, as often we did, other female crew.

When we left Calais, it was decided that we would go up to Rochester via the Swale, as that would then make it easier to get back to Bradwell. We also decided that the next day—to save me going all the way from Bradwell to Ramsgate to get my car—that we should go from Rochester. The day was a Sunday and it rained, so I dressed in my sailing gear and off I went at about six-thirty am. Sunday being Sunday, there were no buses to get to the railway station, so in the pouring rain, I walked to the station. No trains until nine o'clock, so I decided to try and hitch a lift.

It was a further good half-hour to get to the main road, and just before I got there I flagged down a police car. Although they were going a fair way along the road, it was not possible for them to give me a lift, even with the way it was pouring. They suggested I go back to the railway station.

I eventually got to Ramsgate and drove all the way through the Dartford Tunnel into Essex, then on to Bradwell. It must have been about two-thirty in the afternoon when I arrived there. Why had I not gone straight home? I had promised two young ladies a lift back to London. They had come to join us at the outset at Ramsgate.

When I finally arrived at the Bradwell Marina, I asked the owner, as I was rather hungry, if I could have a sandwich or possibly make myself some soup, but before he could reply, up pipes the sullen lady, "You can't. Everything's put away, and anyway, we are going to lock up and go."

"Are you the new deputy skipper that I have not been told about? I've had damn all since six this morning, bar a hot chocolate at Ramsgate."

The owner said he would delay leaving. It was of course still raining hard, and would not take but minutes for me to have a sandwich. I felt like taking my gear and calling it a day. "Thanks, but it doesn't matter. Any future trips, if this madam's aboard, you can count me out."

I phoned Mr Clarke Lewis and explained that I was deeply but deeply hurt, and that woman was lucky that she did not get the language from me that she would have had if she had been a male crewmember. "And I am sorry to say that I will not crew with you, which has been, apart from this woman, an enjoyable experience."

He tried to persuade me to stay and sail only when madam was not coming, but that was that. My mind was made up.

Next, I got in touch with a boat owner looking for crew, whose boat was at Danbury, not that far from Bradwell. He was preparing for the season in April, the boat being ashore, so I was given paint and brush. I had not expected to be working but I got on with it, I was also kitted out with clean overalls, Wellingtons and gloves.

There was the owner, his wife, two other crew fellows and myself, so we all got to work. I had a bad cold and it was bitter cold there, the wind coming up the creek straight off the North Sea only about twenty-two miles away.

In early May, the owner and his wife plus us three crew—all on trial for the first time—went for a sail down the creek to just beyond Bradwell, then the tide turned in our favour. Tides must be used, as at low tide, the creeks virtually dry out and boats cannot get back to their moorings. So we arrived back and it was agreed that I and the other new crew would come down in two weeks' time for a weekend trip. However, about eight or nine days later, the owner phoned me to say that he was having some others to try, and that with some commitments he had as well, it looked very likely that he could not fit me in until sometime in early June. I duly thanked him and said that the season would be virtually well on and I would not wait for potluck, thank you.

Next time I saw him was in the river Deben a few years later, when I was in my inflatable boat, just drifting down with the tide in that beautiful Constable country. I recognised his boat, as it lay at anchor as I gently drifted past using the oars to control my dinghy. He spotted me and said hello, nothing else. No 'Come aboard, have a drink.' Oh no, as if I gave a hoot. I politely returned his hello with a grudging hello of my own.

I go regularly to the many Suffolk rivers in the summer. I have friends in Aldeburgh, and I will come to them in time.

Time passed and I decided one summer that I would go to a Royal Yachting Association recommended Yachting course. I therefore had a week at the Solent School of Yachting at Warsash. After speaking to the instructor it was decided that I only needed a one week shore course, as the second week's sea work—in his own words—after a bit of questioning, was not necessary.

Therefore, on 1st August 1989, I qualified on paper, after the stringent exams of course, as a day skipper, day and night watch leader and competent crew. I regret not having taken the three-week blue water long distance course. Anyway, after that, when owners asked if I had qualifications, I said indeed I had.

Many people, some like me who had not got any previous qualifications, were good on boats. Others, well some who knew it all had done it at yacht club bars and I don't mean bars where rivers meet the sea. I could write reams about some right ones I have met. Sad to say, but true, I have gone to meet owners from Suffolk to as far away as Cornwall, but on seeing the poor condition of their boats, politely declined to sail with them.

I feel I must mention the fact that, even with wealthy boat owners, as a crew member, one has to contribute to the yachts and their upkeep and it is positively expensive. The amount could be anything from fifteen to thirty pounds per day, and do not think that that is a cruise lover's holiday; it's far from it. You muck in (so to speak), cleaning, polishing, cooking, sailing the boat, course, speed, distance, and of course my speciality, motors.

It is quite true that one is always learning about different boats, and above all, the ever-changing mood of the weather and the sea, and to say that at times I have not been apprehensive, even worried, I would be a blatant liar. Any honest boater will tell you the same story.

A phone call from a boat owner, who had been repeatedly let down by crew was not uncommon. Some crew members were either late turning up and missing the tide— as it waits for no man—or simply not turning up at all. One could understand if there were family problems, etc. That was ok. But some just did not bother even to send a phone message and that is just not on. A few times I have sailed with various owners and instead of a total of say three or four crew plus owner and even owner's wife, I have even sailed with the owner and I when the other two or three did not show up. I always, if I was ill or had urgent work, notified in advance that I could not go.

Going back in time slightly, I have not mentioned that eventually my parents got a flat in North Finchley, very near to that street of traumas. Unfortunately, my mother passed away in April of 1969, and my father too in 1983. Here I feel, was yet another case of serious neglect which I believe stems from the *couldn't care less* attitude of the National Health Service. I was in the throes of ME and tried to get those in charge of the NHS involved, but all I got was whitewash sympathy and that was that.

It all has to do with the time when my father was living in sheltered accommodation in a flat of his own. It also had a warden there. This was situated in Rectory Close, Finchley Central. Many of the elderly there, like my father, were unwell from time to time, and one of the harrowing things should have been given serious thought and careful consideration, especially as I have said with the elderly and unwell. The problem was that right next to the flats was a church, whose clock struck the hour and every quarter. Now, during the night, this was a serious problem and caused distress, I hasten to add, not only to my father, but other residents also. It was therefore requested of the minister and the church authorities if they could stop the chimes between midnight and six am, or at least stop the quarter chimes. One does not need a degree in psychology to realise how this constant tolling every fifteen minutes, all night long can affect people, especially the elderly.

My father, in desperation, asked to be moved, as the church authorities refused to help. I restrain myself in what would be a dialogue of naval foul language, so come to your own conclusion. Caring people, I don't think so.

I fared little better with the useless council. I approached local councillors, the Department of Health, Age Concern, and what have you, even the Prime Minister, Members of Parliament, etc, etc, etc, all to no avail. As my father was diabetic, he had to take medication and I did not see him daily, sometimes not even during an interval of a few days. The warden rang us one day to say that my father was ill so we immediately went to see him. The doctor had evidently been to see him and that was that.

But things soon went from bad to worse. Once more we were called and promptly went to see him. The warden also phoned Barnet General Hospital, and the next morning a doctor and a social worker came to assess my father as to whether or not he should be taken to hospital. We were not present at that time, and believe it or not, it was decided that he was not going to hospital. What utter nonsense! I do not for a moment think that they checked to see if he was taking the required medication, as it turned out later—and too late—that he had not. That is the so-called NHS and how they treat you when you're old, and that is an indisputable fact. I too have had NHS failures.

My father was very ill indeed, but—and here is a big ridiculous bit—unless the warden found my father collapsed on the floor, he had no authority to phone for an ambulance. We told him in no uncertain terms to damn well phone for an ambulance.

When we got to Rectory Close, the ambulance was

going to Barnet General Hospital. When we arrived there, my father was already being examined in a cubicle. I remember most vividly the young doctor who was examining him, as he could have been the film star Sir Anthony Hopkins's brother. It turned out after a while that my father had even missed some of his medication altogether. Furthermore, this doctor, who certainly knew what he was doing, stated that my father should have been admitted at least two weeks previously. "I'm afraid it doesn't look good." he said.

"Well doctor," I said, "you can tell that to his doctor and the doctor and social worker who came to see him at the start of this problem, and that no tests were done on my father."

"Oh," he said, "I cannot believe that."

And then I recall most vividly how freezing cold it was, bitter, my father was put on a trolley of sorts, no springing, made of wood and as old as the hills. I'm sure that it was used for carrying coffins around. Covered only in an old blanket, he was taken for at least five minutes across cobblestones from one place to another. The scenario had to be seen to be believed, better suited to a scene from a Dickens novel. Needless to say, we lost my father.

I kicked up hell, but it did no good whatsoever, I got nowhere. The medical profession is a closed shop, a total brotherhood. I wrote to all and sundry, national and local press who informed me that they get letters like mine by the mailbag full. I wrote also to the then Prime Minister, local MP, council and councillors. I wrote to Help the Aged, Age Concern and the General Medical Council. Now there's a right little den of the medical boys and girls club; sorry mate and two bags full. Stonewall is not in it, more like iron curtain. I am bitter to this day; all those smug, smiling politicians of any party could not care less, patting and

kissing babies at election time is enough to make anyone ill.
They are cold-hearted monsters and two-faced and they live
behind a veil of secrecy that no one can penetrate.

My father, since being a widower, belonged to a
social club—and why not, indeed? He had a lady friend
there who struck me as a pompous bit of a madam. This
lady was on holiday at the time of my father's death, and
when she got back she tore into us, saying that we had let
him down and so forth. She blasted us for all she was
capable of doing, "I would have had him in hospital and he
would probably still be with us," etc, etc.

I tried in vain to explain the whole situation to her,
but to no avail. I am convinced that my father had no doubt
told her of our love-hate relationship. The truth is the truth
and so be it. Pity my mother was not there to put the record
straight.

My sister of course came from Israel for the funeral
but I had nothing to do with her; it only brought back the
bad memories, so I only saw her at the funeral. As I said
earlier my wife, ever so forgiving, did communicate with her,
but the wounds that my sister inflicted on me are deep, open
ones and still very sensitive.

I did not get to know the contents of my father's
will, or even if there was a will at all. I simply could not care
less. I did know that my father had little savings, as he
wisely spent it on good food and holidays. I think my sister
and her two daughters were left something and as far as I
was concerned they were welcome to it. My wife told me the
lady friend got a big percentage. Needless to say I did not
get the proverbial bean. Again, I say ok by me, and even if
my father had been wealthy or super-rich, I would have felt
the same.

I am no macho, full of guts and no feeling sort of
fellow, but what really cut me to the core and stopped me in
my tracks was that my father never even left five pounds

between our two boys. This most definitely brought a tear to my caring wife's eye, who went very regularly to see my father, as did my youngest son, who my father adored, and who, after a hard day's slog as a trainee chef at The Dorchester under Mr Mossiman, would often call on my father, even very late in the evening when he should have been at home and resting. Now that really hurt my wife and I. The boys just tried to pass it over as 'Papa probably didn't leave any money,' but I know they were both hurt, especially Andrew.

So having had an occasional sail with various people who had commitments and hardly ever used their boats, many just started using their boats as a cottage for the weekend. Plus of course there was the fact that boats, just like property, were a sound investment. That little boat I owned cost me in 1971 the sum of £1,200. I have seen similar boats in 1999, built in 1973-1976 going for around £9,000. That is of course with engine and all the fittings. So today, a small boat similar to mine would cost probably in the region of £28,000, new of course.

In June 1986 at a marina in Suffolk, I had the opportunity, through the CA, to meet a gentleman whose name now eludes me—could be Lindsay or Lindell—but his boat was what is known as a Rolls Royce of yachts. A Nicholson 33 with wheel steering and roller jib sail. The owner and I went out into the North Sea for a trial sail. These Nicholson boats were not that fast, as they were of heavy construction, but they were extremely seaworthy and very safe crafts. We returned to the marina at last, having been out for six hours. "Reckon you've done a fair bit of sailing," he said, "Can you come to Lymington's Marina in two weeks' time? I will have my young nephew, a good man with yachts, as well as a crewmember who can only sail from here to Lymington. Subject to the weather, we are planning

161

to go to Cherbourg and then on to Guernsey and Jersey. The total sailing time would be two weeks."

The plan was that the boat would be left in Jersey for his son and young children to take back stage-by-stage to Suffolk. We had a most enjoyable trip; the tides across the channel in Brittany run at great speed, and an engine breakdown has been known to be catastrophic there for some. We met the owner's son and family at the ferry port in Jersey and we sailed back to England on the same ferry they had arrived on.

At the end of July, with the yacht back in Suffolk, I had a few day trips. They were very pleasant, and the owner and his nephew were very nice chaps, but I wanted to get out into the blue waters, away to sea, down Brittany, to Spain, to the Mediterranean and possibly even beyond. Nights at sea—of course I had nights crossing the Channel to Cherbourg and onward—but I wanted something more. The owner of that great Nicholson understood and wished me pleasant sailing in the future. In a way, I feel that had I not been ambitious as regards longer distance sailing, I would no doubt have been with him for some time.

I was recently looking at my sailing log and I must record here an interesting item written by my youngest son, Andrew: -

*Sailing by Andrew Kress*
*Sailing is a good clean sport, if you know how to do it.*
*First of all you buy a boat, the type with an engine, in case your sails rip or break. I don't advise outboard motors because they're not suitable for fighting strong tides and currents.*
*Next you have to get a life jacket, flares (must be in good condition), life rings and then strong ropes.*
*If I was a man in my first trip, I would take an experienced friend. Sailing can be dangerous and especially if your mast collapsed or broke.*

*You should have a dinghy and if possible a small outboard. Sailing can be fun, but don't go without knowing a thing about it.*
THE END.

And my comments thereon: Yes, very true.

Here is just one of the records in my log for 1976, August 5th, Thursday: -

*Left Maldon on the evening tide at 8.30pm. Motor sailed to the Marconi Yacht Club's mooring's (as there are a few unused in mid-summer, boats away). Had a quiet night there.*
*Left at 7.30am, hardly any wind. Motor sailed with tide against me for a short while. Reached the Bench Head Bay (14 miles from Maldon) across the shallows, now deepening as the tide had turned and was rising.*
*It was very calm, hardly any wind, so had to use the engine. Past Clacton the wind increased a bit, sails filled lightly, still had engine slowly working. Arrived at Orford at about 6.00pm, went ashore and phoned my wife. She's not well it turns out. I'll come back then, I said, but she insisted that I stay (Orford in the River Alde Suffolk).*
*I spent a very peaceful night, not a murmur or a move. Birds woke me at dawn and then went back to sleep until about 6.00am.*

*Saturday 7th, I left Orford on the flood tide and on engine very slowly all the way up the Alde, tricky in places, as the Channel twists and turns. Came up to Iken Cliff and the lovely smell of flowers and the countryside, the sheer beauty of this small beach and mooring.*
*Here truly was utopia discovered. I can see why the painters loved this part. Motored on to Snape Bridge, where the famous Snape Maltings festival of music is held. Just touched*

the mud on a bend, moored by a barge and rang my wife. Then left on the first of the ebb tide. I ran onto the edge of a mud berth on a bend, very narrow up here. Tried engine full speed, but once on and the tide was ebbing. I was there, unable to move for nearly eleven hours. As the time wore on and as the mud was exposed, I could see grooves and marks where others had gone on and stuck.

About eleven at night the tide nearly at high water finally lifted the boat clear and with moonlight, I picked my way down three-quarters of a mile to anchor at Iken Cliff.

Finally called the day at quarter to two in the morning. It was not a peaceful night, as the wind kept up.

Finally at 7.30am, sorted a few things out, left Iken on the tide at about 10.30am. Motored against the flood tide, as to go on the ebb would have been the same as yesterday and possibly get stuck once more.

Stopped at Orford to await a friend who was coming to sail with me. As the wind was now about force five, we motored down river to look at the Bar. I decided not to cross into the open sea, therefore we went back to Orford and lay on a mooring until the next morning.

It has eased and so we went to the Deben River. Some breakers on starboard side there, but had depth of about eleven feet, up to Waldingfield. Had lunch there, then back to the Ramsholt. Saw George the Boatman (he looks after the moorings). Terrific man, one of the best.

We left at 8.20 in the evening with about ten feet of water, not so rough as when we entered here earlier. Wind now totally gone, just a swell. Motored.out to the deepwater channel where there are buoys to mark the channel.

We worked our way through the buoys and the Moonlight to Pin Mill in the river Orwell, which goes to Ipswich.

We arrived at Pin Mill at 11.00pm. It was a lovely calm night, really worth the time of night, restless night as big ships go up and down.

*We left at 7.40 in the morning and motor sailed to Pyefleet Creek (near Brightlingsea). Arrived there and anchored early afternoon, very calm, hardly any wind, a rare and lovely stay it was.*

*Next morning we left the creek on the last of the ebb tide to assist us down to the Bench Head Bay, where as the tide started to flood, it assisted us on our trip to Maldon. We had to wait there for two hours as the tide was still coming in, to allow us to get in to the mud berth. All in all a very memorable trip.*

So it was yet another new owner that I met and discussed sailing matters with; this boat was another one that was kept at Bradwell Marina, a nice thirty-six foot centre cockpit yacht with two masts. That is, a main mast and the rear one—a mizzenmast. This boat was another heavily built one. I am not a lover of the lightweight flyers, as events have proved. When the going gets rough and tough, I want to be in a heavy boat that has got plenty of it in the water, not a skimmer with very little in the water; the modern trend seems to be lighter and faster boats, but not for me, thank you. One can only reflect a few years ago in the Fastnett Race, when there were horrendous mishaps, but an Army or possibly ex-Army man in an old, very heavy sailboat plus engine of course with his family aboard stood by at the scene, co-ordinating the rescue services. He eventually got a medal for his efforts and deservedly so.

So it was arranged that I should come to Bradwell for a weekend's sail. Weather permitting, we would either go north to Walton backwaters or to Burnham on Crouch.

The day duly arrived and we met up at the marina. This was early evening and as we had planned to sail early the next morning, the owner asked me if I would like to go up to the clubhouse for a drink. So off we went, and I offered to pay, but after much debate and near argument in a pleasant sort of way, he insisted, saying that it was a nice gesture on my part, and that he was going to tell me one of these tales about a fellow who came to crew for him.

Here once again I have no hesitation in saying that this is yet another tale of some people who come to crew on yachts, and have I met some myself, haven't I just. In fact, if I gave every detail of such persons, male and female, that would be a book in itself.

The fact that we were in the clubhouse reminded him of this scenario and he told this story. A well-spoken sort of chap had telephoned him regarding crewing his boat, so it was arranged for the chap to come to Bradwell. Well, when he arrived, he looked just like a bit of a tramp. His denim trousers were torn and ragged and he wore a leather jacket of some sort that had seen better times; he had no deck shoes, so he dug out a pair to lend him.

"You told me that you worked in the City for a large company." The boat owner said.

"Oh yes, indeed I do, but a few years ago I was mugged, so now in my leisure time I dress down like this. It puts yobbos off attacking one."

So off to the clubhouse they went to chat over a drink. The fellow never offered to buy the drinks, so the skipper ordered the drinks, the chap then said he wanted a sandwich. So the skipper put a fiver on the bar and said, "I'm going to the toilet."
You will not believe that went he got back, that so and so had pocketed the change!

"Hope you don't mind, skip," he offered before he could ask him where the change was, "I'm afraid that I've come rather short, having had a taxi from Maldon. Of course I'll repay you, but actually can you lend me a tenner?"

The skipper went on to say "I've had some types on board, but this fellow was way over some I've had the

166

misfortune to meet up with. He said he had done dinghy sailing and had been with some friends on a charter yacht in the Aegean. Well, I wasn't very confident in this chap. I felt that I could be a reasonable judge of character, so we set off just to potter up river for a few hours. That short trip was the first and the last for this City gent. He felt too unwell to go below to put the kettle on, wasn't the least interested in the working of sail or motor, didn't bother to look at the chart, and sat reading a tatty old novel most of the time. So to hell with the kettle, I got the only sail I had on down promptly and returned back to the marina, where I told him that I considered him not in the least bit interested in sailing. The chap pleaded that he felt unwell. So I told him, 'I can't take you on here because as you say yourself, you're feeling unwell. So I'm sorry to say I simply cannot have you aboard.' I told him that he was not the first that I had refused. And that was the end of that saga, thank God."

"Well," I replied, "this is nothing new. I've seen some that have sailed here, there and damn near just about everywhere. These people, if it came to the crunch, would be a gross liability. Even before mooring lines were secured, they'd be off to the pub, and no doubt return half-stoned."

Next morning we set off and decided to go to Burnham on Crouch, as the wind would be heading us if we went north, and with the wind that way and the ebb tide flowing against it, in those shallow waters unless one had to go, would have been a bit wet, even in this thirty-six footer.

We just made our way down very slowly, and the skipper said, "Hold her on course as we are. I'll get some breakfast going." I offered to do it, as it was cereal, coffee, toast and jam, but he insisted, adding, "I'm sure you won't do what that fellow did. When I wasn't looking, he let her jibe. Luckily the wind was light, or we could have been in trouble when that boom swings round."

We got down to a channel, called the Spitway, as it

runs between mud and sand spits. There is a navigation buoy at each end and from there it is all buoyed all the way into the river Crouch. We had sailed all the way, but now as we were entering the river, we started the motor and stated taking the sails down. Of course, there were yachts and powerboats moving about, plus umpteen dinghy sailors and many closely moored craft on swinging moorings.

The skipper engaged the engine at just idle speed, but with the tide pushing us in slowly, we did not realise until we turned further up the river to pick up a mooring buoy, a boat must be turned against the tide to finish off the securing to a mooring, this meant more drama. I went forward to pick up the mooring line, which usually floats on a small float. Skipper increased engine speed but she was not driving the propeller, and the tide was taking us backwards. "Hell Walter, forget the mooring, we've got no drive and we don't want to hit this big one moored behind us. Help me get some of the main up; that should get us out of trouble."

"What's gone wrong?" Just at this crucial point we got the sail up quickly, just enough speed to get us out of the line of moored craft. "I'll go down and see what's happened. Stop the engine." I lifted the floor and saw lying in the bilges the four bolts, nuts and washers that connect the gearbox to the propeller shaft coupling. "I've found the problem. Are you managing all right up there?" I called out. I told the skipper, "I'll slip in two bolts and nuts fairly tight and that'll give us drive." This was done in seconds. "Start her up."

That was that, temporarily solved. We then picked up the mooring and I fixed the drive coupling.

"God," exclaimed the skipper, "can you imagine this scenario if I had only that other chap with me? I think he'd probably have jumped overboard and swam ashore.

"You know, I have the engine serviced before the season, but you simply cannot trust them. £286 it cost. I don't begrudge it, but I feel that the so called service engineer didn't bother."

This drama also proved another point, which is that even the most experienced sailors can get into unexpected difficulties. As events later turned out, never was a truer word spoken, and I have got a wounded sciatic nerve to prove it. I hurt my back off Beachy Head one time but I will explain that later.

The skipper and I got on very well and he said to me one day, "It appears that we're on the same wavelength. How d'ya fancy Falmouth in August for a couple of weeks or so?"

Of course, being self-employed, it posed no problem whatsoever, as I have worked many a weekend on top of a full week, so my conscience was clear, and above all, I had the support of my wife.

We continued to potter up to Walton backwaters and the Orwell River at weekends, and soon it was time to leave for Falmouth. There would be another two male crewmembers joining us as far as Brighton Marina. We were doing it in stages as opposed to doing it in one hop. Then at Brighton Marina two female crewmembers would join us when the other two left. One of the chaps who sailed with us had sailed quite a bit and knew the ropes, so to speak. The other one had a small motor sailer on the River Medway, but admitted he had not long owned it and had only pottered in the Medway and the Thames Estuary. Having no experience was not a problem in itself, the problems occurred when they tried to hide their inexperience.

Now, very clearly there comes to mind an episode that my son Andrew was witness to. The skipper and I and the other crewmembers duly arrived at Bradwell, and my son came with me, as he was to drive the car back to London. The skipper had agreed to let Andrew stay aboard for the night, so Andrew and I got the small but comfortable after cabin in the rear of the boat. We got our heads down, as we were going off at 5.30am with the morning ebb to the Spitway. At 5.00am and skipper calls below, "I've miscalculated the time of the tide. We have to go right now or we'll lose the advantage of the tide."

Andrew was on the jetty in about five minutes. I threw my clothes on over my pyjamas, and Andrew said he would watch us go off, so he went up to the car park to get a better view. The engine was now running, we check the oil, pressure, temperature, cooling water pumping out all right. Just about to cast off in all this panic to get away, when lo and behold, skipper declares, "Sorry chaps, I've just realised that at this time in the month, the tides are bigger rather than the other way round, and I didn't want to get stuck at the marina entrance where it is very shallow. We have some time in hand."

So the engine is stopped and all is quiet now. "I'm going to the showers," says skipper, and off he goes. Meanwhile, Andrew, watching at the top of the gangway leading down to the floating marina walkways, came back and asked why we were not leaving. I explained that the skipper had made some detail calculations that were not right and as we now have three-quarters of an hour spare, he has gone to the showers.

"I saw him go there and wondered why, with all the rush to go. Thought there might have been an engine problem. Anyway, I'm going now, Dad."

Well, that is how it goes, I suppose. The others were not at all pleased, rushing up and then not going off as planned, but these things happen at sea, its all part of the joy of sailing!

We were off then by about 6.30am. It was a nice, warm morning, a bit hazy, but very peaceful, and no wind. The river was like a sheet of glass. What more could one want on such a morning? Onwards, slow but sure, cruising down to and through the Spitway; once more using the flooding tides to assist us. I should point out that at this part of England there is a formidable coastline. There are shallows, ever-shifting sand and mud banks. In fact, yachtsmen and women who have written in yachting magazines state that if you can get around these parts without getting stuck on an ebb tide, you can sail the world. All the way to Ramsgate, charts and navigation buoys and depth sounders were rigorously kept under scrutiny. We even passed the towers that had aircraft guns positioned there during the war. These were set on shallow water mud spits, some were even leaning.

We got to Ramsgate, but could not enter as the signal of lights meant that there was a ship coming out. It was a cross-channel ferry. Quite a few crafts were waiting to go into the marina there, so I reckon it was about 5.00pm when we finally tied up.

We went out drinking at various places, juice, beer; the evening was warm and pleasant. The crew member who had a boat on the Medway asked the skipper, "Are you going to sail between here and Brighton at night at all?"

"Oh yes," he replied, "I'm coming to the decision that I think we will leave here at about two in the afternoon and sail through the night to Brighton."

"My wife doesn't like the idea of me out there in the shipping lanes at night, and as you know, I've only pottered in my boat; never been to sea at night." Well, as I have said, we all have to start somewhere.

"I wish you'd told me before we arranged for you to come with us. Anyway, it doesn't matter. I've even sailed myself to the Orwell in the middle of the night. So it's up to you. Go if you feel you should." So that was that then, and home he went.

We got into shore-going clothes and went to a fish and chip restaurant at about 9.00 that evening. Skipper insisted on paying. Fair enough. As it was, we crew paid our way at £15.00 a day for food, fuel and mooring fees, etc.

After the meal, skipper said, "There's a nice little pub up top of the hill not far from here I've been there a few times."

"Let's go then." I am not into pubs, but when in Rome...so we trooped off to the pub. Skipper was not much of a drinker, although the other crew fellow put a few pints away in an hour or so. I could not bear the cigarette smoke, so I excused myself and said that not only was it too thick in there for me, but we had been on the go since five that morning, so I went back to the boat and turned in. It was now nearly eleven at night of course. We were tied up, the third boat from the walkway with two other boats outside us. That is a total of five boats side by side, with people trampling over ours to get to theirs, singing and shouting, as some merry boaters do. I was in my snug little after cabin, the other crew had the big centre cabin and the owner had the forward front cabin. I think it was just after midnight, when the merriment finally came to an end and with that I finally went to sleep. Next thing I know, there was a gentle tap, tap on the top of my cabin. I woke—though I do not think I had been asleep really. "Come on Walter, we've decided that it's such a nice, calm night that we're going now."

"Aren't you tired at all?" I said, "I've had no sleep because other boaters came crashing and banging about." I was nearly, as one can well imagine, in a pack up and goodbye mood, indeed. And who can truly blame me, I ask you.

I wasn't the only one to be put out that night because of course, to get the other two boats on our outside moved, caused at that time of night, as one can imagine with many of those merry souls the worse for drink, a bit of a kafuffle. The fellow on the very outside asked really angrily—and I do not blame him in the least—why had our skipper not moved to be on the outside much earlier, and not at this time of night, for God's sake. Some of that chap's language can only be imagined.

Our skipper explained that as it was a nice night, he had decided to go, and we finally left. As we came out of the harbour, the other crewmember was stowing things and tidying up, squaring things away as one might say. Skipper was at the chart table with the cabin lights full on. Of course, as we left the fully lit harbour marina and went to sea where it was absolutely pitch black, the navigation buoys were flashing and twinkling there, as it is a very busy and tricky channel. "Skip, please turn off those cabin lights and switch on the dim reddish light [used at night in the cabin] 'cause I just can't see a thing." I said.

"Oh sorry, I'll switch over." Which, he did. It took at least a good minute for my eyes to get fully accustomed to the pitch dark, now that the cabin light was off, which mercifully had been done in the very nick of time, for dead ahead was what I thought, on looking back to those years, was a completely blacked out police or customs boat waiting to catch someone. I swear that it was not more than ten lengths of our boat ahead. "Skip', switch off the chart light, up here quick!" I shouted.

He came up right away as did the other member of our crew. It also took them a few seconds to regulate to the pitch dark. We were now just a few yards away, but thankfully clear of it. "Hell," I said, "it's an unlit harbour entrance marker, a dreadful danger to the unwary."

The owner immediately—by the VHF boats radio—informed the harbour watchtower and Thames coastguard. "Oh thanks," the tower said, "We are aware and it's going to be fixed shortly. Good of you to report it."

Thames said ours was the first report and said they would put out warnings to shipping and small craft. It is of course a mariner's duty, whether commercial ships, liners, sailing boats or small private craft, to keep listening on the distress frequency, as is the custom of the brotherhood of the sea.

"Well," said the skipper, "They certainly didn't say anything about that bloody thing, as we turned the transmitter receiver on upon leaving our moorings."

Of course, I was still high with regards to the early morning fracas at Bradwell and now without sleep going overnight to Brighton so I didn't say anything in reply. The skipper went on, "It will be light by about 4.30am, if you're really that tired, I'll take the wheel in about half an hour and you can get your head down."

I refused his offer for several very good reasons. I must herewith state that, especially at night, and needless to say in a major world shipping channel as that was, I have never, ever, or ever will go below to sleep, and it is the recommendation in every seaways manual and boating publication that at night, two members of crew need to be on watch together, to speak to each other, drink hot drinks regularly, eat chocolate or other food and to watch that the other does not nod off. Plus, the warmest clothing and wet weather gear needs to be worn, as well as a lifejacket and distress high intensity light, self-activating when in contact with the sea. Serious watch must be kept at all times, compass heading, speed, depth, navigation buoys, etc, listening to the distress frequency, writing up the log every half hour. Each watch has two hours on then two hours off, and where there are more crew the time off is more, depending on the number.

Of course, I have often sailed across the channel at night either from east coast or south coast, and Cornwall to Brittany many a time with just the owner and myself or perhaps three of us. The object of a night crossing is to arrive in the daylight at our destination, especially in rock strewn Brittany, where the depth is enormous in places. Even some local boaters and fishermen will not venture close to the shores at night, and I can see why. The tides run at frightening speeds too.

I have even sailed from Cornwall to Brittany with just the owner, but we rested most of the day, had marvellous food in restaurants, slept in the afternoon in beautiful, usually peaceful St Mawes Creek, before departing in the late afternoon. We prepared hot food in flasks and containers in case it was not easy to cook, should we encounter rough weather. I will write more about those trips later on.

When approaching major parts such as Dover, one must stay very close to the navigation monitor buoys, so as not to hinder commercial craft, and of course, the constant comings and goings of the ferries. Well in advance, Dover control must be contacted to give your position and receive permission to pass the harbour, in relation to the ferry operations.

Usually, depending on the weather and the visibility, people have a small radar system on small crafts these days, but the decision to proceed or wait rests with the control centre. We got the all clear, but we should be ready for any change in our permitted onward journey.

This passing of Dover harbour must be done as quickly as possible, and strictly within the buoyed channel, as anyone failing to obey these regulations can be in serious trouble.

So we passed clear as fast as possible, mainly with the engine, as there was very little wind that night. It was reasonably warm, good visibility, and by dawn's early light, we were off Dungeness Nuclear Power Station.

We started the breakfast going. Here it was now slightly misty, and we were in water that was not deep enough for big ships, but we still kept a visual and radar watch for small craft and fishing boats.

Naturally, although I had a few catnaps when I was off watch, I was extremely tired. Of course, when I and the other crew member were on watch, the skipper slept for one hour only, having set his clock to wake him. He would then check that we were all right, what craft were around, radar and log check, position of our boat, etc, then, he would sleep for another hour. And now, as it was daylight, he would come and take over, and thankfully we turned in, the engine was stopped and we just eased along gently on a fine little breeze. Another boost was that the tide was in our favour, helping to push us along. I was asleep in record time.

It was about three hours later when the skipper woke us with a mug of freshly made hot chocolate, and boy did it taste good! We were almost off Eastbourne with the modern tower structure navigation lights and radio beacon, known as the Royal Sovereign Tower. This was formerly a lightship moored there with huge anchors and chains. We calculated that we would reach Brighton Marina by late afternoon. However, we were about six miles off Beachy Head when the engine started slowing down and seemed to be unable to pick up speed. We tried all the angles but to no avail. One of the things we discovered to our horror, and situated in a very cramped and almost inaccessible place, was the fuel filters, which we suspected were the problem. The fuel filters are of absolute importance on a diesel engine. I managed to take the tops off both the primary and secondary filters, and the skipper—who was passing me spanners—and I could not believe what we saw. The filters had no elements inside them, and the sediment had to be seen to be believed. Skipper produced the spare inserts while I cleaned out the filter containers. This operation did my back no good and I damaged the sciatic nerve. While this was going on, up top the other crewmember was trying to sail us away from Beachy Head, as the tide and currents were nudging us towards the Head. That would have meant disaster! Thankfully he did a great job. We got the engine going, and it revved up all night, but when either forward or reverse was engaged, it simply slowed down and would barely rev. It was at that moment we discovered that there was something trailing under the back of the boat. Later, in Brighton, a diver brought up a thick industrial plastic sheeting, four feet wide and sixteen feet long, which had wrapped itself round the propeller, and on this type of yacht, it was not possible to use a boat hook to untangle this thing. We therefore very slowly, and with the sails drawing nicely, made headway towards Brighton. If it had been evening by now instead of about two pm, skipper said he would have asked the coastguard to send a small tow boat or even a fishing boat at a pre-arranged price. Ok, yes if you do not agree a price beforehand, they can say that they rescued you and claim salvage. This is a very grey area of the law.

So at about 9.00pm we finally limped into Brighton Marina, a place I would not dare enter in anything of an onshore wind. In fact, I had been there by land transport many years before, just to see this Marina, and watched the lifeboat go out on an exercise, against a force six to seven onshore wind. They went out, the boat bucking up and down some and rolling heavily. They went out for about twenty minutes, and when they entered between the breakwaters, the boat was carried on a wave, and did it surf! The speed was unbelievable, but they held her straight all right, a great spectacle of seamanship.

We went ashore to eat, and the diver came the next morning and got that plastic sheet off the propeller. Skip' went ashore before the diver came to us and rang the yard where the engine was supposed to have been serviced and gave them hell, but of course, the engineer was not working with them anymore, etc, etc. So skipper decided that a local engineer would come and give the engine a good going over, he had little choice really as the boat had to be made seaworthy.

The weather forecast was not good at all, so us crew

decided—with the owner's agreement of course—to go home by train and continue the trip in a few day's time, as the outlook for the next few days certainly looked bad. Who would wish to go out and fight the elements in a boat that wasn't fully seaworthy? Only foolhardy people do so and unfortunately there are more of those folk than you might expect.

There was a tale in the papers a few years ago of a chap, his wife and two young children who had done some river power boating, got a thirty foot speedboat, I believe it was, and decided to follow a ferry out of Dover to Calais, yes it is true. What he did not realise was that the weather in mid-channel with the tide going against the wind was, to put it mildly, not very pleasant. But to top it all, the ferry he was trying to follow was too fast for him and it was going to Ostend, not Calais. The result was that a trawler saw their distress signals nine miles out. They were all seasick and distressed. Then out came the lifeboat and ended their epic voyage and of course saved their lives.

A few days after leaving the boat, I had a phone call from the owner to say that he was getting a local chap that very day to assist him to move the boat to Poole, and I should join him there on Saturday. It was, it seems, that the bad spell of weather had passed on, but the sea state was still rough out there.

Now here comes yet another episode that just about decided that I should call it a day here. At Bradwell, I had remarked to the owner—the day that I arrived there and assisted him with various jobs—about the weirdest steering mechanism that I as an engineer had ever seen. It was for some reason what can only be referred to as a Heath Robinson contraption; to go into detail is unnecessary. It looked as if some parts of it however were not what I had seen on other craft. The bolts and nuts seemed to loosen after a time, and I had even pointed out on that first day that they were far too thin for the stress that they are being subjected to, but the owner did not seem to be at all perturbed about it. "Well, it's never let me down yet. Actually a friend recently also remarked on the system, but that's as it was when I got the boat. Anyway, don't over-tighten them, as I've snapped quite a few over the past two years."

I duly arrived at Poole and got aboard. The other crew that came with us on the other leg of the voyage unfortunately could not come, but a young lady doctor was coming to crew at short notice. This was how I was greeted by the skipper, "By the way, I went to tighten the steering bolts and they just snapped like matchsticks and when I took them to the boatyard, the engineer said they've been over-tightened; some engineer you are."

He could get stuffed as far as I was concerned and I said my piece, "You bloody well said yourself that you've had problems with them. These damn bolts are not designed for this steering." Of course I was not just talking, I was damn annoyed and letting skip have it, both barrels. Heads popped up in some of the other yachts moored nearby to see what the hell was going on. "As a matter of fact, I'll tell you that since that episode at Ramsgate, I've been in two minds to pack it in here and now."

"Oh well," he said, "it's six of one and a half a dozen of the root of the problem, and I didn't realise just how you felt regarding the Ramsgate departure."

"Furthermore," I said, still with voice raised in anger, "I've done my bloody back in behind the engine," I did not want to make a scene about it, but things needed to be said.

"Really?" he said, then after a brief reflection he conceded, "Yes, that's a damn awkward place to get into. I simply couldn't, I'll admit it."

Then, in an effort to calm the situation he tried to side-step the issue.

"Ah hello, here comes the young lady who is going to join us to Falmouth. Come aboard." he called to her. I cannot however remember her name, possibly because I was still fuming. But I didn't want her first experience with the two of us to be ruined by the scene of us arguing tooth and nail over something she knew nothing about.

So for the moment, I simmered down and had come to the conclusion that I had indeed had enough of these trials and tribulations irrespective of what might have been said later to pacify me. I cannot tolerate these scenarios.

The atmosphere however was by then what can only be described as not conducive to a long trip to Falmouth, and to top it all, further down the Channel in about two days hence, there would be the return of strong winds in the forecast of sixes. That is all right if you are running before it, but to butt into it is not pleasure sailing whatsoever. There are of course many who feel that it is a challenge; some, as the rescue services prove, go to sea in craft that should only be in secluded rivers.

Late that evening, having once again listened to the land and shipping weather forecasts, the skipper decided to go ashore to make a phone call to see if the other fellow that had sailed with us from Bradwell was in a position to join us. When he came back, however, he told us that the other crewman could not make it, so he rang a lady who was going to join us at Weymouth and asked her to meet us late the following day at Lymington Marina. This was all news to me, but that is the owner's privilege. He had—while going to phone I presume—decided against going south and that he would go to Lymington, as he rather liked the restaurants there too. It seems that he preferred to wait there to watch developments in the weather pattern.

"As we now have ladies on board." he announced,

"you'll have to have the centre main cabin, as the after cabin will be a bit of privacy for the ladies."

"That's ok by me." I could see the sense in this decision. I guess it also proved that he could make a sensible decision once in a while!

# CHAPTER 7

Midday on the next day, we decided—with the tide in our favour—to head to Lymington. We had not gone halfway down Poole Harbour when the young lady said that she was beginning to feel awful. She had been on duty in a hospital just before she joined us, and junior doctors were worked like slaves in days of old—we all know that. She even wanted to turn back and go home. Skipper said that she should go below and lie down and see how things went. That only made her much worse, so she came back up into the cockpit. We sat her in a corner out of the wind, basin at hand.

We cleared the entrance and put to sea. Once we got sailing, the boat steadied up considerably and the lady said that she felt a little better. We kept giving her tea and at times she almost fell asleep. The poor girl, she must have been completely exhausted.

Please do not judge me as some intolerant, hasty person as I relate now the next episode that made me decide that I was finished with this owner.

We were by now approaching the Solent—at best a place to show caution. There are tidal streams, crosscurrents, shallows, over falls—some four to six feet high. I instinctively felt—and even checked by looking at the chart—and told skip' that we were too close to Victoria Point on this heading, but one can only give an opinion, and usually a consultation can quickly sort things out, as two heads are usually better than one here. After some thought and checking of the chart and the time of tides, etc, the skipper said, "Yes, I see your point, but I feel confident that as we round well clear of Victoria Point, it'll all come out as planned." So we proceeded, going very well. She was touching seven knots at times.

"If you take a bearing skip I think you'll agree with me that we are being carried sideways little by little towards those shallows. No doubt you know that it's a helluva place to give a wide berth. I can honestly say that I've never sailed so close to this place, and look at those kelp streamers. Get those round the prop here and it's lifeboat for sure. And now look at the echo sounder—it's hardly registering. We have to alter course—there's no alternative." I said.

"I've been across here before," he replied, "I can assure you these weed streamers are very long and the chart shows at least forty feet at this stage of the tide."

I did not reply. I waited for us to hit the seabed. The depth gauge affected by these long streamers simply could not give an accurate reading, and to this day I am convinced that we were in very shallow water. One has only to read the notice to mariners regarding Victoria Point. Good fortune shone down on us that day and we because we did not run aground.

When we arrived at Lymington, the other lady was waiting there. The young lady doctor had now recovered and skip' offered to take us to the restaurant for dinner. I declined and explained that I was not prepared to proceed further, due to his cavalier attitude to obvious danger. And anyway, he had enough crew to sail safely to Falmouth, and of course with the weather outlook mixed into the equation I was calling it a day.

When the others came back at about ten o'clock, I told the owner that it was time to pay him the usual agreed money, but he insisted that he did not want it. But in the morning—in order to catch the first train to London—I had to leave before at six am. Before I left I put fifty pounds on the chart table. I considered that ample for food, fuel, mooring fees, etc from Ramsgate.

183

Let me assure those who may, on reading these records that so readily come to mind and often with unbelievable clarity, think 'he knows it all,' that this is far from the truth. With the ever-changing moods of the sea, the problems with people, with gear, etc, one is always learning. And far better seamen have said the same; they have even confessed to being frightened and on occasions been terrified, especially those men and women who have been to the Southern Ocean. I confess that I have been at times very frightened, and have no intentions of ever going near the Southern Ocean. But the basic principals of good seamanship are the same the whole world over and they are that unnecessary chances should never be taken. And I was not willing to have unnecessary chances taken on my behalf.

Now I will relate the story of an affair with a beautiful all ocean-going American-built yacht, 'Valiant Lady,' a Valiant forty-footer. What a toy!

To start at the beginning, I went to one of the meetings at the Cruising Association's Club at Ivory House. There were many owners and crewmembers there as usual, as I remember it was the first meeting in March of that year. I still have the log of all these trips that I crewed on and all the owners' details are on the lists, as are crews' details. Anyway, we all had our names on stick-on labels on our jackets. The owners did too, but they also had the name and type of craft, etc. The owner of 'Valiant Lady' came up to me and we had a long conversation. It turned out that this gentleman had been planning to sail round the world over a period of two years with long stops at various places en route and crew changeover and I expressed an interest. The final plan as to his departure date had not yet been agreed, and also having spoken to me and checking my records, he decided that a trial sail would not be required. I remember that Valiant Lady was in Villamuera in Portugal. So he would let me know very soon. I offered to go for three, possibly four weeks at the most.

Soon it was all arranged. Once again my wife thought it was yet another great opportunity for me, from Villamuera non-stop to Gibraltar, then on to Moraira in Spain, and then to Majorca, and finally the south of France near Monaco. From there I would return to London.

This trip on this terrific ocean-going yacht was, I think, the pinnacle of my crewing stints. I arrived in Villamuera on a very hot day, and consulted the harbourmaster's office as to where the 'Lady' was moored—walking round that huge marina looking for a boat would have taken hours. I found the boat, but there was no one on board and she was all locked up. A note said that the owner would be back shortly, so I sat down in the cockpit and relaxed. Across on the other side there were shops and cafés, restaurants, etc, and the owner came out of one of the shops and waved to me. I went to meet him as he was carrying about eight bags of shopping.

"Got here ok, I see. Hot, isn't it?" he smiled, "Lovely sailing weather; I've been out just for the day a few times. There's plenty to get ready before we go, so I've been getting it all done, but it's so hot during the day. Later today, the other crewmember, a young German fellow, is going to join us. He has done a bit of sailing, also qualified at a sailing school. I've not met him—he got in touch with me, and he seems keen. That's the main thing."

We went to a restaurant at the marina, one of many there, and I must admit I do like the food in Portugal and Spain, especially grilled sole, the way they do it, and of course, the way they cook rice; that for me is living the life of Riley.

Next day, the other crewmember arrived and we cast off to go to a floating jetty near the harbour entrance, where there was a police and customs office. After securing the boat, we all went to this office to sign a form that we were going to Gibraltar. We were told that should there be any problems and our plans changed we were to radio to them of our intentions, as long as we were in their territorial waters. When at this departure port one is not allowed to go ashore anymore, so we had a light evening meal on board and I just could not wait to cast off at about eight pm and go to sea.

We did not organise watches at that time, as we just played it by ear so to speak. I was far too hyped up about the trip ahead and this 'Valiant Lady.' I say again, what a toy, and what a beautiful evening it was, as we motored along using the sails too. The sight and feel of it all will never, ever leave me.

The owner kept going below to the chart table and using the direction finder, and kept a check on land-based maritime beacons—not that we required these, as we were in the open, deepwater sea. Sailing in warm climates is something else too and well worth mentioning. So we sailed on. What a night! The moon, the stars, distant fishing boats, a cruise liner on the distant horizon, the other crewmember and I were at the wheel at different times, as we felt it was time to hand over. I was not going below to sleep this night. When the owner came up at about midnight, having had a bit of a doze, he was also excited about putting to sea, as it was for him the second part of his round the world trip.

I thought of the Panama Canal, Hawaii, on to the Polynesian Islands, New Zealand and beyond…oh, if only.

The other crewmember went below and made us hot drinks and sandwiches. The skipper set the autopilot and sat down, looking ahead. I tucked myself into a corner of the cockpit facing astern and just sat there taking it all in and considering myself privileged and lucky to be here.

"Did I ask you when we met in London if you'd ever been down these parts before?"

"Never, but I have been as far as Belle Isle in Brittany."

"Now that's a nice little island. Yes, I've been there, but not in this boat, it was many years ago." It turned out in conversation that he got the Lady in the far north of Scotland, where she had lain ashore for about two years; when the American owner, who was going on to Europe and then back to America, had evidently to go back from Scotland urgently and put the Lady up for sale. I was never told, nor did I enquire what she cost, but I hazard a rough guess that there was not much change from two hundred thousand pounds.

This warm and calm night ended all too with the arrival of a misty dawn. It was then—while the owner was once again below having a short sleep—that we crew were in charge up top, so to speak, still on autopilot, but ever-watchful all round, as there were fishermen's boats everywhere out there. It was then, while still semi-dawn and misty that I got a dreadful fright, for there on our port (left) side and at about a quarter of a mile away, in the mist was what appeared to be an old-time naval rowing pinnace, with its oars shipped (that is, the oars held up vertically to facilitate coming alongside a ship or jetty). We were fast approaching the famous Cape Trafalgar of naval battle history. I cut the autopilot, took the wheel and altered course slightly. No problems, as we were well clear of the coast and in deep water. Skipper felt the change below and asked if I was avoiding a trawler or ship. "No, I've just seen what looked like an old naval pinnace with oars shipped. It didn't half give me a turn."

"That is the marker for a set fishing line anchored in the direction of the shore, and that old boat with the sticks set up is to show the end of the seaward line. Gave you a fright, did it?" he said, "Just as well we had reasonable visibility, and not been closer inshore. Get that line round your prop and they'd probably shoot us. I'm surprised it's not got a light on it. It is supposed to by law."

Shortly after, as we rounded a headland steering by hand, it suddenly came to me that I was looking at something that reminded me of drawings and paintings. "Skipper, we're at Cape Trafalgar. I'm sure that's it!"

He had been getting breakfast ready. The German crewman asked me if I had been here before. He just could not believe that I recognised it from paintings. I had also been keeping a close check on the chart through the night, but there it was—Cape Trafalgar. "Oh yes, that is the Cape alright."

"You certainly know your history," the owner said.

What true sailor anywhere in the world doesn't know of the heroism of that October day in 1805 when England's greatest hero Admiral Lord Nelson tempted Villeneuve from safe harbour in Cadiz and routed his fleet? We were at this moment sailing over dead men, broken ships, all those cannons and equipment I could, as I had seen in films of naval battles, hear the cannons firing, hear the commands of officers through the smoke of gunshot and above the din I could hear the screams of stricken men. If that had been my own boat, I would have stopped there for a while just to absorb the atmosphere in the air around us—it was here— right here that it happened. Again, I felt privileged to have sailed over this place.

On to Gibraltar, and over to our right, very clear was Africa, Tangier, as it is not many miles across from the nearest port in Spain. The currents and eddies run very strong in these narrows between the two continents, and the boats swerve constantly in these parts. At Gibraltar, we were met by the owner's brother, who was an ex-naval Phantom Pilot, then a civilian working there, doing aerial photography. The port of the marina that we were moored in was just yards from the runway which was used by the services as well as the airlines. That evening, the four of us went off to a restaurant in a little hire car of the skipper's brother. On a hill, the car stalled, and luckily there was no one behind us, as the car slowly lurched backwards for about five seconds or so. It was still in gear, making dreadful sounds.

Amid much laughter, we stopped and finally got started again. When we got to the restaurant, they obviously knew the brother of the skipper and apologised that they were fully booked. So we set off again all crammed in this small car in search of another restaurant. Around midnight, we finally got back on board and we crew bid the skipper and his brother good night and good morning, and called it a day; the brothers—no doubt—had a lot to talk about.

At about five in the morning, there was the most thunderous roar as six Phantoms took off and as near straight up as one could get them. This was followed by a Canberra and it gave us all a fright to say the least. Skipper's brother later told us that what we saw was done for training aircrew purposes. The plane had made a short take-off light on fuel, for a short flight only. It was already airborne halfway along the runway, flying level at about three hundred feet, when the engines slowed down to where it was barely possible to hear them. We thought that the pilot had lost it as he glided past us, near the end of the runway, and that he would crash into the harbour; it was then he turned on the power and up he went quite steeply, although not as steeply as the others had done.

We spent, I think, at least two or possibly three days in Gibraltar.

So once again it was time to cast-off, the skipper's brother was flying that morning, but as he taxied—and whilst he was still on the far side of the runway and turning to go to the other end—he flashed the landing lights and we all waved like mad;  great days they were, fantastic memories.

Into the night we sailed.  The forecast was reasonable, wind force four with occasional gusts of force five; nothing to be anxious about with a yacht like this one. Also, the wind was behind us, therefore pushing us along nicely.  We could see the coast, at times very clearly lit up as we passed well out to sea. We saw the lights of Marbella, Malaga and Almeira, and as we passed Cape Cabo de Gata and headed further out to sea, the wind increased and we started to move and some!

We two crew were on watch—who cares about turning in, in this possibly once-in-a-lifetime trip? We were not tired; we had lived the life of Riley in Gibraltar and we were ready for the adventure. Skipper was down below listening to see if there were any weather alterations being broadcast.  He checked the wind speed and called up to us that the wind speed was gradually increasing, and of course we were running before it, so deducting our speed of about nine knots, plus the wind from astern of us at 32 knots, this gave us a wind speed of true 41 knots, land speed of about 49 miles per hour. Skipper said he would reduce sail more now, rather than later, should it come on to blow stronger. I offered to shorten sail; we were all dressed, wet weather gear on, lifejackets, harness always clipped onto the boat at night time.  Go over the side at night and it is serious, especially as now with the wind starting to stir up the seas, but running before the wind and sea is totally different from butting and crashing against the wind and sea. Skipper insisted he would reduce sail, which he did quickly.  Then he asked me to take the wheel and asked the other crewman if he felt that he could cope below and make us some soup, explaining that he must hold on and not scald himself, as we were starting—to my delight, I must say—to surf and it was exhilarating! Skipper was watching me. He asked sort of hesitantly, "Have you surfed a yacht before at all? What happens if you let her broach?"

I replied that I had near Alderney, but not in a sea running as big as this. If you should broach—that is, not keep her dead straight—when a wave picks you up and you ride on that wave for a second or so, the boat and sea are moving at same speed. When that wave passes, the boat slows down before the next wave, if you let her turn—either way—and you get the force of the following wave on the side, it can roll you over.

"Ah well, it's evident you've done your homework. Let's have a go. I've not surfed for sometime now, and she flies. You're not apprehensive then?"

"No, in fact I don't even feel like turning in."

Soon the wind eased and as dawn came, we were abeam, but well out to sea, off Cartagena, where Drake had gone in and sacked the place centuries earlier. And near there is a headland called Cabo de Palos, with a huge lighthouse.

Yet another hot day to come; the wind had eased now, but the sea takes a bit longer to ease down.

Actually a few years before, my wife and I had a nice holiday just around the corner from Cabo de Palos at La Manga del Mar Manor. Many years ago I had that ghastly ME and I would simply get a cheap flight and go to the most beautiful out of the way places, not to Torremolinos, Benidorm, Marbella, etc. By train and coach I have at various times been to Seville, Madrid, Cadiz, Huelva, Jerez, Torifa directly opposite Tangier, Algeciras, mostly big commercial harbours, there and away again in two hours, Gibraltar of course and Spanish La Linea on the harbour at Gibraltar. Bevanedena Costa was very nice, but has got very big and commercial since. Almunecear, Calahonda,

191

Almerinar, Roquetas de Mar, Cabo de Gata, Carboveras, Puerto de Mazarron, Cartagema, La Manga Mar Menor and Santiago de la Ribera. I have passed through Alicante, La Villa Joiosa, Altea near Benidorm, Benidorm before it got big over 35 years ago, Calpe which has a rock and is known as the miniature Gibraltar. Morarra, Javea, Denia, Valencia in and out in one day, the heat truly unbelievable there.

Then up the coast—about one hour by car—there is a small place called Sagunto, where many people from Valencia have summer villas and apartments. A Spanish friend and his family that live in London near me, friends that I have known for well over twenty years, have a nice flat a stone's throw from the nice beach at Sagunto. I have been with them a few times. They are going to retire and live there, as they come from Valencia.

Then Benicosin, Coubris de Mar, Sitges, Barcelona in and out in one day, Blanes, Clomett de Mar, Escola. Twice I have been from England by the Valle de Loue ferry and Pride of Bilbao to northern Spain.

So past the huge headland lighthouse and we passed about a mile out from Calpe. The water there is very deep, and as the day wore on the wind and the sea had eased down, at about six pm we entered the marina. It was a case of get changed and off ashore to one of the many restaurants. A good time was had by all once again. I did comment to the skipper that it was a pity that his brother was not here.

"Yes, I'll agree to that. A bit of a character he certainly is without a doubt." He was just one of us, none of that naval officer, top dog business, not him.

It was a peaceful night, and next day we got the dinghy down and cleaned the hull, and with a broom we washed below the waterline as far as possible; she looked nice and sweet when it was done. We had lunch ashore and left in mid-afternoon for Majorca. We had to gently motor, as the wind had gone completely. The sun was hot and the air around us was fresh and still as we motored out. We had gone about six miles when many dolphins appeared, some leaping in unison, others darting under the boat. What a display! We were to see many more before we got to the south of France. What intelligent and beautiful creatures they are.

We made course to leave Ibiza well to starboard, at least fifteen miles off. We did see the lights on the island at various times and we were blessed with yet another moonlit night. Of course, at this time of the year, nights lasted only about six hours at the most. And again, with the exception of the skipper who liked his little forty winks, we kept watch and had the autopilot on. No way was I going to go below on nights like these, as once again we were rested and who in their right mind would not wish to stay up through the night amongst all that natural beauty? It was warm and balmy, and the skipper would occasionally call up to us to ask if there were any craft or big ships around, and speed, etc and we would report by calling back to him…all very technical stuff!

So as we motored on slowly, the sea was now like the proverbial sheet of glass. I leaned over the side and gently, so as not to disturb the owner, patted the stern of the boat, very quietly calling 'dolphin, dolphin, dolphin,' I wondered if they would hear me. The German fellow said, "I think you're crazy."

Yet ten minutes later my new friends arrived. They did not play with us, but went on their way; they had simply stopped by to say 'Hello'. Down below asleep, I would have missed it all.

Dawn came and in the far distance we could just make out Majorca. We assumed that we were looking at Port de Andratx, just off the starboard bow. As dawn merged into day, the breeze got up, so we stopped the engine and got the sails up. We were not in a hurry; we were a cruising yacht, not a racer.

It was yet another hot day, and the dolphins obliged yet again. At about two in the afternoon, we were almost level with Porto de Soller, but stood onto a small creek further up the coast. The wind was now at about force three, but we were sheltered by the high ground to starboard. So as we slowly came round to enter La Calobra creek, the skipper was down below checking the chart for the depths there. I was not on the wheel, as the other crewmember was steering on skipper's course instructions. Then as we cleared the high ground there, the wind in these places has a funnelling effect and we were hit by a mini squall. She started to heel to port slowly, then faster, all in seconds, hard a port. I shouted to the chap at the wheel, and at the same time I let the main sail fly off. She came back up smartly and rolled to starboard a bit.

"Well done, Walter. She wouldn't have gone over, but good thinking."

The crewman on the wheel did not react, but it was not for me to criticise him. It all happened so quickly. We started the engine, took the sails down and motored up to a fishermen's stone jetty. There was a small shop and a guesthouse, fishing boats, nets and gear everywhere, there were also a few small yachts, and that was it. A more peaceful little place you might not find again. We moored up for the night and enjoyed the peace and tranquillity of a place that modern life had passed by.

Next day, after a visit for some provisions—mainly ice cream and beer—we set off for the south of France, no set time for our arrival, as time was not important. The forecast was good with some early morning mist or fog patches. Of course we had a radar unit, maximum distance sixteen miles, so the forecast posed no problem. Also, the waters were very deep in these parts.

The owner was at the wheel and I was sitting down, letting the world go by. The other crewman whose turn it was to tidy up and wash the dishes had, without telling us up top, removed the steps which led down eight feet into the cabin. He had to get into the engine room, the door of which was behind the steps to get the gallon container of washing-up liquid. Skipper set the autopilot and went to go below. Of course, you do not expect to step into a void. And by the grace of God, I say yet again, the owner was quite broad across the shoulders. He banged his head and his left arm got a gash. I tried to grab him, but I could never have held him. He was all of fourteen stone, very fit indeed. The language was what that fellow deservedly got; if the skipper had gone down he may have got killed or been very seriously injured in which case we would have immediately put out a distress call for a helicopter or a high speed naval craft.

We got the first aid kit and gently felt that no bones were broken or fractured. There was blood everywhere in the cockpit. We put on some disinfectant stuff and bandaged him up as best we could under the circumstances. He was definitely in shock, but not badly so. However, he was huffing and puffing.

The other crewman didn't breathe a word. He was washing the blood away down into the sea through the vents in the cockpit floor. "Skipper," I said, "I think it would be wise to do a Pan Pan call [an advice call, this is not an SOS call] or would you like to go back to Palma or Porto Soller?"

"Thanks, but we'll see how it goes." I think that if I had not been there, there would have been a new tale added to the repertoire of old sea-dog's tales; that of a German crewman that went strangely missing while the owner was asleep.

Much later—on the last day of this trip—the owner

told me that this crewman was hoping to join him somewhere in the world at a later date, but that was simply not on anymore, he was becoming a liability. I had of course at the outset in London told the owner that I simply could not come to the other side of the world, due to my work and of course the money involved.

But before this tale is finally closed there is yet another incident with this fellow crewman. He may have been to a nautical school as I had been, but he simply did not have the experience. I was sitting near the bow of the boat and skipper was in the cockpit looking all around with his binoculars, when the fellow did the unforgivable. We do not throw anything into the sea anymore; it goes ashore to the rubbish bins, but he threw an empty jam jar from below. It hit the top of the first step and splintered everywhere. I stayed put where I was, but the skipper went, as they say these days… ballistic!

"Christ, and may my father [who was a minister] forgive me, why the hell are you trying to throw that overboard? Give me patience dear Lord. Don't you know that nowadays it's got to be kept until we get ashore and put into the bins there? Nothing's to be thrown into the sea."

The atmosphere was by then electric between the two of them. Plus the skipper was on pain-easing tablets. Turning to me he said, "You know, Walter, if I cave in—no, I'm not going to—but on the assumption of any eventualities, what would you do?"

I thought for a few seconds, "Well I'd call for immediate assistance."

"And when I've gone, what then?"

"You'd have to tell the other chap that it's all down to me or the two of us to decide on the next move. I would not proceed to France as I've never been there, but we could call a pilot boat, as Majorca is nearer and Palma is big and easy. I'd take her there."

"Yes, that's what I'd have done." He called the

other chap and told him that if he had to be taken off, the two of us had to take the boat at full speed to Palma. "Is that understood then?" It was clearly understood!

We arrived near Nice three days and two nights after leaving Majorca. On the early dawn of the last day at sea we received the shipping forecast of fog and a big ship on the radar was crossing ahead of us at about one and a half miles away. That ship had us on her radar and she constantly blew her horn. Skipper was having a nap, so when I replied with our handheld compressed air cylinder foghorn, skipper was up very quickly. Yes, that is right, we must, as you know, reply to his signal. So he blew and we blew back, then he was clear of us and the hooting got weaker and weaker and in three-quarters of an hour he had gone off the radar screen. I reckon that was a cruise liner or a big one anyway.

A few more dolphins and we were at the end of this trip. I cannot remember the name of this place but it was not that far from Nice. We met an Englishman there who lived on a boat, but also had access to a flat. He was on his own, into his late fifties. He had originally a few years ago intended to putter round the whole of the Mediterranean for a couple of years, but when he got to this place, he being a shipwright by trade and also having built this great lovely wooden yacht of thirty feet, he did a small job for someone and he has been there ever since. He looked after a villa for a German owner and had the staff flat when they were not at the villa. He repairs boats, and when time allows he goes for a day sail or even to Sardinia. Reckons he'll end his days here, and good luck to him, what some people wouldn't give for just one year of such an uncomplicated life.

Next day we departed. The other crewman went first. I had to get a coach to Marseilles, where I got the night train to Calais and on to London.

What a milestone it was for me. I can recall virtually every part of that fantastic trip. The owner did complete the round the world trip and gave a lecture on it at Ivory House. I say again that the 'Valiant Lady' was some yacht.

Naturally it was not all me at sea, indeed not. All of us had holidays as a family to various places, mainly in Spain and Majorca. We did have some holidays in Devon, but the weather there was never conducive to a nice holiday. And I say yet again, as I worked all the hours that there were, my wife insisted that I should go sailing when I had the opportunity.

The next yacht was a twenty-six foot yacht from the Medway in Kent. The owner sailed regularly to Jersey and I had a weekend's trial sail with him and an employee of his. I think that he was also his nephew. It was only a ten-day stint and it included a night crossing of the Channel. This craft, whose name eludes me, was of a class known as a Twister; very sea capable craft they were, heavily constructed, not very fast but built on older boat lines.

On the way back from Jersey to Cherbourg, there is a place on the French mainland virtually opposite the island of Alderney, called Cap De La Hague. There are shallow rocks, eddies, currents and tides that rip through there, so one has to work with the tides in one's favour otherwise the craft would be going backwards. The forecast was about force four, but at that dreaded place the conditions are not always as forecast. We had the tide and wind pushing us over the area of the current at seabed at fourteen knots. Our boat speed was eight knots but with the force of the currents and tide it was a true fourteen knots. The Sea State at Cap De La Hague was what is known as a confused sea, waves breaking at all angles and directions. Although we were well out from that headland, the sea level varies due to rocks and ledges and shallows. In fact, we saw two yachts foolishly trying to go the other way, and when they eventually turned and got to Cherbourg well after we had arrived there, it turned out they had chartered the boat. They must have been experienced otherwise the charter would not have let them have the yachts. They were all young chaps, strong, but they were totally exhausted. Even with all their gear on, they were soaked to the skin. If they had had a hefty powerboat, a ferry, a naval ship, a coaster or a trawler, they would have made headway, but to try and ram the Cap with tide and wind against you is total madness as they found out to their cost. That would be a valuable lesson for them to add to their experience.

Two days later, as we were approaching the Thames Estuary in a wind force four to five; we heard a strange sound that I had read about, that people had heard on old yachts with heavy rigging in a strong wind heard. It is known as the mermaid's wail, and wail it was indeed. "Eerie," the owner said to me, "That's the mermaids in the rigging. We're nearly home and they are trying to lure us back out to sea." I have never heard that strange phenomenon since.

So it was into the Medway, up to the moorings and the end of another experience. People that have sailed off Cap De La Hague all tell the same story. Even when there is little wind, the conditions there are to be respected.

The year was now 1988 and I had been contacted by a retired gentleman doctor who had a thirty-six foot yacht at St Mawes, Falmouth. So t is on the train to Cornwall and then by car we go to the club moorings. We get the dinghy and outboard, load up all the gear and motor out to the 'Artful Dodger.' She is another beauty with a beam width that would take some sea to roll her over; a lovely painting of the Artful Dodger is on her stern. This was yet another yacht and a half, to coin a much-used phrase.

Our short trip was to go to Mevagissey and stop there for lunch. However, when we got there the wind was blowing into the small harbour and a bit of a sea was running on the bar shallows at the entrance. We were then on motor only. We timed our run into the harbour between a gap in the waves and went for it on full throttle. Once inside, it was still rough and the wall where we should have tied up to was solid with fishing boats and trawlers. The owner said we shall lie alongside the trawler and go for lunch.

"Don't you think they may want to go out before we get back? And anyway, it's going to be hard on the side of this boat, even with twelve fenders out." I said.

"Actually, I'm glad you've thought that one out." The skipper said, "I think I'm coming to the same conclusion myself. I didn't want us to miss out on lunch, and I'm sorry to say there's hardly anything on board. Perhaps it's best to head back out."

We turned her round and eased up to the entrance to await a favourable gap in the waves, as coming in we were pushed. Going out was a totally different situation. We got our chance and let her rip. We were just between the breakwaters and probably right over the bar, with plenty of water beneath us of at least thirty to forty feet when we took a big one. Right over the foredeck it came, thinned out a bit as it ran over the cabin top and dispersed itself on us in the cockpit, and we were out and clear.

"That was one of the worst ones I've had round here for a while, but she rides nicely," the skipper said.

I agreed, "Yes, she certainly threw that one off quickly and didn't even slow down as it hit us."

Skipper found a tin of soup which was still useable and some biscuits that had been well wrapped up, and we survived on that until we got back to St Mawes Creek. Once into the creek with the high ground all around, it is pretty calm there. We went ashore to a restaurant there for dinner and went back to the boat for the night. Next day we sailed up to Falmouth and some way up the Helford River and that was it.

"How do you fancy Brittany shortly? Can you make it? I Gather you've done nights." the skipper said.

"Definitely," I said, "Give me a ring and I'll be down." And that was that.

This was to be the first of the season's trips to Brittany and the Channel Islands. It was now early May and the skipper rang me as arranged, and I met a lifelong friend of his and this friend's son of about twenty-six years old.

From Truro in Cornwall it was next to no time before we were at the moorings in St Mawes Creek. We got everything on board by late afternoon and departed for the Channel Islands, across the Channel by night, so as to close the coast on the Islands by daylight. The Dodger sailed nicely; the owner—a man of vast sailing expertise—let us all have a turn steering and checking the radar and other instruments. This boat had virtually all the necessary electronics that a boat of this size could carry; a weather fax also—and something really new for boats—it had a small unit which could detect a vessel's radar over the horizon. If the vessel it picked up was far away it would bleep at thirty second intervals, and if the ship was going away from us the intervals of bleeps would get progressively longer, but should the ship be coming nearer, the bleeps would become quicker and louder, a marvellous gadget, a great safety improvement.

Of course, the Channel as often said, must be treated with the utmost caution and a sharp lookout at all times must be kept. The son of the skipper's friend was a fair hand at cooking. As is the norm when at sea we only do tins of food, ordinary potatoes and such; nothing fancy. We eat well when we reach our destinations and go ashore.

That is what it is all about. But he did us proud, considering the motion of the boat. We certainly had a good meal about ten in the evening as we sailed at a fair speed. The skipper and his friend then went below to tidy up, check the weather fax printout and to listen for shipping movements, especially if any large barges were being towed or if the navy was around on exercise. Also, we listen continuously on channel sixteen for any distress calls or urgent information as we hope others listen, should we have problems, but of course the coastguard monitors any calls. We often hear ships asking the latest weather, or if the pilot could come and meet their ship at such a time and area off a harbour, etc.

We did the usual two hours on and in this case two hours off. The owner and his friend came up at midnight while the friend's son and I went below for a sleep, dressed in all the gear, even lifejacket on, as at night in an emergency, one has no time to put clothes and equipment on. At two am therefore, it was our turn once again to take the watch. It had turned cold and the wind had increased and we were certainly tramping along nicely. The radar showed a few craft, some very big, as did the bleeper go off most of the time, so we switched that off, as the radar picture was good and visibility was also good. Soon as the dawn broke we saw the lights on Guernsey and took the jib sail down as we did not wish to get there until about ten, so as to catch a favourable tide to assist us. It grew ominously cloudy, started to rain, and we then had a short thunderstorm with hailstones the size of cherries. The noise as they struck the plastic boat was deafening, but as soon as that was over it began to feel warmer and soon the sun came through and it became a different picture.

The Channel Islands have fast tides and are notorious for its rock-strewn coastline, plus the usual hazards of fishermen's floats and even a line of many, many hooks set between two floats some distance apart. Get that lot round the propeller and it is trouble in a big way. Then there are fishing boats, big ferries, local hydrofoils and small ferries, other yachts and motorboats. One has to be constantly alert to the dangers.

So we duly arrived at St Peters Port, entered the mooring and went to the showers, after which we trooped ashore for lunch at a fish restaurant. On the way back to the boat we got some very nice pastries to have next day, plus fresh bread and milk

The weather was pleasant, especially in the shelter of the mooring. In the evening we had sandwiches aboard and then went for a walk up in the town. We found an ice cream parlour and promptly sat ourselves down there and partook of their wares. Later we went back to the boat and it is worth remembering that in some marinas it is not always peaceful, especially when some hooray Henrys come back to their boats after what can only be termed as having had a good skin-full, and usually well after midnight, as well as the usual coming and going of craft at all times, especially just before dawn when the fishing boats with their powerful engines put to sea.

Next morning we left to proceed to Jersey, but as conditions were not good, the skipper's friend felt unwell, as we were butting hard into it. So we turned back to Guernsey and sailing with the wind behind us, it felt immediately easy. We had another night there and as it was now Sunday evening, we had a relatively quieter night. Monday was dull and overcast but by late afternoon the sun came out and the forecast was good, so it was agreed that we would go to Dartmouth. I hasten to add that this owner did it by the book at Falmouth coastguard and on departure here also did he report us—names, how many aboard, destination, etc. About seven in the evening, with the help of the tidal flow, we crossed the Channel silently through the night. The skipper and his friend's son did the first watch, and I and the father did the next watch and so forth through the night. We had of course the usual amount of shipping to watch for and at about five am the English coastline had started to appear on the horizon.

I had been to Dartmouth many years before on a small yacht that some friends I knew had chartered out of Poole, and the following year a bigger yacht out of Portsmouth. That boat's name, believe it or not, I remember despite the passage of time—Sortilege it was—a French name, I believe. One of my friends whose car I used to look after was a chap by the name of Ken Thorne, he was big in film music. He did the orchestra at the Albert Hall with the American crooner Andy Williams and he eventually settled in Hollywood and did music; I believe he did the music for the film for Superman, but that's another tale.

So we motored up to the visitors' moorings pontoon, saw the charge-hand there and went ashore for a brunch style meal. We stayed the night and left early next morning bound for Plymouth. It was a nice warm day; a gentle breeze soon had us on our way, and as we came into Plymouth Sound, to the right behind the high ground there is a river called the Tamar, with fantastic scenery. The Tamar valley is a place of outstanding natural beauty. It also has a narrow port once into the river where there is a ledge, and it fairly boils at that port, but there are small buoys marking a channel, then further up there are many yachts and a pontoon to tie up to for visitors, and then it is into the dinghy and off to the restaurant there.

A very peaceful night we spent there, and at first light we were once more on our way. I would gladly have stayed here for at least another day; it really was a very special place.

An uneventful trip back to St Mawes, passing the Bishops Rock lighthouse, where the remains—just a stump—of the original structure that was destroyed in a gale a long time ago can still be seen there.

We arrived back late afternoon, put the yacht shipshape and left at about seven pm. I got the overnight train back to London.

# CHAPTER 8

Very soon I was back at St Mawes, and this time it was to be at least a week to ten days on a cruise to Brittany. There are places there such as the Raz de Seine and others where if the tide calculations are not correct, it is not only impossible—unless it is a very powerful powerboat—to go through here, but extremely dangerous to try. We had been through there a few times and once we arrived just as the tide was beginning to run against us. At one time—taking a bearing on the large lighthouse and the land behind it—we were stationery and just very slowly going backwards; so we increased engine speed and steered off at a slight angle. We finally got through to calmer and deeper water and skipper said that had we been say ten minutes later, we would have had to go back and try with the next tide. But then that would have been early evening, and it would definitely have been out of the question.

We sailed on and saw a French Nuclear Submarine on the surface off our stern. It simply ploughed through the Raz; at times half covered in water and spray. We did not photograph her as it is strictly prohibited but it would have been some shot. The penalty can be to have the boat seized by the authorities.

The weather was what summer sailing was all about; the further south we went the warmer it grew, and yes oh yes we were now in the Bay of Biscay. What a feeling that was; nearly blue water sailors we were, so keeping well out to sea, as that coast must be kept well clear of. There are rocks, shallows and ridges known as spines that can run from the land to a considerable distance out to sea. They are all on the chart, plus wrecks that are not always marked on the chart and of course fishing floats, a real hazard at night.

Of course when we just sailed without running the

engine, the propeller was a two-bladed one and it was so designed that with the forward movement of the yacht it folded one blade into the other, thus it would not catch any lines, etc or even discarded nets or other flotsam that is unfortunately ever present in the sea. We have seen half-submerged oil drums, telegraph poles, even at one time a huge brand new piece of a wooden jetty, at least thirty feet long by about twelve feet wide it must have easily weighed a couple of tons. Hit that with a glass reinforced plastic yacht in the middle of the night and the most dreaded of the dreaded would surely follow. Modern containers too are a real unseen menace. Containers that have fallen off a container carrier, full of stuff usually lurk just below the surface and like an iceberg have just a bit showing above the water. There is many a tale of boats striking one, and the only chance is if you are in a steel boat, but they come very expensive. Many famous yachts-persons, men and women, have had the misfortune to either hit one or graze it. It has been estimated according to recorded losses from ships that there are literally hundreds in the seas of the world, indeed a sobering thought.

Here I must recall what an elderly fisherman in Aberdeen told me when I was about eighteen. I only knew him as Raushin John. Now Raushin in Scottish means rushing about, and this is what John always seemed to be doing. He was in fact the last traditional fisherman in Aberdeen with a boat known as a yawl. She was a lovely fishing boat with a hatch where the man stood in, so if a sea hit her it would run off the deck and little would go down the hatchway as it was so small.

He had a great spirit and sense of adventure and lived with his wife and son in a tiny fisherman's cottage on the quay there where I finally kept my boat at Old Torry dock. It is all gone now, the oil industry has seen to that. Anyway, he said to me one day—and I will forever remember it. "Laddie," he said, "you must have respect for the water, but ye could be sittin' at home and the ceilin' could fall on yer head and kill ye." That is it then in a nutshell.

We sailed through the Bay of Biscay further south. The next haven was Lorient; then on to Quaberan, then over to the appropriately named Belle Isle—the Beautiful Isle—as indeed it was. From its high ground—where we rode on the bicycles we had hired—the spectacular view was outstanding.

Then on to St Nazaire; I found this place rather depressing, for it had there a massive submarine pen that had been built by slave labour during that horrendous war that we all know about. The French, we were told by the harbourmaster, had decided to leave it as a lasting memorial to those that perished there, having been worked to death. I was not at all sorry to depart from this place, where so many of my blood brethren had perished. Even the sea birds seemed eerily quiet and sombre in the skies above.

At the end of our journey south it was now time to retrace our steps and we did a day and a night motor sailing at a good speed, arriving at Camoret opposite the port of Brent. The skipper said to us, "Go up to the old fort at the marina here and shout the English are coming."

Evidently, the English navy came in there at one time and sacked and burned the place down. We did not go and shout. It was all history now.

We would—when ashore—usually phone home to see how things were back there, and it was the owner who was the first to phone his wife; I heard him say, "I'll tell him," and "You say Portishead has been trying to contact us? Yes, I'll write down the hospital phone number. No, it's not serious, a foot fracture. Yes, thanks for now then."

Then he said to me, "Walter, I'm afraid your wife's in hospital, having fractured her foot. Would you like to fly home or go by train and ferry?"

I phoned the hospital and actually spoke to a sister who lived just around the corner from us. She assured me that everything was in order and there was no urgency for me to get back. I said that I would be back as soon as possible, so we decided to leave at dawn, because as I said before a night out in those waters was not on the cards. In fifteen hours we were back in St Mawes, having really pushed on as fast as we could; with a fair breeze and the engine we covered the distance in good time.

I took the night train back to London and my first stop was the hospital. But my wife had already been discharged. When I eventually arrived home she said, "I suppose it's just one of those things; all a bit of a mix up really with people trying to be helpful. Andrew had got on to Portishead Radio who had put out a call."

The problem was that being in the marina, we do not listen to the radio and I missed their call to us. So my son Andrew rang the skipper's wife in Cornwall and that is how we got the message third hand. Still the main thing was, she was fine and all's well that ends well.

The next year was yet another milestone in my sailing life, a very big milestone indeed, for it was now the five hundredth anniversary of Columbus leaving Spain and there was to be celebrations and yachts were to retrace the route that Columbus sailed. In one of the big yachting magazines I spotted an advertisement for experienced crew wanted for the Columbus 500th trip. I was sixty-two years of age, and my wife in her wisdom pointed out to me that at my age who would want me. She had a fair point but I was determined anyway to chance my luck. So it was off to the Southampton Marina where I met the owner and his wife. Their yacht was a new forty-five footer Oyster class. We did not go for a sail, which rather surprised me. After at least two hours of chatting about yachts and yachting, he said that he would take me as crew. I pointed out that I could not go all the way to the Caribbean because of my work, and the expense involved, as one once more has to pay for the privilege. I feel that once again, being an engineer was a factor in having been accepted but whatever the reasons I was delighted.

The plan was that the owner and his wife, plus their daughter and her boyfriend would take the boat to El Puerto de Santamaria in Spain, where eventually I was to join them. This was near Cadiz. But before joining them there for at least three weeks or longer if necessary, I had ten days with the Artful Dodger to Brittany and Belle Isle yet again, and various ports en route to northern Spain where I left as other crew joined to sail the Dodger back. Among the places we visited was Les Sables de Olonne with its medieval village, then on to La Rochelle, which must be one of the biggest marinas in the world. There were some super toys moored there.

Then from there we went non-stop to northern Spain to a beautiful little harbour west of Santander, but unless I can find my log, I cannot unfortunately remember the name. The hills and mountains, and even the little houses looked just like the colourful hillside houses in Switzerland. I left my friends there and took the train to Madrid. I had some time there between trains so I looked around Madrid. I did not stay long, as it was forty-four degrees. I managed to stumble from one Italian ice cream parlour to the next one.

I took the overnight train to join the Columbus yacht as arranged. When I got there it was a very modern marina. So modern in fact they were still constructing it. I met boaters from various countries, and one of the biggest yachts that had a full time paid crew was ACTIII, a yacht of at least 150 feet in length, owned by an American theatre owner, hence the name.

After a couple of days here we left for Huelva, from where Columbus had set sail. All the other yachts were to meet here and of course we were lavishly entertained. This was a big thing there in Spain, and there were bands, dancers and a huge fair, the whole spectacle was very grand and the Spanish did themselves proud. I think we were in Huelva for three days and we were all taken to a large memorial to Columbus and all who had sailed with him. There we signed our names and the names of the boats we were with. We were told it would be there forever. Well, well, I am in a large book there in Spain… immortality, just like Columbus!

Then came the day when the Spanish royal family joined the celebrations, His Majesty and Her Majesty the King and Queen of Spain boarded a frigate and waved to us all as we left that early evening—a sight I shall never forget; boats everywhere. We had a big speedboat come alongside us with some charming people, we shook hands all round, shared a crate of beer and then it was, 'adios amigos'. It was terrific. Brethren of the sea, converging together like that is something truly to behold.

The river down to the open sea took us about an hour or so to navigate, the sun was sinking in the west. It was all very clear, planes and helicopters all around, and as night approached, we all took different courses to our next port of call, as Columbus had done, which was the island of Porto Santos, not far from the main Canary Islands. It had a nice beach, the water was warm and as is the custom on the harbour wall, many people paint a slogan or name of the boat that had passed that way, and there I found a painting and names of all on Valiant Lady that had come this way.

Once again, the local council took all of us to a restaurant on the harbour where we had musicians and dancers, great food and the wine flowed freely. Our boat, having used the least engine hours to get here, was awarded a small stainless steel model of a yacht. We all had our photos taken, each of us in turn holding it, standing by a large model of the same that had been erected to mark this milestone in Spanish history. It was just one big party after another. Of course, sailing in these warm climates is just great. We were here for two days and then proceeded to the main island. On the way we once again had a visit from the dolphins, and also saw what had once been a very large volcano just above sea level. Half of it had exploded evidently, so it looked wide open and there were boats inside the half part fishing.

One of the other crew on our yacht was a young Dutchman, ex-naval officer. I felt as did the owner that this chap thought he was on board for a cruise, in the true sense of the word. It was statutory on this trip, as I laid down in the safety regulations that any cabin skylights were to be closed at night or in bad weather. However, this fellow did have his skylight partially open and one of the jib sheets happened to ease off and, when it took up in the strain again, hooked itself under the lever on the outside of this aperture and promptly snapped off the handle. The skipper went mad, I can tell you. We had to seal it up and log it as well, as required by the safety people who had inspected all the boats at Huelva. It doesn't sound like much but something even as tiny as that can be the difference between being seaworthy or not.

We were about six miles from Puerto de la Cruz, and I and our ex-naval man were on watch. The steering was on autopilot. The skipper and his wife were below sorting out things for lunch, etc. The daughter was lying down facing the sun so she of course was not on watch. There appeared directly ahead what looked like yellow plastic tubing floating, and where was my buddy watch-keeper but lying aft with his head on a sailbag reading a novel! It was not my job to tell him that he should be keeping watch as well as me, so I beckoned for the owner to come up and I pointed ahead to the yellow tubes, and to my supposed companion watch-keeper. "Is this how you keep watch in the navy?" he asked our ex-naval man.

"Oh I do look up from time to time. Anyway, Walter is capable and we are well out to sea anyway."

"I suppose you have seen the stuff ahead then?" skipper asked.

"What stuff ahead?" asked our novel reader. He raised himself up and sheepishly said, "Oh yes, some sort of piping and a lot of it as well."

The skipper told me to disengage the autopilot and steer off a bit in case there were parts of this mass of tubing just below the surface which would catch our propeller. Any potential hazards were avoided. When we got into harbour, not much was said by either the owner or his wife to our ex-naval man, and when the question arose about departure, he said that he would go ashore and see about a flight. He came back, got his gear and without a handshake or thanks just said cheerio and was gone. I stayed for another night and went ashore early next morning, got a flight for two that afternoon, bade the family farewell and thanked them for having me.

"If we get stuck or let down for the next stage, can we contact you?"

"I'll be honest," I said, "I'd love to come all the way, but I simply cannot. I'm sure you understand."

"Well, pleasant flight to England. See you again one day perhaps."

I heard that they arrived on the other side before Christmas, having stayed for about six weeks at Puerto de la Cruz, but left the boat and came back to England, as the hurricane season had to pass before the boats continued to proceed across the Atlantic. When they had all arrived, I was told that they had a party that lasted about three days. I can well imagine that. Columbus had no knowledge of hurricanes and nearly lost both boats. He was not simply a visionary and an adventurer; he was also a very able seaman.

Before next season came, the owner of the Artful Dodger rang me to see how I was placed regarding sailing once more with him. Of course I could come; it was for at least two weeks, down to Brittany again. The owner as usual met me at Truro railway station and off we went to St Mawes. Waiting in the car was a female crewmember. She had this peculiar thing that before she started to speak; she did this odd and irritating half giggle or laugh, and the same when she stopped speaking. It certainly was not an impediment; it is something that some high-class people do evidently. I had never heard anyone doing this before, and I suppose I got used to it. However, this female was a farmer's wife and apparently she had sailed extensively, but she also had another irritating habit and that was her constant boastfulness about what they had and what they were going to get etc, etc. The lists and the bragging were endless. I was definitely not too keen on this one, but it is not for me to choose who sails with us. Later events were to prove my suspicions.

This female did everything in what is known in the army as at the double, dashing around at speed. I asked her if she had done a lot of racing, and she said, "Why do you ask?"

I answered, "Well you seem to dash around as if you're a racer."

"Yes indeed, I have," she said, "a fair bit."

I left it at that.

We left at the usual time of late afternoon. I felt deep down somehow that I was not going to get on with the lady, nothing to do with class or any of that holier and better than thou; it was simply her nauseating attitude.

214

The first leg as usual was to head for Camarett, which we did for the remainder of the next day and night. Of course, having a female aboard does pose problems, as with an all male crew you can dress or undress without pulling curtains across or closing communicating doors, etc. One cannot do that when there is a woman aboard, and the occasional expletive cannot be released.

So it's the next lovely morning and we are off to see how the Raz de Seine looks today. We went in company with other southbound yachts. This part was to be a through the night trip, well offshore and once again we were in the Bay of Biscay. We had to resort to motor sailing, as the breeze eased off. Come nightfall us two crew did the midnight to three am watch, the skipper having turned in at midnight. As usual, I was too hyped up to sleep, so when I got the owner up, the lady went below to her cabin up in the front of the boat, and I tucked myself into a corner by the cabin, but still in the cockpit, to keep the owner company. I did occasionally nod off, but the ever-faithful ship radar detector kept bleeping occasionally throughout the night. Food had been prepared by the skipper in the evening as well as hot drinks and soup in flasks, always a precaution in case it gets up rough and unless you have to cook, it is no pleasure, so the thing is to prepare it all before night closes in.

The lady crewmember came up at about five am to see if the skipper would like a rest, after all he was a few years my senior. But like me, he said that he did not want to go below. He was making the most of it, and he was not at all tired, the yacht having been on autopilot for most of the night. I couldn't understand why anyone would want to come on such trips and then sleep through the best parts of it.

Dawn comes early at this time of the year and I recall an incident when we two crew were on watch again.

The time was about seven am and madam was on the wheel looking ahead and I was leaning easy on the cabin exterior, when a French twin-engine plane came from behind us very low and with power cut to a minimum I could see the plane coming. She, looking ahead, could not, nor did she hear it until it was nearly on top of us, opened up and zoomed upwards directly above us. She got a fright and a half. "You must have seen it coming. Why didn't you warn me?" she shouted.

I simply said that I had not spotted it until it was on top of us.

The skipper said that the plane always swoops low like that and photographs craft all the time to catch smugglers, so if they see you very regularly they send a high-speed naval or customs boat to check you out.

On most yachts there is carried a large sail known as a spinnaker. We had never used it as it is a performance and a half to rig it up and more often than not more trouble than it is worth. It is used to its best potential only during certain conditions. The weather conditions—as it was on this day—with little breeze was warm and the outlook was settled. So madam talked skipper into getting this huge thing out of the bag. She tore up and down getting all the lines fixed up, and at one stage I thought she was going over the side in her eagerness, dashing up forward and back to the cockpit. There were lines everywhere.

I remarked to the owner, "We won't be much faster even with this lot up."

"Well let's see." he smiled, "I wouldn't have bothered with it as it entails a lot of work, as you probably know."

So the boat was now fully rigged with the sail up. And we observed as the boat speed increased ever so slightly; the sail would billow backward and half collapse, then fill with a jerk and so forth and so on, rather like the forward motion of a kangaroo. The other problem was that it made forward visibility rather difficult, and I emphasise once again, a watch all round must be kept at all times. Relax completely and ignore a good lookout and you could be in trouble. The skipper finally suggested to madam that this constant collapsing and picking up of the spinnaker was not doing the rigging any good, and it was decided to take it down. This action requires at least two persons to hand it in so that it does not drag in the water. Some people I have heard have let it down so quickly that it has gone half under the bow of the boat and then you have got problems getting it aboard. So the owner helped get it down without any problems.

I did not hear what was said while the owner and madam were up front, but it turned out that she was keeping a RYA crews logbook of recorded trips, etc to be signed by an owner. I have never bothered with this type of record of sailing. She required that the owner signs her logbook that she was competent in handling a spinnaker, as I grant you and as said, it is not that easy. The skipper agreed and madam was happy, I might have know that she had some

Ah, but comes the next episode in the tale of this every sentence that starts with this infuriating giggle cum laugh, very wearing it is, as far as I am concerned.

So it now turns out that she has talked the skipper into letting her be mate, not just ordinary crew, but mate, as she wants to qualify for open sea, long distance skipper, and therefore required at least another sixty hours in her log and signed for evidence as a competent mate or acting skipper. This was not on the cards, as far as I was concerned and I was therefore just waiting for madam to tell me to do something, and she could put in her log that she had a mutiny on her hands, for I was not having any of it. We eventually got to Auray without any problems. There we decided to go ashore for dinner, so we left the boat at about five pm. It was very hot that day, and I was in shorts and a sleeveless shirt. We strolled around a bit, all three of us, and at about seven we went to the restaurant. This was at least three-quarters of a mile from where the boat was moored in the marina.

To cut a long story short, we did not leave the restaurant until well after nine o'clock, and it was now quite chilly, and as I said, we had a long walk back to the boat. By the time we got back there I was cold, but the others were not feeling it as much as I was. It took me some time to get warm and I even put on my heavy cold weather underwear before turning in as soon as we got aboard. I had definitely got a chill with going ashore so lightly clothed.

Next day we decided to go back. A short trip it was to be to Lorient, a very pretty place it is, with a massive old fortification at the entrance. Madam had been on the wheel for most of that day, and I had done about an hour after the skipper took us out of the marina. Madam had done the casting off of the securing lines and I will make no comment on that, after all who in this world is perfect? So she was at the wheel, giggling and jawing, as was her norm. The entrance is well buoyed for at least two miles from the entrance as this area has rocks, shallows and depending on the tide one must keep in the marked channel. We were gently sailing along and had the engine going but not yet in gear, just in case we had to manoeuvre quickly for any reason. It therefore gave me the greatest pleasure in telling madam that she had not paid proper attention and had gone on the wrong side of one of the buoys.

"Look, it is on the other side." I said, "If you'd been paying attention, instead of forever jawing, you'd have seen it."

The owner did not say anything to me at that point. He looked at the depth gauge and said, "Ah well, there's good depth this side of the buoy at this state of tide, and I feel at a rough guess even at low water we wouldn't have touched." He was being overly kind and I think it was wrong of him.

"Anyway," I said with a not to well disguised hint of sarcasm, "it's no distance to swim ashore from here, had we had the misfortune to strike the rocks and there are a few boats around to pick us up."

I must add that by then—because of the chill I had picked up—I was feeling most unwell. Not seasick, but the chill had the hallmarks of turning into a bad cold, and what with  madam I had just about had enough. I decided and told the skipper there and then that I was going home.  I told him it was because I was not feeling well and I told him—again sarcastically—that I felt that madam was able to carry out crewing without my assistance, and I felt sure that therefore I would not be missed. We tied up in the marina, I said goodbye to the owner who tried to talk me out of leaving, and I had no hesitation in politely telling him that madam came as crew and as crew she should have remained, not as mate, and lucky for her that she did not once tell me what to do because I would not have stood for it.

That then was that.  Tales of woe, facts are facts. The RNLI has all the tragic facts.


There is yet one more saga that beggars belief, but during my time I met some people who could best be described as some right monkeys.  Please do not presume that I am exaggerating these things.  I have spoken to many people that go to sea, but even owners I have been told, besides some being eccentric, others can be rather odd and unrealistic.

My friend, referred to as R way back in this story of my reflections, finally got himself a thirty-eight foot motor cruiser that he kept in a marina up the Thames. We, that is my wife and I and our children and sometimes a friend or two would go and help him to use the boat. To me, this landlocked River Thames, with its locks that I have seen people nearly coming to blows at, was not my type of boating, but what are friends for if you cannot help them in their pursuit of pleasure?

We even got as far as the Medway one summer, and eventually he decided, as I had often tried to persuade him on the Suffolk rivers and the Walton on the Naze backwaters, to sell this motor cruiser of his and get a motor sailer type of boat. His mother was now actually living at Frinton and I said that I would always crew for him. We went to many places to see boats, and finally way down in deepest Cornwall, the name of the place eludes me, but it was near Penryn, and I remember there was a seal sanctuary there; my friend bought a thirty-six foot Catamaran. I personally felt—and even told him so—that to part with money without having it taken out of the water for a proper inspection and report, which is the norm, was foolish. However, he wouldn't listen and went ahead and was pleased... until we found lots of problems. Among the many was that the engine needed a bit of work and the rear of the craft needed attention. All the plastic water piping right through the boat had not been drained at wintertime, resulting in all the pipes fracturing, and had to be renewed.

Another part was that the previous owner, who had promised that he would come and assist us to get the craft ready for sea and also to come with us to Falmouth, was never—not that I can recall—present when we required him.

Luckily a fellow who lived in flats nearby got talking to us and he helped us get the rigging up, etc. Well, here as this tale unfolds is yet another of a chap with whom I would not go across a duck pond with let alone a real stretch of water, and it nearly ended the friendship that I had with R. Furthermore, if this fellow should read this and if, as the saying goes, the cap fits, then let him sue me. It turned out that he was, so he told us, an ex-RAF pilot on planes that actually carried a nuclear bomb. So much for that, but he had in his possession something that I will not disclose here. No, it was not a nuclear bomb, but it was something that he should not have taken with him when he left the service.

I took—as this saga developed—an instant dislike to him. He really thought he was the Bees knees and he did just as he pleased. My friend and I had been looking for at least another crewmember, and I had even written to the commanding officer of the Royal Marines Boat Squadron at Poole, pointing out that we needed crew from Falmouth to Walton on the Naze Marina. I explained that I was an ex-National Service sergeant and that R had been in the Navy, and we could not get crew from the Cruising Association. I had a reply saying that they were sorry—they were rather busy.

Now my friend and I had agreed that with or without more crew we would cast out by day and stay in harbours or marinas at night, a leisurely sort of trip cum holiday. The plan was, subject to the weather of course, to go from here to Plymouth then on to Portsmouth then to Weymouth or even on to Poole, then Lymington or the Isle of Wight, on to Brighton Marina, on to Dover or Ramsgate and finally Walton on the Naze Marina. We had all the charts and my friend had arranged to take this do-or-die fellow on as skipper. Ok it was his boat and he could do as he pleased, however, this created more friction between my friend and I. I would not be taken over by this other fellow. For the proverbial two pins I would—had it not been for letting my friend down—have walked off at Falmouth, and the reason, oh yes our do-or-die chap had told R that he did not have time for this harbour every day caper. No, he was going to press on and my friend accepted that. One can understand my feelings of course because I was there for different reasons.

The day came for us to make a start and we left Falmouth; the weather was slight rain. Once clear of the estuary I said to our skipper, "Aren't you going to radio the normal procedure to the coastguard with the details of name of the boat and our destination?"

"No, I've never bothered with that sort of thing." he said nonchalantly.

I said to my friend, "You know that this is not the way to go about things."

"Oh don't let's cause problems with him," he replied.

He was soon to realise, however, what a specimen of the human race we had here, an utter idiot as far as I was concerned, and a nuclear bomber pilot to boot! Dear Lord thank you for not letting him destroy us all! If that was his attitude on a boat, who knows where his bombs would have landed when—as he says—he was a pilot.

"And what about listening on the distress frequency?" I asked.

"Oh I can't stand that crackle and chit chat." was his unbelievable answer.

"Well I'll tell you," I said in no uncertain manner, "if a lot of boaters adopt that attitude, what happens if we need help and no one's listening?"

"Oh," says our skipper, "the coastguard always listens, all the time."

I did not press him further, as it was a sheer waste of time. The rift between me and my friend got ever wider. On reflection, I should have created hell. There is a code of the sea and everyone who takes to it should either abide by it or stay at home where they can't cost other people their lives.

Next thing, this fool goes for a nap. "By the way, I've decided," He states, "that we will go into Salcomme for the night."

222

By the time we got there in late evening, it was calm but the rain on the cabin roof sounded like marbles thumping into us. Sleep was impossible. R and the skipper decided to take the dinghy as we were on a mooring buoy in mid-river there, and go ashore for a drink. I declined and tried to go to sleep. No such luck, however.

It was soon dark and I heard a motorboat and it very gently bumped against our boat. I heard someone say, "I reckon they've come across as they haven't recorded passage. I think we're onto a winner here."

Bang, bang, bang on the cabin top, "Anyone aboard? Customs boarding!" Yes, you've guessed it, it was all down to our nuclear bomber man.

"I'm crew," I told them, "the owner and skipper are ashore."

"We are going to search the craft." One of them said in a no-nonsense manner.

The others having seen the launch alongside were soon back. "You mister," I said pointing to the skipper, "can sort this lot out, and it bloody well serves you right for not getting in contact with the coastguard.

"And R," I said, "I've had just about enough. For all I care they can rip this boat apart."

They were aboard for nearly three hours. What with the rain and the launch gently bumping against the very area where my bunk was it made sleep impossible. Finally about two in the morning, Customs left. But that is far from the end of this sorry tale. At five am we were off. Oh yes, it was going to be non-stop to Ramsgate, this critter had decided. He did not have time for the pleasures of cruising. He seemed to be on a delivery mission and that was that. I have no hesitation in stating that our friendship—to quote a nautical term—was heading for the rocks.

"Well," says my friend, "I think it's a good idea." He changed his mind during the night, but before that we had two navy helicopters come while crossing Lyme Bay, one of which called us on their loudhailer to tell us we were encroaching into a reserved training area, and had we not got a chart showing so? So bright lad—captain Pugwash—waved and we altered course out of trouble. During the night a bit of a blow came on from astern, so we were with sails and engine, fairly tramping along. I also felt that this catamaran had had a seriously hard life as she groaned a lot. I told my friend during the night to just listen to her. "I reckon she's not that safe. You damn well ought to have had her surveyed and checked over properly."

Just then the dim light for the compass packed up and we had not got a spare bulb, so we had to shine a torch from time to time. There was no autopilot; the steering was by wheel by hand only. Then to add to our woes a big ship came up behind us, blew its siren and flashed its searchlight. I tried to contact them by radio but could not. The coastguard cut in; "Yes you are off Swanage, about twenty miles out. You have no stern light, the ship behind you reports."

"Thank you and understood. Out," I said.

I was not going to lean over this or any other boat in these conditions to replace the bulb, but it wouldn't have mattered if I had because it later turned out that the whole thing was rotten with seawater having got in. That was also our bright lad's business as skipper to have checked everything before departure and again at nightfall—but no, not this bright one. It leads one to think that someone with a similar character was perhaps the brains behind all the military catastrophes that hindsight and history have assured us could have easily been avoided with a little common sense. Yes, that was our nuclear boy up at the helm.

Sleep for us—as you might imagine—was out of the question. At times we semi-surfed, as I said, when the wind was behind us. Had the wind been heading us, I would have insisted on us going to Poole. I was totally taken aback regarding my friend's attitude, but he later told me he was feeling seasick and the sooner we got to Ramsgate the better. I was sick too, sick to death of our illustrious skipper and his dangerous bungling.

Having been on the move for a day and night miraculously there came the dawn of another day, and we were between Eastbourne and Dungeness, having passed the very bright beacons on the Isle of Wight, well out I hasten to add, during the night.

Now once more we add another saga that could have well got us killed, and I do not exaggerate, not one bit. This was at Dover.

Our lad decided to creep close to the outer breakwater. I told him and also pointed out to my friend, "You are not allowed to be so damn close. You've got to be at least a mile out, and you've got to get permission to cross the entrances due to the ferries. You bloody won't listen, will you? I've been here a few times. Hell, look at this, just look! Turn hard at starboard!"

No sooner had the words left my lips when this huge ferry put its bow out of the harbour entrance, we were I swear no more than three hundred yards from this huge ship. Pugwash never uttered a word. "R," I said, "for two bloody pins I'd take her in here, asking permission first and leave you alone with this bright fellow."

The fates must have been on our side that day because we escaped being dashed to pieces by luck rather than seamanship. We had not gone very far from this entrance to the harbour when I recall the opening lines of a poem I wrote to the Cruising Association:

Then out of Dover Harbour there came with a roar
a large powerboat doing thirty knots or more.

"Hello. You ain't half going to cop it. I wouldn't be surprised if they take us in and impound the boat. You just know it all, don't you?" I said. It was the harbourmaster's launch, all forty feet of high-speed craft. When she stopped and reached us, he said, "What idiot is in charge here?"

Nothing was said, so I replied, "He's the skipper and that's the owner. I'm crew and I've been telling him the rules and regulations and if it wasn't for my friend here, I'd have left this boat back in Devon. I'm going to pack it in at Ramsgate, that's for sure."

I was most surprised that they did not take us in.

"The captain of that ship near had a heart attack due to your bloody ignorance. Where are you bound for?"

My friend told him Walton on the Naze.

"Right matey, we'll be watching you every inch of the way from now on, just remember that."

Those few words were music to my ears.

Now the approaches to Ramsgate are very well buoyed, because of shallows, shifty sandbanks and other dangers, but our boy decided to go the short inner route as we did not draw much in the water. Catamarans sit with virtually little in the water; their stability relies on the twin hulls or even better with a three-hulled trimaran. They skim the surface rather than cut through the water.

Late afternoon we finally made Ramsgate Marina. "We'll go ashore for a meal," said my friend.

"Count me out. I'm having a snack and getting my head down." I said. My intentions were to leave in the morning and let them sort themselves out to Walton.

So off they trotted, and I had not even got into my bunk when three people came aboard. Bang, bang on the cabin top. "Customs!" A sergeant major type voice shouted. *Here we go again! It's getting grimmer by the moment. I think I'll go and stay in a guesthouse tonight. I'm just not taking any more.*

"Where are you from then? And where's the other two?" The customs man asked.

"They've gone to eat. I'm too bloody tired. We've

been on the go a day, a night and all day today."

"Oh yes, we've been following your movements since you left Salcombe."

"For all I care you can dismantle her, or I'll go ashore and try to find the owner and this mad bastard of a skipper. He's a menace. Ex-bomber pilot he says he is, carrying a nuclear bomb. What a nutcase," I said, "you wouldn't believe it."

"Oh we would. We get charlies like this all the time, matey."

The customs officers had a good search and the senior one said, "There is a possibility that we may have to hold the boat for a very detailed examination. Did you know—I suppose you wouldn't as crew, and you did say the owner has only got it recently—that this craft has been across the Channel very regularly and coming back always very late at night. We don't miss much these days. And as for going ashore to find the others, I'm afraid you must stay aboard. That's the regulations, matey."

"Fair enough," I said, "For all I care you can haul her ashore and cut her up. That's how I feel about this situation." I went on to say, "If you want to know, I've been in boats since I was four years old, owned several and have a certificate of competence. And I've been telling this bright spark about the usual procedure with contacting the coastguard but he doesn't bother with that, won't even listen on channel 16—would you believe that? He didn't contact Dover and wasn't the regulation distance out from the entrance."

"Oh, we know it all," said the senior one.

I went on to say, "My friend, the owner, seems to have a 'couldn't care less' attitude about the situation. All he wants is to get this boat to Walton. And I'll tell you something else, all this is about to end our friendship. Before he got this bright spark on board, the two of us had it all planned as a leisurely cruise; stopping off for the nights and sailing during the day. I daresay I could have handled the situation alone without any problems. I've covered over 20,000 miles in total sailing so far."

The officer nodded, "I'll have to leave one of my officers aboard until they come back." Then he looked out and said, "Oh, looks as they're here."

Before any questions were asked, in fact before they had come aboard, when I went right over the top—and I have no regrets—I recounted the whole episode regarding the customs search at Salcombe, etc., the lot. "And R," I said, "I think you've lost your brain.

Anyway that's my bit said, and I'm bloody well going in the morning, like it or not. I've had more than enough. I've sailed with some twits, but this one tops the lot."

Our man never said a word. The customs men took it all in and just waited for me to finish. "And I hope they take this boat out of the water and cut her up in search." I said.

"Right then, let's get down to business," the senior officer said. While he was questioning us and was writing it all down, the other officers continued searching. At one stage they thought that they had found evidence of drugs, but R explained that this whitish powdery stuff was the residue from using a small hacksaw to cut out the fractured plastic water piping. They had a good smell of it and took a sample in a small container. About one in the morning they departed. Not a word was said. Had this scenario not ended at this hour, I would have gone without a doubt.

Once more, as is the norm in a marina at the height of summer, especially like Ramsgate, boats and fishing boats go off at all hours, so getting a good sleep was out of the equation. Especially with all the aggro, it just was not easy to get to sleep.

In the morning, R said to me that he did not want me to go, as the final port to Walton is across the Thames Estuary. He need my experience with the shallows, the currents, the sand and ever-shifting mud banks that the estuary has to offer.

"Yes, yes R," I said, "I know all that. Well it'll be a test for this specimen."

"I'd feel confident if you would stay for my peace of mind." R pleaded.

For the sake of our friendship I gave it some thought and said, "R, the best bet as I see it is to pay him off here and now, leave the boat and we will sort it out in a few days time. I'm clapped out."

Well, my friend finally got round with the promise that we would have great days on the Suffolk rivers and all that, etc, etc. I never spoke to the skipper. We left immediately and the bright one said that he was going to take the deepwater channel, as used by big ships, as having studied the chart, he realised the problems of the other alternative. I never said that I could handle the shorter but trickier way. *To hell with it,* I thought, *let him get on with it.*

We duly arrived in the late afternoon at the Walton Backwaters Marina, and in a matter of minutes—with the exception of the owner—I was ready as was this skipper to depart. He got £400 for his fee, plus I think first class rail and taxi from there to the local station, and a first class overnight sleeper to Cornwall. That came to about another £140 or so.

"I think you've definitely lost your marbles, R I'm convinced, it's goodbye, yes that's it R." On that note we parted company.

It wasn't until I was on the train that I suddenly remembered on the way home that my inflatable dinghy, outboard motor, tools and a few bits such as lifejackets, oars and the floor for the dinghy were still on board. So when I got back home, I phoned R's sister in Frinton and explained about my equipment that I'd left on board.

"He's here anyway, you can talk to him. I've told him what a chump he was to get involved with this skipper, as he's told me all the grim details." she said.

"Hello, I've remembered my dinghy and bits, so can you make a point of being aboard next Friday about eight pm, as I'm going to Suffolk for the weekend." I said.

"Yes, I'm going to be here all this week anyway," he said. And it was left at that.

However, with the traffic delays, I finally arrived at the Walton Marina after nine-thirty. I got my dinghy off the boat and deflated it so it could go into my estate car, I carried it up to the car park and came back for the other bits.

"By the way, the engine's at Frinton, as I was going to bring it all to you next week." R said.

"Well that's all I need. Being late, I should be in Aldeburgh at my friend's place about now," I said. Talk about problem after problem. "The least you can do, after I've been for my motor is to let me stay aboard for the night. I can't go knocking these people in Aldeburgh up at midnight."

"That's not possible. I've got my lady friend aboard. She's not feeling well and would prefer privacy."

I did not give him a reply. No doubt my look said it all. I gathered up the remainder of my gear and departed.

"Let me help you," he said.

"I can manage perfectly well." Perhaps rather stubbornly, but I had had enough.
So that was definitely that. Not a hint of an apology.

I arrived in Aldeburgh just before midnight; and at the small boatyard where I launched my dinghy, I parked between some boats that were on the hard ground waiting to be sold. I spent the rest of the night sleeping in the car.

# CHAPTER 9

My friends Peter and Diana usually get up early, so at seven in the morning I went off to their delightful bungalow in a private lane.

"We expected you last night." Diana said.

"I did phone about nine-thirty but got no reply."

"We were out until nearly ten." Peter said.

I explained that I stayed in the car at Sloughden Quay.

"You should have come, even at that hour," they insisted.

"I was well wrapped up and it was no hardship, really."

I would like to explain how I first met Peter and Diana Hinves.

When I was young, while at the Grammar School, we covered the work of the famous artist John Constable, and of course Constable County. And then having read and studied various boaters' experiences of the Essex and Suffolk areas I suppose that lead to a deeper interest in general—that was now my love affair with these parts grew and grew.

So when I sold the boat I had, I kept the nine-foot inflatable and had spent a lot of time on the rivers of Suffolk. Of course, I had to find a guesthouse to stay in, and on looking at an advert, I saw a photograph and details of this imposing house in Golf Lane.

It turned out that this lovely house had a large lawn with several sheep in an area surrounding the lawn. It also had chickens, doves and lots of things growing and it was two houses away from the late Benjamin Britten's Red House. It was truly a place of great natural beauty and tranquillity.

One day very soon after finding this haven, I came back early in the afternoon as the wind was chilly and I did not fancy getting afloat. Peter and Diana were into country dancing and it was their turn to host that afternoon's dance. So when I got back, I offered to help, as I could see that the dishes were piling up, and that they needed some assistance. So I started to gather cups and plates and put them into the dishwasher. Then I went round with tea and coffee, juices, cakes and what have you; I generally made myself useful.

Peter unfortunately suffers from Alzheimer's, so from then on I even helped Peter with various chores in the garden, piling up wood for winter and cutting the large logs with a big axe. From then on, they refused payment for my stay, and I became an honorary member of their circle of friends.

Some years ago, they retired and sold this beautiful house, and where once there had been a tennis court, they had a bungalow built. They kept the land surrounding the place and I still to this day I devote at least a day every year to help out. Do what I can, wash up the few dishes, etc. I like to do my bit.

Diana is always telling me not to, but I say that I am not treating their place as a hotel, and therefore I feel justified in doing what I can. Even in early spring or late autumn I go there, without my boat of course at those times of the year, and before my problems of Sciatica hit me, I would walk a fair distance to relax and enjoy the beautiful surroundings.

One day I decided to walk along the shingle bank to where there is a large notice. I did not intend to pass it, as it was Ministry of Defence property, with a large building and some smaller ones, and some high aerials. I had heard rumours from locals as to what was going on there, and nowadays it is open to the public, and they are told a story that differs form the truth, but it is not for me to state what

I have heard. Also remember that I signed the Official Secrets Act at Honiton on joining up in 1951.

So when I came to this notice, I had seen it all before, as on the riverbank on this side, they had similar warnings, and in addition these stated that landing was not allowed, nor was mooring allowed. An M.O.D. policeman drove up to me in a Land Rover. "I'm afraid you can't come any further, as you can see." he said.

"I have no intention of doing so. I'm just out for a walk. As a matter of interest, I've signed the Official Secrets Act."

"Really? What was that all about then?" he asked.

"I'm afraid I can't tell you. It was while doing my National Service in '51, and I'm committed for life. Don't you know that, working here as you do?"

"Suppose you're right. Never gave it a thought. Cheerio." And off he went. I reckon I gave him food for thought that day.

Moving on now to further recollections regarding my family; our two boys went to the Jewish Sunday School. Of course, they could never be of that faith, as my wife was not of the faith, and I belong to a reform, modern type of Judaism. It was decided that when the boys were old enough to choose what faith they wanted to follow, that was alright by my wife and I. We certainly would not stand in the way of their choice, one less problem to surmount; that was our point of view. As it happened, both boys married Christian girls and we have three grandchildren, one of whom was recently baptised.

I had an interesting conversation with the young minister there after the ceremony, when I told him about the four fingerprints and a thumbprint on a haddock. He said he had never heard of it, and that he was certainly going to check it out, and coming from a Jewish man—"really astounding," he said.

233

Having been brought up in Scotland with fisher folk it is part of their folklore that the haddock's marks were the fingerprints of Jesus Christ; it was the fish he threw into the waters. So I had known the tale all my life and never questioned it.

The ultra-religious of the Jewish faith by the way tell us all the time now that we of the Reform Judaism are not Jews. That is their opinion, and as column after column appears in Jewish newspapers, we do not care. People are entitled to their opinions.

When I tell them that they should not be eating haddock and tell them why, I am—according to those 'holier than thou' lot—committing the most dreadful sin of sins, by mentioning the name of Jesus. They immediately shun away from me, as if I was a leper or a carrier of some other ghastly disease; so much for the understanding and tolerance of the religious faiths and the beliefs of our brethren on this world of ours.

If there is a second coming, I pray to God that it may be soon, very soon.

I relate now the experiences that have befallen me in regard to health problems, and I have not the slightest hesitation in naming the guilty parties, none whatsoever.

In early 1996 as a member of the Manor House Healthcare Organisation, I had an athroscope at their hospital in Golders Green, North London. It is an examination of the inner knee and removal of any loose particles. I was only in barely two days and the very next day after discharge from hospital I became ill. Here once more, if I described the full events of it I would need about sixty extra pages. So we called the hospital because my problems got worse. I was very ill and we phoned at least four times a day.

"No, we can't take you back in. Go to an NHS hospital." was their sympathetic response. I had bronchial pneumonia, and yes it is possible after this type of operation and furthermore, when we eventually saw at that MHH hospital a Mr Romeo Vecht, he told us that is what I had, and I have it in writing. I took it to law myself but got nowhere. But thank goodness for another medical scheme that I belong to. A hospital and staff therein that is hard to beat. I refer to the Benenden Hospital Trust at Benenden Cranbrook in Kent.

They have done marvels without a doubt and in later revelations I am totally convinced they have given me another lease of life, as I had been inside the gates of hell with very serious illness.

While in the throes of the result of the knee operation I did have one stroke of luck but it wasn't to last long. It was at the Keats Surgery in Edmonton that I had a real doctor cum gentleman from the old school, by the name of R. M. Ezzatt. Unfortunately, he passed away suddenly. One of the other (so-called) doctors was one by the name of Kattan. He constantly refused to come to see me. I was indeed very ill, and on about the fourth day of my traumatic experience the secretary at the surgery suggested that I take paracetamol. That so-called doctor steadfastly refused to come to the house. He got my wife to pick up a prescription without seeing me—a dangerous practice if ever there was one!

On the fourteenth or fifteenth day, he came to see me and diagnosed a chest infection. I honestly felt that my time had come. I do not exaggerate when I say that I thought I was going. My youngest son Andrew—second after the head chef at London's very famous Ivy Restaurant—decided that the time had come for me to be admitted to the private Kings Oak Hospital, as getting to Benenden Hospital required written proof from my lousy doctor and time was of the essence.

I have all the details of the time I was in that private hospital. We had no cover and therefore we signed a statement that we would pay. I was only in three nights and two days. We paid £1,800 for the treatment.

After a few weeks of trying to get back on my feet, I went to Edmonton County Court and completely on my own without a solicitor, as the citizen had rights and now has even better rights, took out a summons against the said doctor Kattan for the hospital fee, plus £1,000 for the horrendous suffering and trauma that I had endured. However, the GMC simply were not interested. After weeks of his solicitor's letters to me, they finally offered me an out-of-court settlement of £1,800 plus £500 without of course admitting liability, so I accepted their offer.

A retired gentleman—who is no longer with us unfortunately—told me, as he had been connected with the medical profession, that I had not had a cat-in-hell's chance of bringing a medical case to court, especially without a solicitor.

There is at the time of writing this story a case of yet another medical nature in the hands of the courts, and I am awaiting developments. I am not one to give up against big odds, never.

As I have said I have received tremendous support from various friends of ours on the subject of this book, but my dear wife thinks I am no author and is a bit dubious as to the success of my efforts. Time, of course, will tell. So now, whenever the mood takes me, I sing, "In Spain they said he was of mind unsound when Columbus told them that the world was round."

"Oh do pack it in," she says, "I'm sick of hearing that."

We will see who has the last laugh.

"And just because you've been on television for a few minutes…"

Ah well, that is to be explained next.

It was in mid-2000 that a friend of mine whose car I

had looked after up to my retirement—but always contacted me since for an opinion on various problems—once again got in touch with me, and not to discuss car problems either, but something totally different and unexpected. This friend of mine, about thirty-six years of age, by the name of John Gordillo, had been, along with our eldest son Simon, into amateur dramatics, since they were about sixteen and onwards. However, John went on to what he was best at—comedy and satire. He started at the very foot of the ladder, in pubs and clubs, a few small parts in television, and gradually made it to a programme of his own on BBC digital television.

Before I continue with this part of my tale I must tell you something else that happened a while back. A few years ago, I relate now to when I was in Edgware General Hospital, I began to wonder if I was going to do vehicle engineering again. Now I have always had ideas about writing and decided that I would write a story about disgruntled servicemen who had been discharged through the cuts in Defence-spending and what some of these fellows were going to do—not in relation to getting work. No, they intended to do something that would make headlines to bring their plight into the public eye. However, I never got anywhere with it, to this day.

But John Gordillo read it years ago, amongst others also, and he thought that it was terrific and had kept it in mind.

Then out of the blue I received this surprise phone call, "Walter matey," his actual words, "I'm at the TV centre Shepherds Bush doing a program of my own. And I've always reckoned that you're more than just a good mechanic, especially having read that story about grabbing a bit of nuclear reactor from that shut-down power station. So how would you feel if I asked you to come down here and bring that story with you? You can think about it."

"Well that's nice of you," I said, "and I don't need time to think it over. When do you need me?"

"Ok, say three pm next Tuesday."

Of course, my ever-cautious wife did not really feel that I should take it on. "They'll probably make a fool of you or something similar."

"Well I reckon when it comes to it, I can act the goat," I replied.

I am not boasting when I say that I was raring to go, and had a good feeling about it. I was not a bit apprehensive, and as it turned out, I was absolutely right. I was made most welcome. After going through security screening, I was led through a complete maze of passages, looked into various studios where John's office and his team of assistants and programmers, typists and other staff were working. They were an extremely pleasant lot. I was introduced and John told them not to laugh at my name, as 'Watercress' has been my nickname. A few of the people there, male and female, were Scottish, and one of the young ladies piped up and said, "I've got an odd sort of name as well. It's Honey."

So much for that then, she broke the ice. *This is going to be a ball,* I thought.

John also had his lovely big white dog with him there. It was a bit of a husky cross and I got on well with 'Charlie', as he had been to our house many times.

So I was to go with the director, a cameraman and a lady who was to write on my progress as we went. First stop was the staff car park where they asked me various questions, all being filmed about the different cars there, and then, whilst still being filmed, we walked back slowly to the office. I was asked more questions about myself and where the name Kress came from. So I adopted a typical continental, very broken English accent, and said, "You see, my fader voz Austriaan."

238

They had a good laugh and said it was terrific. John certainly can pick them.

When we got back, the film was put on a TV monitor and I was surprised how my Scottish accent came through. One cannot guess how one sounds until a chance like this happens. These were only tests, and the next one a few weeks later was in a small studio. I must now explain that present at that take was a critic from some paper or magazine, but firstly to explain what by and large this programme was about; it dealt mainly with day-to-day happenings, with the various people, peculiar goings on, etc. That is why there were stacks of daily, weekly and local newspapers all over the place.

So that afternoon, one of the things was to do with the star Madonna's shopping trip. Our man spotted Madonna and her bodyguard out shopping, and when he approached them to take a photograph, she promptly held her large shopping bag up to her face, but naturally she could not hide her tummy bulge.

When it came to my turn, last but not least—they later told me the star is always last to appear—I was to read about twenty lines from any part of my story that I had written. Well, here I was, this is what I had come for, piece of cake. So I read out from a page that I chose at random, with full-pronounced actions and feeling, etc; they all applauded. Of course, this was just a step towards a take for the real thing. The critic gentleman had been keeping notes on the procedure, and having given them to the director, the camera people and technicians and others who had parts that day, he came to me. "Now," he said, "we come to Walter, who I understand was your car mechanic, John. He does not work here; he has not done anything like this before, therefore I have not the slightest hesitation of giving him four out of five. Well done, Walter."

Ten feet tall was not in it. There was wine, beer, cake, biscuits, juice, you name it. Even had I failed, it would still have been a great adventure for me at the age of seventy. No, not seventy years old, but seventy years of age, there is a difference. "Surely,"—and I feel that they were not just being polite—they said, "Well you certainly don't look it, and don't act your age either."

"I don't," I said, "necessarily believe that a person has to act the age that they are at." I told them about my sailing as far as the Med and the Canary Islands, that I still went on the rivers in Suffolk with my Avon proper sea-authorised inflatable boat, usually at about six in the morning in the summer when it is all peaceful and tranquil, and hardly another soul around.

For days and days afterwards I went around the house singing, "There's no business like show business, no business I know. Everything about it is appealing..."

And as far as I was concerned, that song was true. I was on a high. Show people are definitely something else, and I am not in the least bit conceited when I say that maybe I did miss my vocation in life.

A couple of weeks later, I got a call. Was it possible to come that very day, as they were putting together at short notice a bits and pieces programme of something in which I was definitely the person for it. It was to be done in a big proper studio, at six pm to go out at eleven pm, once it had been edited, and I have got a tape of the show. There were about a hundred people or so in the audience. When I got to the studio John explained the whole take from end to end and that it was a walkover.

"John," I said, "even if it was live, I don't have any qualms about it."

"Well you're not having my job," he said, laughing.

So it was time to go to the studio. I was wired up as they say and was going on last. John did the usual bits of satire of the day's events which included three out-of-work actors who did sketches. They were very good. John rang a company to complain about something and only got an answering machine, so he gave it a piece of his mind. Then in an upstairs studio, he introduced three young Jewish girls and each showed a brief few shots of their homes, lifestyles and work.

"Now last but not least," John said, "my friend and former car mechanic, please meet Walter Kress."

So on I trooped and held out my hand to John. Also I had noticed in front of his desk an exact size model of Charlie—John's dog. So before I sat down and while shaking John's hand, I said—and the whole four minutes was done without rehearsal or script—"I'm sorry to see that your dog has passed on."

"Oh no, it's so cold in here the dog's frozen," he said. That certainly went down well with the audience.

I sat down and John looked up at the three young ladies and said, "Walter is Jewish."

"Yes indeed, and Scottish to boot, I'm proud to say," I said.

I had my story with me as it was agreed that I should read a few lines from any part of it, but we never got around to it for lack of time.

One of the young ladies in the studio upstairs had recently passed her driving test, so I called up 'Mazeltov,' Yiddish for 'Congratulations. 'Mazeltov,' that went down well.

"Do you have a car now," John asked.

"Yes," and she mentioned the make and model.

"What do you think of that car," John asked me.

"Very nice little car, reliable. They've got a good record."

"Time's running out, so Walter, I have a cake here that we'd like you to take upstairs and present to the young lady who has recently passed her driving test."

One of the staff took me up this steep, steel stairway

241

where I presented the cake to the lady, and as she gave me a kiss on the cheek, I said, "Watch my makeup." But this was now a few seconds over time and was cut for the later viewing.

Afterwards, back in the offices, there were refreshments as usual. Well it all went down very well and I was definitely top of the pops that day, they all thought so. In fact, one of the three out-of-work actors who had done a sketch came up to me. This chap I would envisage was about forty. He was well spoken but had the features usually associated with a gangster. "I reckon I've seen you on telly," I said.

"Oh yes, I've been in a few things, usually the villain, robber, getaway car driver, and situations like that. You can see why by my features. Tell you what Walter, I reckon you've got what it takes. You're a natural."

"Oh you're all kidding and hyping me up," I said.

"No, I mean it, and I reckon we all do. You were good."

As seems to be the tradition when a series comes to an end, they hold what is known as a wrap party, virtually meaning wrapping it up. I was invited, but did not stay to the end, as most were smokers, and with my problems I simply cannot take it, it is pure poison for me.

I go back now to the girl with the coal bucket who became an arts teacher as described way back. I decided to contact the school in a bid to make contact with the arts teacher, so that if it was at all possible for her to give substance to my story; that would be television stuff all right. I had a letter in reply from the administration, but with regard to the Data Protection Act, and also as it was so long ago, they unfortunately had a serious fire in an area of the loft a few years ago where they kept the records, and many were lost. I rang the school and explained that I would write and give them details of the whole episode, and why it was of some importance to try and find this lady. Within a few days, I received another letter, and here are the sad details. The lady had passed away just a few years ago. On my many visits to Aberdeen since I left there, I never ever thought that I would be writing this story, but perhaps her brother may still be alive—who knows?

My memory, as it does from time to time, goes back and suddenly an event that needs to be put here just to prove how the establishment will hound a person, irrespective of the fact that the person at the heart of the matter is in a desperate plight with ME, and at the same time is trying to support a family and continuing trying to work, when the following day was worse than the day previous.

The Inland Revenue at Capitol House, Winchmore Hill decided that I owed them £141 or a figure near that, as it was so long ago I have not got records, but I remember the scenario clearly. I had of course with ME had periods off work—three weeks then two months and so forth. The last one lasted from a December until the end of March, and being self-employed, say no more. The pittance from the state was not adequate. My wife fortunately had a part-time job; therefore the state in its wisdom decided that there were sufficient funds coming in for us to survive on. That episode left what one would describe as a very bitter taste in my mouth. Is that what we work for, to simply survive in our retirement?

I had an appointment to report to the local tax office, where they insisted that the figure was correct and had to be paid immediately. There and then I offered them monthly post-dated cheques, I couldn't be bothered to argue my case anymore.

"Sorry," they said, "that cannot be accepted until the matter goes to court, and then on the outcome we may be directed to accept those cheques, but that's not our decision, it's the law." It would seem that even when you offer to pay they are not satisfied.

So I went to Kingmaker House in Barnet. I arrived in good time and parked my van—which by the way of a protest to the government's extra stamp levy on the self-employed, I had in large letters printed on both sides that the self-employed should not pay the extra levy and all should refuse to do so. I sat in the little waiting room next to the main office and you can clearly hear what is going on at the counter there.

In swaggers a fellow with a black briefcase. I thought he was a judge, but no, he clearly, very clearly told the clerk, Paul Spaul or Spawl, Inland Revenue and produced identity.

"I've got a usual 'been ill' bloke again. They don't try anything else; a mechanic, name of Kress."

Now, I am not the 'wade in and sort him out' type, but I felt like slapping that arrogant pig; apart from and despite the fact that I was indeed very ill. So in we went to a small office and sat down, the clerk, myself, the smart know-all from the Tax Department and a Court Official (or he may have been a Judge).

In three minutes flat, it is all over. The Court Official told the smart-boy that this matter was a total waste of time and to accept the offer. I had my accountant's figures, all my weekly expenses, bank statements and building society book, etc. To top it all, I was charged £46 for the court's time; good ol' British justice!

I complained to the Inland Revenue about the statement that Paul Spaul or Spawl had made on entering the office, but of course they said that he would not have said it, and on being asked about it, said it was untrue and that I was just trying to cause trouble. We do get complaints like yours frequently, and they are completely unfounded. What chance has your average citizen against morons like that? NILL – NONE!

It took a very long time for improvement to my health, as motor mechanic work is very demanding, and to add more problems to my problems at that time, and even now in 2000, many doctors still do not accept ME. According to those disbelievers, it is a virus known as Yuppies Disease or Malingers Disease.

I had at the time another so-called doctor by the name of Patel. His attitude was that I should GET A GRIP of myself. I gave him some very loud verbal and told him that if I treated my clients' cars as he has treated me, I would be sent to prison for dangerous workmanship. He struck me off as a patient and that was that; good ol' British medical profession!

There are many people that have and are suffering from ME. It has definitely been the thin edge of the wedge as regards the slow but further decline in my health. One of the people who have ME is the famous writer and yachtswoman, Claire Francis. She has had more of her share of that dreadful disease and is still at this very time having bad days with it.

And I can say without the slightest hesitation that at the time of a depth in the pit crisis with this ME that were it not for my wife and the fact that I had two young children, and the outlook on life was bleak, I would have gone to a lovely little marina or jetty, taken an overdose, wrapped chains or anchors or a mooring block to myself and jumped in. So only the Lord is my witness to my feelings at that time—total despair is not an adequate word here.

Here once again I am about to give details of one of my innermost feelings. There are of course some things in a person's life that simply must remain that person's only— not that I have done anything criminal, unless you count doing 33mph in a customer's car in Finchley way back about 40 years ago, when the police cars were Wolseleys with a bell concealed behind the grille on the front of the car. Yes,

Creighton Avenue, East Finchley it was officer.

A few years later in Salmon Street, Wembley, I had just overtaken a learner going very slowly. I was in a customer's car again and at the point where I safely cut into the left side, I ran a very short distance of about 25 feet on a double white line. Out pops a panda car. I stop, "not your car eh, mechanic are you?" I got the full treatment, "You ought to have a letter of authority from the owner."

"Oh yes," I said, "I could write one myself for that matter. How would you know it's authentic?" I was fined for both offences and it completely altered my view of the police. Never before has the term—bad to worse—been more apt! And that's not only my view, as time has proved my views to be correct, absolutely so.

The next part of this story regards the unidentified flying objects theory, and yet one of the deepest of my feelings and views that I have regarding them. I have never seen an unidentified flying object—a UFO—but I am ever hopeful that one day I might. There are many stories of such sightings, of people from other worlds; of people who claim that they have been abducted and so forth and interrogated on board ship by celestial creatures, as well as reports and sworn statements by senior people in the Forces. Of course, governments will tell you this, that and the next thing. There are documentaries on the subject where there is proof of extremely high-speed objects in our heavens, speeds that at the moment with our knowledge would simply crush a human with its velocity and pressure.

Now, I quote from the bible all those years ago that they ascended on a pillar of fire. What about today's rockets? Is that not a similar pillar of fire? The mind boggles. Were those biblical pillars of fire people from another world, so far away that even with today's advanced equipment that can see further into the strata than ever before, their world has not yet been seen. We know the unbelievable distances involved. It is therefore in my humble estimation as a mere human being on our planet that if they had rockets then, why should they not have advanced in the thousands of years since, or other worlds also further advanced, when we here have in just over one hundred years, excluding balloons, gone from flying what were merely kites with motors to the sophisticated planes of today, the space flights plus secrets of flight that regularly come to light as we have seen, all in a very short period of time.

Air Force personnel and records of radar stations are not abnormal weather, satellites, space junk re-entering our atmosphere, chunks of other planets and what have you, as often has been stated, we are not alone. And furthermore, I feel that they do not wish to make contact with us super-duper lot here; and why so? Because they have been watching us since the dawn of time and are aghast as to what man has been and is still doing to his fellow man on this miniscule dot in the galaxy. And that is a view held by many, not just by me.

Not so very long ago, there was a documentary on television about UFOs. One such documentary was of rather greater interest to me than any other, as it was when the American Air Force Base was still a fully operational one at Woodbridge in my favourite county of Suffolk. In fact, Andrew and I borrowed a tent from our scout unit when Andrew was about twelve and we camped in a campsite next to the end of the runway at its end pointing in the direction of the sea.

When I think what happened in the forest there, Rendlesham Forest, a few years later, I feel sick, really. And yes, I will confess that I do not go near or even drive anywhere near there in the dark. Those who want to laugh, please do so. The base is now closed down, no Americans there now. I think it is being developed for industry.

To make the tale short, during one night, according

to the documentary—of which I am prepared to accept every detail—the radar at this base, plus Heathrow's confirmation, showed that there appeared over Rendlesham Forest at some time in the night a UFO. The commanding officer along with many armed personnel went to investigate this thing all lit up with pulsating lights etc. It was at treetop height, and they (that is, the Air Force personnel) had strict orders not to shoot. There were sworn statements, but the authorities said that about nine miles away as the crow flies was Orfordness Lighthouse, and that that was the culprit. The American authorities at first thought when they saw it over the forest that it was some sort of a surprise exercise by our services to check the security at the base. But how can one account for Heathrow's statement that they lost it at 96,000 feet at incredible speed? Some helicopter, that is all I can say or perhaps a lighthouse on a pillar of fire?

And that is not all. The documentary goes on to tell us that lots of samples from trees, earth and rocks and anything at all there was taken in heavily sealed containers to America, and a small house that Andrew and I know very well, as we used to watch the comings and goings of the planes, helicopters and things, this small house was looking at the runway well to the left and clear. The perimeter fence was so built that the house, inhabited by civilians, was not inside the base as such, but do not take my word—the documentary stated that next thing the perimeter fence had engulfed the house—and it was now technically in the base. The occupants were sworn to secrecy.

As I have stated, I have not been anywhere near there since. I have, however, been told as with the empty base, the house is now empty. And I have read a book from the library by some professor or other. It did not state what religion he was, but dare I say it, these were his thoughts, not mine.

He had come to the conclusion that Israel as it was thousands of years ago was the nearest to some other world and went for it, and that we Jews had come from there, as the majority of us evidently had a fraction more up top than other people of this earth.

I do not, however, consider myself to be brainy, 'chitzpah.' I've got a bit, yes, but I am definitely not one of our 'holier than thou' brothers.

Some friends of ours—the Smiths—Andy was born in Glasgow, and she says that I am just a wild 'Heelan' man—Highland man. I am never backward when it comes to being outspoken. Anybody that runs down us Jews I will give a piece of my mind. But they get naval language thrown in if they start on the Scots.

I can now elaborate in some detail that phase as previously outlined with the health problems as a direct result of the knee operation, and I have not the slightest hesitation in once again stating that were it not for the Benenden Hospital Trust, I most definitely would not be here today, as the National Health Service in the dreadful mess that it is in does not know; and what is more, with the overworked staff, just cannot cope.

I cannot at this time, owing to another court action which I have on my own initiative again without a solicitor, started against a hospital, where I was in casualty for ten hours, all night, and sent away with bronchial pneumonia. I was sent away because I was old (67), and that is an indisputable fact of our times. Being old seems to automatically put one in a special (low-priority) category

I was referred back to the then new doctor that I was given by the health authority that may yet possibly go to law, and why one may ask? The reason was that I made no secret when I went to this new doctor and told him, as if he did not know already, that I had successfully taken a court action against that (so-called, I say once again) doctor Kattan. Of course, how can I prove that he adopted a 'couldn't care less' attitude to my serious illness – or is pneumonia in an elderly person not considered serious in these times?

I have records to prove that the time was fast approaching Christmas. In fact, I got to see a senior specialist of the Benenden Hospital Trust at their London clinic in Wimpole Street, and finally got to the hospital in January, so it was sometime between November to January. Was I ill—it was absolutely grim for my family and I. So I have every reason to go to the law for the gross negligence that seems to be the norm today. We see and hear and read about it virtually every day. Our babies are dying up and down the country at an alarming rate due to cut-backs and staff shortages and nobody seems to raise an eyebrow.

At first at Benenden they thought that with the extensive tests that I was having, which included x-rays, being put into a scanner twice, bronchoscopes and umpteen other tests that it looked as if it was recurring pneumonia.

I was in for a week, then a few days, then ten days, so it went on and on; two days, five days, two weeks and so forth. They even took me down in a small sitting ambulance and at other times sent a car for me. I simply cannot praise that hospital and its staff enough, and I make a point of always sending a cheque for the staff Christmas fund.

So as time went on, it was discovered that with the constant pneumonia, my system had been seriously weakened and if I had been a smoker or into alcohol, there would not have been much chance for me.

I had contracted a disease that can only be stabilised and not cured, and very few medical people have even heard of it. It is called Wegeners Granulomatosis, and if, as I have had serious problems, hey presto it attacks the body's immune system, say no more.

And here at this point I can say to those when I make the following statement that they can believe it or not, that the dreadful state that I was in now made me think that I was on my way out of this world.

I looked back at my life; I had not crossed the Atlantic but I had got a third of the way, and so forth. And at my age, I truly felt that I was going for the inevitable, and that was that—I was on the last voyage—I was dying. But it held not the slightest fear for me. That is how ill I was. I will swear to that—I was at death's door, but I was way past caring.

I have been on steroids and other drugs of course. I am not half the man I was but I accept that. I regularly see the doctors at either Wimpole Street or even at Benenden for any problems, and it's no delays, while my local doctor, who by the way is a marvellous understanding man of the very old-school of doctors, writes a letter. If at any time I have been instructed on my doctor's advice to get help. I phone Benenden and I am on my way there. Beat that, I say, and I have had to use this system a few times when problems have arisen.

My love of sailing is a thing of the past. And now at seventy I find it nearly knocks me out to hump my deflated but still heavy inflatable dinghy in or out of the car, pump it up, put in the wooden floor bits and all the other bits, fuel can, cool box with food and drinks. And then if the tide is out, bit by bit I lift the front round, then I lift the back round, so forth and so on until I get to the water. The mud at times comes over my Wellingtons, although in the summer it is no problem. But all-in-all it is a long laborious process these days. Before going back up to get the outboard motor, which is heavy as well, I have to stop for a breather. I don't think this pleasure will last much longer. But by the time I finally get rid of the mud while the dinghy is still in the shallows, I sit in it for a while and just drift as the breeze or tide takes me.

Of course, even on the warmest day, I wear a proper boater's lifejacket without fail, as I now recount a tale of when I capsized.

On a pleasant day in late May, about seven years ago, on the River Alde in Suffolk, I had not filled the small fuel tank to capacity, but I always had a gallon spare with me. I was using the last two hours of the ebbing tide and wanted to get to the mouth of the River where it meets the sea, and then use the incoming tide to slowly drift back up the River. I was running at half speed and about two miles from Orford, which is down-river from Aldeburgh, the engine stopped because it had run out of fuel. I refilled the small tank, but did not set the throttle back, so when I started the motor the bow went up like a rearing stallion. The wind, which was not really blowing hard at all, but a breeze, got under the flat bottom of the dinghy. I tried to throw myself forward, but it was now vertical and the lot fell on top of me. I was underneath but not in any problems, as the dinghy was well spaced inside when it's upside down. I had my lifejacket on, of course. I was extremely lucky that the propeller did not hit me, as when it comes out of the water, it is completely free of water drag and gets up to terrific speeds for a second or so, until the engine hits the water and stops of course. I came out from underneath the upturned inflatable and lay alongside it. Was I frightened? Not at all; I did, however, consider myself very fortunate not to have made contact with the propeller. I then started to swim slowly, dragging the dinghy with one hand, towards the nearest bank. To add to my troubles it dawned on me after a few minutes that I simply was not moving toward the bank. What had happened was that a very small anchor that I carry had of course dropped out and was securing the dinghy to the muddy bottom. So being fully supported by my lifejacket, I pulled the rope and anchor up, put it on top of the upturned dinghy and finally got to the bank.

Then I thought, Lucky day—here's an American helicopter on its way to Woodbridge, very low as usual. So I did the two-handed distress waving of the arms. I thought he must have seen me, but he did not stop. So later, when I reported myself to the coastguard lookout at Aldeburgh, in case I had been reported, they said no one had seen me. The coastguard told me, "No, no he will not stop and pick you up, as some bright young lads and lasses, even in the summer, get down-river and then when they see the chopper coming, they get in the water, and turn their dinghies upside down. Believe it or not! But the Yanks have got wise to these capers. That's why he didn't pick you up lad.

"Anyway, thanks for reporting yourself, OK."


I took off all my clothes and lay in the warm long grass. There is of course very high anti-flood banks build all along this river. After a while, I put on my clothes that were reasonably dry. The other clothes I threw into the dinghy after I turned it the right way up. All I lost was the bellows for pumping the air into it. Everything else was tied on. The engine of course was full of water and was fixed later at Aldeburgh.

With the last of the ebb tide I rowed down to Orford, where I left the dinghy at a small dinghy sailing club. I hitched a lift back to Aldeburgh by some very nice and understanding people, and he even went out of his way to take me eight miles away from the direction that he was going, as I explained what had happened. "I can see by the dried mud on your face and hair, you've obviously been in the water."

So at arriving at Slaughden Quay boatyard and slipway where I had started from, Mr Upson, the owner, said, "Heavens, are you all right? You've been in the river, haven't you?"

I explained.

"Anyway, you're not the first nor will you be the last."

So I took my car to Orford, deflated the boat and

went back to my friends' house. They were horrified to see the state that I was in, but I assured them that I had it all completely under control.

At the time, of course as it happened early, around 7.30 in the morning, there are not always boats about. I must say that it was within sight of the secret MOD depot, but obviously no one was there except the security personnel, and I was not spotted or the inshore small semi-rigid three-man lifeboat would have been alerted and it would not have taken them more than twelve to fifteen minutes from getting a call to get down there to me.

However, all's well that ends well.


In conclusion, I feel that now is the time to relate four episodes that come to mind regarding our money extorting councils and their traffic wardens. All four I have rigorously fought and against all odds I have survived and got those so-and-sos to eat humble pie.

Episode one: as stated previously, I have to attend appointments with Dr J Dibble of the Benenden Hospital at Wimpole Street very regularly. So as my eldest son was on holiday I was keeping his car running, and my wife and I parked it in Golders Green by the lower part of Hampstead Heath. It clearly stated on a notice that the parking was for residents and non-residents. We parked behind a big minibus. I did not see further up the road, hidden to a certain extent by bushes or similar foliage, a ticket machine. So we took a bus to the West End. When we got back to the car, there was a warden's ticket on the car. Now hold your breath. I wrote to the authority and evidently it is not the driver of that vehicle that is liable, it's the owner. They do with the law as they please. I wrote to Jack Straw, but had no reply of course. I decided to take photographs of the instructions on the notice, but for two weeks the weather was bad and I was unwell. Eventually I went there and lo and behold, new signs were there—brand new—with helpful instructions for paying, etc. I took photographs and wrote to Barnet Parking Ltd. Phone calls and letters went unanswered or ignored, they tried to wear me down. Anyway, they were adamant that my son as the owner was responsible. We asked them for details of the dates when these new signs were put up. After more whitewash, they finally gave us the contractor's details.

Do you think for one moment that we got anywhere to establish the dates of when the new signs were put up? Never! Not even something as simple as that; the excuse was that they have many people on these jobs, even subcontractors, and it would be impossible to say exactly when the work was done, we had all that rot. But at the end of the day that shower at Barnet caved in and the fine was cancelled. If they don't know when the work was done how can they check on the invoices for the work having been done?

Episode two: I occasionally go to Golders Green to buy a few bits and pieces. This by the way was just days before I got the orange badge. I paid for half an hour on a meter and was back in twenty-two minutes. There was a ticket for sixty pounds, not the thirty as usual; and why so you might rightly ask? Well I will tell you, I was supposed to walk down the road where 3½ feet off the ground there, against the garden wall of a block of flats, was a notice that between such and such a time this was for residents parking only. That shower had done ten cars there. Of course, it was Barnet once more, and I had the whole rigmarole all over again. At the end of the long trauma, the fine was cancelled. At what cost to the authority—the public purse—who knows?

Episode three: I have what I refer to as a distant

aunt who is in a nursing home in Bushey. This elderly lady I have known since my days back in Vienna, and to me she was Auntie Elizabeth. She came from a wealthy family and my mother, when she was young, was maid at their sumptuous place in the city. When I was about four, I remember Elizabeth giving me the most fabulous fire engine. It was big, and the ladders extended to four feet. I regularly go to visit her, as does my wife and on occasions we even take the grandchildren. So about ten months ago, when I went to see Auntie, there was no room in the car park. So I went to the lane where there is little traffic, but there were two vans parked there, so I went about a foot up on the pavement so as not to block the lane or get the car damaged—as one is now recommended to do in the Highway Code.

I had my orange disabled badge at that time due to my problems, which was clearly on show. I came back to the car and hey presto, warden's ticket. That was another uphill struggle with that diabolical shower. In the end they cancelled the ticket. Does anything sound familiar? However, there are people who—rather than stand up for their rights—simply pay up.

Episode four: I was unwell but had to go to the bank. I took my orange badge and my wife drove me there and parked on a perfectly legal yellow line for my badge. When we came back to the car, yes a damn ticket was there, and why? There was a notice stating no loading or unloading and some faded yellow marks on the pavement.

My wife, not liking to protest or have a go at Enfield department of showers, paid the thirty pounds. I nearly went ballistic, so to speak. I got on to a most charming Indian lady at the central office. She asked me to send a letter of explanation. I gave her the facts about my state of health, my wife's diabetes, etc, and offered written medical proof. Hey presto, a cheque for thirty pounds was sent with an apology. I can not stress enough that we must challenge what is wrong every time. If a thing is wrong, it doesn't matter what power or organisation is behind the wrongdoing it must be challenged otherwise we are nothing more than voiceless slaves to the big brother system.

While working at Henlys Garage at Henlys corner, Temple Fortune, a young lad straight from college came as an apprentice mechanic. He was going to be my assistant, and I have no hesitation in naming him—and let his family sue me. I have some very interesting proof of how some people that you have absolute faith and trust in can let you down.

And here is a story that shows exactly what I am saying. This chap, Tony Hubner, lived in Golders Green and his father had an antiques shop in the West End. Tony's father, with his knowledge of Yiddish and his style, even looked Jewish but was not, although he spoke broken English. I never asked nor was I told his background.

Soon Tony left and went to work at Bibsworth Garage in Finchley, about a mile up the road from Henlys. We kept in touch and one day he said, "Come to the house, my father wants to discuss something with you."

So I duly turned up. His father said that as I had been good and taught Tony all that I knew, he was going to buy Bibsworth Garage and make me a partner. I said that I had no money to put in this project. "That doesn't matter," he said, "all I need is your expertise, and you will get a third of the profit after all expenses and outgoings." *Generous offer!*

Time went on and Tony seemed to be getting to be what I can only describe as being the boss at the place. There was only one elderly mechanic there. Nothing seemed to happen for some considerable time.

And now once more fate with a big 'F' comes into the equation in a big way.

It was July 1969 and a sort of friend/customer of mine, who was manager at the gas company in Finchley Central, a Danny Toms, who had often come on business to Bibsworth Garage, and made a point of  seeing me there, just to see how things were progressing. Then one day, as Danny knew the facts about me going to be working there as a partner, said to me, "You know something, you can forget about that lot letting you in as promised.  His father bought the place in March and if you don't believe me, ask Tony or his father and also get in touch with the Registration of Business Names."

And so I did, and have written proof that Bibsworth Garage, Motor Engines and Petrol Sales, Bibsworth Road, Finchley N3 was owned by Anthony Joseph Hubner, British, of 955 Finchley Road, Golders Green, NW11, Antique dealer, commencement of business March 1, 1969. Dated May 4, 1969, signed by A J Hubner.

So I took the copy of this document to their house. Would you believe that they tried to tell me a load of rot? Mrs Hubner was in tears, she knew nothing of it she said. She was in total disbelief. What a shower.  I could have probably done as good or even better, as I had had many offers of going into business with some of my very wealthy customers.

Therefore, if it had not been for Danny Toms, I would probably never have found out the facts.

A few weeks on from the row with the Hubner lot—yes, what a rotten lot, I say once more—I met Tony. "I only now realise," he says, "that I should have told you some time ago that the old man decided, but hadn't got the guts to tell you, that he was not going to let you into the business, and the reason was, if you remember, I asked you to go to Muswell Hill to look at a Sunbeam Talbot."

"So," I say.

"Well," says slick Tony, "You needn't have been so bloody honest as to the state of that heap. The owner went livid evidently, and rang the old man and kicked up hell regarding the way that I ran down the state of his car. Evidently the owner of that heap was a friend of old man Hubner and what have you."

"Well you c***! I wish to bloody hell you had told me! Right bleeders you've turned out to be."

"Not at all," he says, "You shouldn't have condemned his car. That's not the way to do business!"

"F*** you! If you think that way, then I'm better to be out of a business than think like that."

So here I now relate the Muswell Hill car report, direct at the time both verbally and in writing.

"Don't tell me you've actually been driving this and not been stopped by the police."

"Well," says the owner, "I have up to last week when it refused to start."

I have pride in my work as well as honesty, so I told this fellow that the front bumper was about to fall off, one headlamp was cracked, and the bonnet would not close as it was damaged and out of shape. There was rust and illegal, jagged and torn edges on all the wings; the front wings, where they were welded to the body, had come adrift and the windscreen was gouged by the metal on the worn out wiper blades. The car would have acted like a butcher's mincing machine if a child had been hit with it! The doors had dropped and would not close properly; the engine oil dipstick showed no oil whatsoever, there was lots of oil under the car and on the lower part of the engine. There were leaking coolant hoses, three illegal down-to-canvas tyres, the driver's seat had collapsed, the back part frame was broken; the foot pedals had no rubbers on them and by their shiny appearance must have been used like this for some time in the past. All of this amongst various other faults.

So after giving the owner of this death-trap my honest professional opinion, to my amazement he said I was nothing but one of these garage crooks making a mountain out of a molehill, and that his car was not all that I had said it was. He said he would speak to Tony's father regarding my attitude. I politely told him that was not true and the written report is what I had found. "I'm sorry you don't agree with me," I said, "but that's that."

I went back, I remember, to Bibsworth Garage and told Tony and he went, as they say today, totally ballistic. "Christ! It's a scrapper, but you should have humoured him. Sure as hell he'll phone the old man!"

"That's up to him entirely." I felt that this was the thin end of the wedge. Nobody pushes me around. I will not be a 'Yes Man' for any reason, or any person, however it may benefit me. That's me, but especially so when people's lives are at risk.

Well, the rest is history. The old man Hubner—so Tony told me—said, "We are not letting Walter into our business with his damn honesty." Says it all, doesn't it?

And so as my story comes to a close, I reflect on these events that are part and parcel of life's journeys of course. Nearer to the present, I truly thank yet again Benenden Hospital in Kent, who, as stated, brought me out from inside of the gates of hell.

The court case has not gone well at all, due mainly to the claptrap legal jargon that Chase Farm's legal lot have tried to overwhelm me with. The main stumbling block is as stated. The medical profession is a club, closed shop, boys and girls society. They will not say anything about each other—w e all know that—or as the expression aptly puts it, witnesses to the disgraceful goings on that often devastate whole families will not put their heads above the parapet or stand up and be counted. It was decided as expected that there is a lack of the necessary medical evidence. I have pointed out that this is not, and will not, be forthcoming, so it was decided that it would go to the most senior judge at the court.

Please do not hold your breath when I say that his decision to disallow my claim was taken without me being asked to come to court to defend myself or put my case and why that decision was taken is a matter of a date on a hospital report. That, unfortunately, when at the time that I got the said report, did not register with me that the date of the diagnosis of the Wegeners Granulomatosis was not the date that it was actually diagnosed; hence more problems.

So I have protested in the strongest terms to the court's senior administrators not only of my case but—as very regularly comes to light—of the dreadful, sometimes total, failure of the NHS. The very Chase Farm Hospital has had horrendous problems, and I read story after story of yet more letdowns by the hospital in question. One in particular of a woman whose wristband of her details was not checked and she was given an injection that was meant for another patient. The result was that the lady passed away. I sent all these details to the court and now that it has come almost to a stop, I have contacted the European Court of Human Rights. Without a doubt, I have been seriously wronged, and I have about forty-six statements from friends and acquaintances that, since November of 1996, I have as a direct result of medical negligence had health problems of a serious nature, and I am definitely not near or will ever be the man that I was, both physically and even to some extent, mentally.

I will not give up my legal action. There are people, many people, that tell me constantly to call it a day regarding the court action, but I am not the giving-up type. No, never. I do truly feel that as I am bringing the case on my own and that they know that I successfully sued that so-called 'doctor' Kattan, therefore, it is all loaded against me, they have closed ranks as they have on so many other unfortunate people; so hopefully, the European Court of Human rights will come to my help and see that justice is done.

This July (2001) we are at now, I decided that it was time once more to go and see my friends and as near family (and true) that I can honestly say, up in Aberdeen; the sea was calm and the sun sparkled on it just as if I was in the Med.

So I rang K, my first love, if you recall, way back. As always, she was genuinely delighted that once more I had come to Aberdeen for a few days. "You've certainly brought this beautiful weather with you. We would like you to come to lunch tomorrow if you can, Walter." she said.

"Well K, that's nice of you, it really is, and I look forward to it."

So, duly the next day, ten feet tall, with a beautiful bunch of flowers in hand. I went by taxi to their house at 12:00 on the dot. The door was open and K and her sister E were in the hallway as they had seen me arrive. I cannot recall ever a time when a person has hugged me and cried, as did these lovely and ever-beautiful ladies that day, one on each shoulder, hugging me and crying. Yes, I cried as well, from ten feet tall I was a humbled creature. After all, I was not blood family. All they kept saying was, "Walter, oh Walter," as K's hubby looked on, then he shook my hand and put the other one on my shoulder. "Right glad to see you again Walter. Come in and sit yourself down." he said.

To say that I was indeed, 'Wimy Ain Fowk,' puts it in true perspective. We had a great couple of hours and a lovely lunch. I love those ladies, as ladies indeed they are; properly brought up and of course serious Christians true.

The clock seemed to move like lightning as it always does at times like that and before we knew it the clock said two-thirty and K apologised saying that soon they were to go and see a friend in hospital and would give me a lift to the town centre. Meanwhile, her sister E had to go round the corner to her house for something to take to the hospital, as K's husband was getting the car out of the garage onto the road. I was standing with K on the pavement, and I said to her, "You know, I've often thought that if I had not left in 1954 to go to London and we were of course adults by then, I feel sure that by that time your parents' views regarding our religions would perhaps not have come into the equation. You see, K, you know that you truly were my first love and I think that had I not left in 1954 and of course perhaps you were then already engaged or married, I feel that things would possibly have been different. I was unattached, yes, even at 24. I had not got into girlfriends, ridiculous but true, boats and cars as you know."

Looking at me straight in the eyes, she told me, "Well Walter, now that you mention it, I've often thought the same. Says it all, does it not?"

We went round and got her sister, and off we went up to town. The ladies were in the back, so I got out and K opened the rear door. We kissed and shook hands; of course I also shook her husband's before I got out. I thanked them once again, and was told yet again how delighted they were to have seen me again, "And remember the next time you come back, do come and see us." I'll never forget that day and those dear, dear people.

Yes, I have told my wife all about it, of course. She knows all the facts. What is there to hide? All our close friends know the story from the very beginning.

Recently, we had our other granddaughter, Elise, christened at the Catholic Church of her mother's, and why not? I never have and never will say anything against other's decisions.

So now it is October again, the date the eighth; and I am going downhill fast, as is of course the curse of Wegener's Granulomatosis. As the details of its side effects clearly state, it is a case of here today and possibly gone tomorrow, there are no guarantees; a fact that I have faced up to since it was properly diagnosed. So from bad to worse, but I have at least some protection that many people don't have. Having been told many a time by Dr Dibble and Dr Ahmed that if I have any problems whatsoever I must simply tell my GP and get on the phone to them. Having that sort of support really is the tops as far as peace of mind goes. You try an NHS hospital with that and see how far you get.

I do not contact them at the drop of a hat; only when I'm down really bad, when all local medication has failed. Then it is with great effort with my wife takes me by car to Charing Cross station then to Headcorn, where we usually get the waiting minibus to the hospital.

I have on Tuesday 16th October been once again admitted to the hospital. This is going to be, I really feel, another long haul, but as a realist, I am facing up to it. What else is there to do? I have lived a full life that most men can only dream of, I have a wonderful family and I have always been surrounded by some wonderful people, for that I will always be thankful.